Social Media Strategy

To the insightful and thoughtful students I've had over the years, as well as to my lovely and wonderful wife whom I will cherish for years to come

Sara Miller McCune founded SAGE Publishing in 1965 to support the dissemination of usable knowledge and educate a global community. SAGE publishes more than 1000 journals and over 800 new books each year, spanning a wide range of subject areas. Our growing selection of library products includes archives, data, case studies and video. SAGE remains majority owned by our founder and after her lifetime will become owned by a charitable trust that secures the company's continued independence.

Los Angeles | London | New Delhi | Singapore | Washington DC | Melbourne

Social Media Strategy

Tools for Professionals and Organizations

Phillip G. Clampitt

University of Wisconsin at Green Bay

Los Angeles | London | New Delhi
Singapore | Washington DC | Melbourne

FOR INFORMATION:

SAGE Publications, Inc.
2455 Teller Road
Thousand Oaks, California 91320
E-mail: order@sagepub.com

SAGE Publications Ltd.
1 Oliver's Yard
55 City Road
London EC1Y 1SP
United Kingdom

SAGE Publications India Pvt. Ltd.
B 1/I 1 Mohan Cooperative Industrial Area
Mathura Road, New Delhi 110 044
India

SAGE Publications Asia-Pacific Pte. Ltd.
3 Church Street
#10–04 Samsung Hub
Singapore 049483

Printed in the United States of America.

ISBN: 978-1-5063-4624-3

Acquisitions Editor: Karen Omer
Editorial Assistant: Sarah Dillard
Production Editor: Bennie Clark Allen
Copy Editor: Karen E. Taylor
Typesetter: C&M Digitals (P) Ltd.
Proofreader: Sue Schon
Indexer: Molly Hall
Cover Designer: Anupama Krishnan
Marketing Manager: Jillian Oelsen

17 18 19 20 21 10 9 8 7 6 5 4 3 2 1

Brief Contents

Detailed Table
of Contents

List of Tables and Figures

TABLES

FIGURES

PREFACE

"Alice laughed. 'There's no use trying,' she said: 'one can't believe impossible things.' 'I daresay you haven't had much practice,' said the Queen. 'When I was your age, I always did it for half-an-hour a day. Why, sometimes I've believed as many as six impossible things before breakfast. . . '"

—Lewis Carroll, *Through the Looking-Glass and What Alice Found There*

Many of the great pleasures in life are rather simple—reading a good book by the fire, engaging in a scintillating conversation, or eating a sumptuous breakfast. I wrote this book with the first two pleasures in mind, fueled by the last one. I've read countless books in my career. The good ones were well written, informative, and prompted me to think about something in a new way. That's what I've attempted to do with this book. But I wanted to do something more. I wanted to prompt engaging conversations. Most conversations are rather utilitarian (e.g., "What would you like to order? How do I get to your house?"). The special ones, though, couple a respectful clash of ideas with a thoughtful flash of insights. Fortunately, I've had many of those conversations with my students and colleagues as I wrote this book.

The conversation started with a simple challenge gleaned from one of my favorite tales, *Through the Looking-Glass*, the sequel to *Alice's Adventures in Wonderland*. The idea of "thinking impossible things" (only *after* breakfast, for me) always intrigued me. This book represents one of those "impossible things." To be specific, how do you write a book that has enduring value when the subject matter (social media) changes almost daily? Social media platforms, algorithms, and trends can shift with the mere tap of a finger on a distant screen. The reasonable answer to my impossible question might be "You can't, so just pay attention to the daily social media blogs and go along for the ride." But as a college professor committed to providing valuable thinking routines that can last a lifetime, I simply couldn't accept that answer.

So this book and related website provide an answer to the impossible question. If forced to answer the impossible question in a word, it would be *strategy*. Why? Good strategic thinking about complex issues will transcend time and social media platforms. There are plenty of social media specialists who are tactically competent—but strategically clueless. Their expertise will endure for a time, but inevitably they will run into challenges for which they are unprepared and ill equipped. And ultimately, they will fail. What they need are tools to think strategically about the ever-shifting social media landscape. That's what we seek to provide in this book.

That said, you can learn a lot about effective tactics that work today by reading blogs, posts, and articles from successful tacticians. I encourage that, but it is not enough. Why? Too often, these tactical superstars breed an imitation mindset driven by the faulty logic of "It worked for me, so it should work for you." Maybe. Maybe not. For instance, posts from an entertainment superstar may create buzz but may foster a backlash when used by others. So, yes, read the blogs of tactical superstars—usually they are quite eager to share—but be wary of learning the wrong lessons. I love case studies, for instance, but I prefer to look at them through a strategic lens. Without that lens or framework, people tend to see only tactics to copy not tools to illuminate thinking nor enduring lessons to learn. In fact, in Appendix 3, we provide five case studies filtered through the strategic framework developed in the book. That should make the lessons learned applicable to a wide range of organizations while offering lasting insights about strategic thinking.

Some brief history: I didn't know it at the time, but this book started when a group of students implored me to start teaching a course on social media. I was intrigued because nobody on the planet was teaching such a course at the time. But I was perplexed about the "impossibility" of creating something that was both timely and timeless. So I decided to seize on the intellectual challenge. After all, grappling with "impossible questions" is fun, stimulating, and illuminating.

But it is even more so when done with valued friends, thoughtful colleagues, and engaged students. I have all of these, in abundance, including Adam Halfman, Danielle Bina, Amy Martin, Elizabeth Hintz, Karli Peterson, Taylor Thomson, Katelyn Staaben, Julie Sadoff, Laleah Fernandez, Ryan Martin, Jena Richter Landers, Ben Kotenberg, Steve Schmitt, and Rachel Veldt. Fittingly, this book could not have been completed without these social and professional relationships. Thank you one and all. And I was privileged to work with the very best copy editor on the planet, Karen Taylor. Even she humbly admits that "it's too bad there is no *American Idol* show for copy editors." I couldn't agree more. Finally, I want to thank my wife, Laurey, who tirelessly worked on making this book more accessible, readable, and understandable. She has an amazing capacity to bring out the best in dogs, people, and my books. Hugs and kisses—not just the social media kind—to her!

Reading Tips

- Visit the book's website (www.amazingSMstrategy.com) for further exercises, quizzes, and reference material.

- Check out key terms that are in bold and defined in the glossary.

- Deepen your understanding of the core ideas by completing the exercises ("Deep Dives") at the end of each chapter.

- Sign up for complimentary social media tips at www.drsowhat.com (or Twitter, @drsowhat).

Acknowledgments

SAGE Publishing gratefully acknowledges the following reviewers for their kind assistance:

L. Simone Byrd, *Alabama State University*

Gregory G. De Blasio, *Northern Kentucky University*

Melissa D. Dodd, *University of Central Florida*

Pj Forrest, *Alcorn State University*

Matthew J. Kushin, *Shepherd University*

Patty Lamberti, *Loyola University Chicago*

Bill Mills, *East Texas Baptist University*

Peggy O'Neill-Jones, *Metropolitan State University of Denver*

Brandi Watkins, *Virginia Tech*

Scott D. Roberts, *The University of the Incarnate Word*

PART I

Understanding the Fundamentals of Social Media

CHAPTER 1

Who Needs a Social Media Strategy?

"Many people intuitively understand the 'social' dimensions of social media, some appreciate the 'media' properties of social media, but only a few fully fathom the unique synergistic possibilities and perils of combining social sensibilities with media capabilities."

—Dr. So What

Picture yourself at the dawn of the golden age of electricity. Alarmists rage about the dangers of putting lightning into wires. Leaders wonder if electricity is a fad or a game changer. Prognosticators debate the fate of AC or DC power sources. Innovators salivate about the possibilities of a world without candles. What would you do? How would you respond? Would you wire your home? Would you wait to see what the neighbors are doing before you decide?

Similar questions arise as we enter the golden age of social media. Alarmists, leaders, prognosticators, and innovators respond in predictable ways along a continuum of fear to giddiness. Organizational leaders wonder if social media is just a fad. Prognosticators argue about which platform has the most potential and staying power. Eager innovators jump in with both sides of their brains to use social media in novel ways that platform providers never envisioned. What do you do? That's what this book is all about.

Defining Social Media

We need to start by defining social media. That sounds easy and perhaps even unnecessary. After all, almost everybody can name a high-profile social media player such as Facebook, Twitter, Instagram, Pinterest, and Snapchat. But a good working definition of social media can 1) highlight key features that distinguish social media from other forms of communication, 2) help us translate the conceptual shorthand of the "social media" label into something more meaningful, and 3) foreshadow many of the key issues discussed in this book that rarely surface in the daily cascade of social media blogs.

For our purposes, we define **social media** as *an electronic form of communication that is governed by the rules of platform providers; it allows users to share images and text within their selected communities.* This definition highlights five distinct features of social media:

> *Electronic form of communication*: Social media uses the Internet as the technological means for facilitating communication. Two friends talking face to face in a restaurant, for instance, are not using social media even though they may have agreed to meet using Facebook.

> *Governed by the rules of platform providers*: Platform providers such as Twitter and Facebook set the communicative parameters. You only have 140 characters, for instance, to share something on Twitter. These limits are designed to shape the community dynamics by cultivating unique cost-benefit relationships for users, consumers, and marketers.[1]

> *Users*: You don't have to be a celebrity, a newspaper editor, a government official, or a TV personality to communicate on social media. Anybody with the right technology can participate and become an instant social media celebrity. That's one of the key distinguishing features of this new age of communication; the media gatekeepers are receding into the background.

> *Share images and text*: Information, opinions, pictures, graphics, and videos can all be shared via social media. The sharing can be one way or two way depending on the social media platform.

Selected communities: Social media users form communities of various sizes and of assorted interests. Some communities are large, like the followers of a pop star, while others are small, like those connecting neighbors. Some communities are geographically oriented, e.g., Nextdoor, a neighborhood social media platform, while others are more subject-matter driven, such as those devoted to people suffering from a rare disease.

This definition underscores the complexity compressed into the "social media" label. In fact, we will be exploring many of these issues in this book. Consider, for instance, the seemingly easy choice of selecting images and text. How do you maximize the utility of those choices? That's an issue we discuss in depth in the content chapter. Here's a more perplexing question: Why are some social media communities vibrant and growing while others are stale and dying? That's an issue we discuss in the connections chapter.

This definition also deliberately avoids identifying particular uses of social media or specific types of users. All too often, the word "social" signals a trivial amusement or a frivolous pastime. That's an overly narrow view of social media. People use social media for a wide range of reasons including exchanging information, soliciting advice, and inspiring action. Likewise, many organizational leaders narrowmindedly relegate social media to just another tool in the marketing toolbox. This book takes a broader, more encompassing view of both the uses and the users of social media. The next section expands on this notion.

WHO CAN BENEFIT FROM A SOCIAL MEDIA STRATEGY?

A wide range of users in a great variety of roles can potentially benefit from the effective use of social media. The sample below highlights a few of the strategic questions they might confront.

Senior leaders: Traditionally, CEOs, university chancellors, and presidents of nonprofits would share information with their employees through memos, emails, and town hall meetings. Today, many are using social media like Twitter and Facebook to stay in touch with employees. Some use an information-rich strategy by tweeting on a regular basis.[2] Others use social media in a more supportive role as a follow-up to using more traditional tools such as a town hall meeting. Still others avoid social media altogether. *Which approach makes the most sense?*

Research and development professionals: Less than 50 percent of companies use social media for research and development.[3] Instead, many companies develop and test new products and services using more costly tools, for example, by assembling numerous focus groups around the globe. *How can social media lower those costs while harvesting innovative consumer ideas?*

Marketers: Marketing professionals were probably the first people to recognize the power of social media. They are uniquely qualified to do so because their day-to-day personal relationships with customers drive sales. *What role can social media play in building or supporting those relationships?*

Public relations professionals: Traditionally, PR professionals crafted press releases, built press kits, contacted the media, and staged press conferences. Many PR professionals assume the role of brand ambassadors, as well.[4] *Can social media replace or support some of the traditional roles?*

Internal communication specialists: These professionals are often tasked with rolling out major changes, building support for organizational values, and getting new employees on board with an organization's culture, policies, and procedures. Many of these professionals embrace social media to either conduct or support these functions. *How can these professionals enhance their usage of social media?*

Human resource professionals: These specialists are tasked with hiring the right people, training them, and supporting them in their careers. Many use LinkedIn or Facebook for some of these functions. *How can social media better support HR professionals?*

Journalists: Many journalists search for story leads and breaking news by following celebrities, sports figures, and politicians' social media posts. Some journalists tweet their followers about an upcoming story or article they've written. *How can journalists make the most effective and ethical use of social media?*

Small business owners: Small business owners clearly don't have the financial resources of Fortune 500 companies, so they are always looking for cost-effective ways to compete. To some extent, social media levels the playing field by allowing local restaurants, for example, to compete against national chains. Clever localized promotions via social media may well trump high-profile national advertising campaigns. *How can small business owners make the most efficient use of social media?*

Celebrities, politicians, and thought leaders: Many people offer advice, promote their personal brand, share their thoughts on current events, and post about their day-to-day activities. This kind of familiarity subtlety encourages followers to attend their events, buy their products, and share their lifestyle choices by exploiting peer-to-peer networks of influence. That is, you tell your friends about a great concert or book, and they, in turn, attend the event or buy the book. Some celebrities copromote their wares and commercial products. For instance, Selena Gomez posted an Instagram photo of herself drinking Coca-Cola with "You're the spark," lyrics from her hit song "Me & The Rhythm," written on the bottle. Her post, with the clever caption under the picture, "when your lyrics are on the bottle," generated an astonishing 4 million "likes."[5] On the other hand, almost every day we can find celebrities, politicians, star athletes, or thought leaders posting something really stupid, offensive, or classless. *How can these celebrities and leaders avoid the downside of social media while enhancing their reputations?*

The list of professionals who could benefit from a social media strategy could go on and on. Regardless of your professional background, social media usage raises some rather challenging questions, such as the ones *italicized* above. Crafting the right social media strategy can help you answer them.

So What?

Fair warning: You are going to see this question a lot in this book. It's my favorite question because it focuses attention on the implications and next steps implied by an idea, insight, or intuition. But, there's another bonus: this question builds a strategic mindset into your thinking that we will use throughout the book.

In this case, the "so what" question allows us to explore the broader implications of our social media definition, especially those relating to our discussion about the potential benefactors and the benefits of a good social media strategy.

First, what works in your personal world may not translate well into the professional universe. You aren't qualified to be a traffic engineer because you know how to drive a car. Sure, it helps, but it's not going to help you optimize the system, smooth the flow of traffic, or prevent accidents. Similarly, just because you regularly post on Facebook, Snapchat, and Twitter, doesn't make you a social media expert. While your social media experience helps, it won't guarantee that you'll know how to use it to deliver business results, promote an event, or prevent PR gaffes. That's exactly what happened to Cinnabon when a well-intentioned—but clueless—social media "specialist" tweeted about the death of actress Carrie Fisher, the famous *Star Wars*' Princess Leia. Cinnabon's poorly conceived and insensitively illustrated "tribute tweet" said, "RIP Carrie Fisher, you'll always have the best buns in the galaxy."[6] Ugh!

Second, most people are victims, rather than masters, of their own de facto strategies and rarely seize on new opportunities. Only in recent years have many mobile phone users started discarding their landline telephones. Consumers wasted billions of dollars on services they rarely used. Why did it take so long? In a word, inertia. The same holds true for companies that use antiquated methods for communicating with shareholders, sharing updates with their customers, and performing a host of other activities that could be accomplished through a robust social media strategy. Hardly anyone talks about their personal telephone strategy because it's something that has emerged over years of unexamined decisions. For ill or for good, this became the de facto telephone strategy. Unfortunately, most social media strategies emerge in the same fashion.

This process of decision making is not particularly helpful because de facto strategies are rarely recognized, much less evaluated. Social media specialists who merely allow their strategies to emerge often miss opportunities. In contrast, consider how Vermont artist, Bo Muller-Moore, fought back against the fast-food chain, Chick-fil-A, Inc. The company claimed his T-shirts emblazoned with the slogan "Eat More Kale" infringed on its trademarked "Eat Mor Chikin" catchphrase. He fought back with a social media campaign that sparked public outrage against Chick-fil-A. He received high-profile media coverage and even free legal representation.[7] This is exactly the kind of novel thinking that great social media strategies inspire.

Likewise, Ashleigh Blatt, aka @mompreneuronfire, excels at developing novel social media strategies for her clients. Her passion is helping women in business realize the possibilities of expanding their revenue streams, along with providing them that extra boost of support in juggling career and family. She knows a blogger with over 600,000 followers who generates almost no revenue, while she has helped one of her clients with only 45,000 followers generate $250,000 annually through thoughtful digital marketing.

Ashleigh even helps her celebrity clients add to their revenue streams through on-line marketing with Facebook, Pinterest, Instagram, and Twitter. She does this by helping them craft messages, select platforms, and manage their online presence.

These activities may not come naturally to many celebrities because they have neither the time nor inclination to learn about the social media landscape.[8] Bottom line: celebrities might be very good at attracting attention but not have a clue how to monetize the attention. That's what a good, not a de facto, social media strategy can do.

Third, organizations and professionals are using social media for a wide array of tasks well beyond mere social chitchat. Years ago, it would have been easy for senior leaders to dismiss social media as mere child's play, something fun to tinker with but not to be taken terribly seriously. Today that is not possible. The broad array of organizational types and professionals using social media suggests that social media needs to be taken more seriously than child's play. Clearly, social media is being used for tasks well beyond social chats at the virtual bar. It's time to start thinking of social media as a strategic asset as important as an organization's brand or any other intangible asset.

Consider how some for-profit as well as nonprofit organizations make creative use of social media. For-profits, seeking to provide financial benefits to their owners by increasing revenues and decreasing costs, realize that a good social media strategy can address each of these goals. Effective social media campaigns can increase market share, decrease research and development costs, and lower advertising costs. For example, in 2014, McDonald's faced the challenge of attracting millennials to its fast-food restaurants. This was at a time when millennials were more frequently interacting on social media, but McDonald's had a limited presence on these platforms. So it beefed up its social media staff, but what executives discovered was that translating a robust social media presence into actual sales was a tricky business. However, it did discover something unexpected: its R & D staff could garner a lot of great ideas for new products and offerings. For example, staff members noticed that many millennials would lament the fact that breakfast items were not available after 10:30 a.m. This insight, along with other data, resulted in McDonald's shifting to an all-day breakfast menu.[9]

On the other hand, nonprofit organizations seek to provide educational, social service, or other humanitarian benefits to the general public, but without the explicit burden of making a profit. Although universities, hospitals, churches, or fraternal clubs may not focus on profits, they still must live within their financial means. Social media can be enormously helpful in providing these benefits in a cost-effective manner. The University of Wisconsin-Green Bay, for instance, uses social media to promote events for the community, disseminate emergency information, recruit students, and recognize university accomplishments. Other nonprofits, such as the Y (formerly the YMCA), use social media to share news and announcements, build relationships with donors and partners, and tell the story of the brand.

Fourth, consensus remains elusive about the effectiveness and ethical use of social media. Many of the questions raised in the previous section revolve around the effectiveness of social media versus more traditional tools. For example, can social media replace direct mail advertising? Other questions revolve around optimizing the effectiveness of social media practices. For example, what's the right mix of inspirational and promotional posts for thought leaders? Unfortunately, these are not yes-no or even multiple-choice questions.

Other questions about the ethical use of social media may be even more challenging. For example, during the July 2016 killing of five Dallas, Texas, police officers, the police department tweeted the picture of a "person of interest" for the horrendous crimes. The person in the picture—aka "the person of interest"—turned himself in and proclaimed his innocence. Shortly thereafter, the police released him and officials tweeted out a "clarification." Within hours, Twitter transformed the "person of interest" from a potential mass murderer to a fully exonerated citizen. Activists, academics, and officials will debate the ethics of this particular use of social media for years to come.

Less debatable, at least by Western traditions, is how the Chinese government pursues a social media strategy of distraction by shifting discussions away from politically controversial issues. A Harvard study estimates that the Chinese government hires millions of people to surreptitiously post 448 million social media cheerleader-like posts each year in support of government policies.[10] On the other hand, there are less nefarious uses of social media, such as American officials seeking to remove from the web the highly effective al-Qaeda recruitment YouTube videos by Anwar al-Awlaki.[11] They are also testing various social media tools and messages to counter the influence of radical Islamic terrorist thought.[12]

In short, most of these effectiveness and ethical questions can be answered by crafting a robust social media strategy.

Fifth, social media touches so many different departments that it requires a strategic mindset to sync communications across the organization. Think of all the traditional departments that could be potentially influenced by social media. The obvious ones are marketing, public relations, and internal communications, but there are others. Customer service, for example, might first hear of consumer or client complaints through social media. Likewise, the legal department might have to weigh in on the potential liabilities of posting certain information.

At the very least, the number of organizational activities and entities potentially affected by social media means that social media managers must coordinate with other departments. Nick Rudd, a social media specialist for Alta Resources, remarked:

> I work with six different brands daily in two different countries. Each has a brand voice and different goals for its social media. Everything I do involves some other department, brand, or other agency. One day I could be working with BuzzFeed; the next day a consumer-turned-blogger wants to partner up and chat. At the end of the day, my success or

failure always comes down to how well I work with everyone. That's why I believe the social media department should really be called the "Teamwork" department.

The social media team has a unique relationship with our stakeholders. The legal department wants to defend the organization against them, while marketing wants to sell them something new. PR wants their stakeholders to do something or think in a certain way. Customer service and fulfillment want customers to have a positive and fast consumer experience. But the social media or Teamwork department is the only one to have the raw level of give-and-take with the public. We team up with other departments to communicate something inside the organization or externally to other stakeholders. In response, they post or tweet to let us know whether we've successfully communicated. In short, our social media messaging and listening is what makes our strategies fly or flop.[13]

If we take Nick's insights to the next level, we might conclude that social media may become the hub that integrates traditionally separate communication functions, such as marketing, PR, and customer service. If so, the strategist mindset will become even more important than it already is for social media managers.

Conclusion

This chapter prompts deeper questions that deserve attention. What benefits does a strategy really produce? How can I create a social media strategy? What are the major components of a social media strategy? How can I translate my social media strategy into an action plan? How do I evaluate my social media strategy and performance?

Great questions. And we will explore the answers in subsequent chapters of the book. But first, let's go back to the dilemma posed at the beginning of the chapter. Let's assume that we are standing at the dawn of the golden age of social media. The murky morning fog conceals both hidden dangers and opportunities. How do we move forward? A good strategy can be your guide and protector. That means we need to define a good social media strategy. The next chapter addresses this issue, thoughtfully lighting our path for the journey into the future.

Key Terms

Social media 4

Deep Dives

These exercises are designed to enhance your understanding of key principles, approaches, and ideas.

1. Using the definition of social media, discuss why email, text messaging, and video conferencing would not be considered social media. Develop three arguments about why it is important to distinguish social media from other communication tools.

2. Craft three arguments you could provide to a skeptical leader about the need for a social media strategy. Provide your supporting evidence with examples, statistics, or testimonials from experts.

3. Describe how the social media strategy needs of a Fortune 500 CEO differ from the needs of a local entertainer. Provide three specific differences.

Notes

1. M. Piskorski, *A Social Strategy: How We Profit from Social Media* (Princeton, NJ: Princeton University Press, 2014).
2. C. Malhotra and A. Malhotra, "How CEOs Can Leverage Twitter," *MIT Sloan Management Review*, Winter 2016, 73–79.
3. D. Roberts and F. Piller, "Finding the Right Role for Social Media in Innovation," *MIT Sloan Management Review*, Spring 2016, 41–47, 41.
4. M. Cervellon and P. Lirio, "When Employees Don't 'Like' their Employers on Social Media," *MIT Sloan Management Review*, Winter 2017, 63–70.
5. N. Sands, "Four Million Fans Can't Be Wrong: Selena Gomez Has Uploaded the Most 'Liked' Image in the History of Instagram," *People*,

July 12, 2016, http://www.people.com/article/selena-gomez-most-liked-photo-instagram-history. Accessed July 13, 2016.

6. C. Mallenbaum, "Cinnabon Deletes, Apologizes for Carrie Fisher Tweet after Backlash," *USA Today*, December 27, 2016, http://www.usatoday.com/story/life/people/2016/12/27/cinnabon-tweets-deletes-carrie-fisher-tweet-after-backlash/95893594/. Accessed December 30, 2016.

7. D. Orozco, "Using Social Media in Business Disputes," *MIT Sloan Management Review*, Winter 2016, 33–35.

8. Ashleigh Blatt, personal interview, February 13, 2017. See http://mompreneuronfire.com.

9. J. Jargon, "McDonald's Turns to Social Media to Draw Millennials," *Wall Street Journal*, October 14, 2016, B6.

10. G. King, J. Pan, and M. Roberts, "How the Chinese Government Fabricates Social Media Posts for Strategic Distraction, Not Engaged Argument," Harvard University white paper, January 14, 2017, http://gking.harvard.edu/files/gking/files/50c.pdf

11. "Halting the Hate," *The Economist*, June 25, 2016, 70–71.

12. J. Bohannon, "How to Attack the Islamic State Online," *Science*, June 17, 2016, 1380.

13. Nick Rudd, personal communication, September 5, 2016.

CHAPTER 2

What Is a Social Media Strategy?

"A good strategy draws power from focusing minds, energy, and action. That focus, channeled at the right moment onto a pivotal objective, can produce a cascade of favorable outcomes."

—Richard Rumelt

Complex subjects resemble a ball of twisted knots. Experts know how to untangle this mess of concepts and isolate the core ideas. So to better understand **social media strategy**, let's start by highlighting what it is NOT:

- Strategy is NOT an action plan, although plans certainly emerge from it.

- Strategy is NOT a single idea, although it often arises from a simple basic notion.

- Strategy is NOT stationary, although it does provide a degree of stability.

- Strategy is NOT abstract, although it may initially appear to be.

- Strategy is NOT a clever slogan, although a catchy phrase might describe it.

Knowing what strategy *is not* helps, but knowing what constitutes its essence helps even more. We turn to that issue in the following section.

THE ESSENCE OF A SUPERIOR SOCIAL MEDIA STRATEGY

Based on an *assessment of the ever-changing competitive landscape*, superior strategists make *big-picture choices* and *coordinate these choices into a coherent path forward*, resulting in an *orchestrated set of tactics*. We've packed a lot of critical concepts into that definition. In fact, we packed so much that the remainder of the chapter will be devoted to unpacking the key (italicized) elements.

SUPERIOR STRATEGISTS ASSESS THE COMPETITIVE LANDSCAPE

Most animals have cylindrically shaped tails. But not the wonderfully mysterious sea horse—its tail is square. Why? This biomechanical oddity creates two major competitive advantages in a tough environment: 1) the shape of the tail provides the superior grasping ability needed to hold onto swaying sea grasses and 2) the tail provides flexible armor to protect it against crushing by enemies.[1] The seahorse's tail embodies a strategy uniquely adapted to its own needs and the competitive environment. And that's precisely the nature of a superior social media strategy.

We will examine in depth how to assess the competitive environment in a later chapter. For now, it is worth sketching the broad brushstrokes of the process:

- The first brushstroke is to collect your facts about your organization, your competitors, the social media environment, and your stakeholders.

- With the second brushstroke, you look for underlying patterns that emerge from the facts. This focus helps you determine your strengths, weaknesses, opportunities, and threats.

- The final brushstroke on the canvas validates your judgments. The finished product? It may look more like a sketch than a perfectly crafted Rembrandt, but that's ok—it shows the fluid nature of the process.

One of my favorite strategists, Richard Rumelt, thinks about it this way: "Good strategy grows out of an independent and careful assessment of the situation, harnessing individual insight to carefully crafted purpose. Bad strategy follows the crowd, substituting popular slogans for insights."[2] That's why you'll never be able to beg, borrow, or steal a superior social media strategy from someone else.

SUPERIOR STRATEGISTS MAKE BIG-PICTURE CHOICES

Superior strategists make big picture or macro-level choices. If you get those wrong, then you'll lose the contest. Consider the following examples:

- Despite ominous war clouds, deadly provocations, and military alliances, the United States was not at war with any other country on the morning of December 7, 1941. That changed when the Japanese attacked Pearl Harbor in the morning of a day "that will live in infamy." The strategic choice facing President Roosevelt was whether to focus the military and industrial might of the United States on Germany or on the one country that directly attacked Americans. A tit-for-tat strategy suggests that Japan should have been the focal point of military action. That's not what Roosevelt decided. Instead, the strategy was "Germany first, then Japan." If he made the wrong strategic choice, then much of the world might be speaking a different language right now.

- In the mid-1980s the CEO of Intel, Andy Grove, could foresee that the market for dynamic memory chips (DRAM) would evaporate in future years, despite the high current demand for the chips. He realized that the company was at a crossroads: that Intel could continue to ride the wave or it could make a dramatic shift to other markets. Grove chose to switch the focus to manufacturing microprocessors instead. If he had chosen to stay the course, his personal fortunes and reputation might have remained intact, but in all likelihood, Intel's fate and status would have suffered in the long run. His approach was best summed up in his notion of "strategic inflection points." He explained, "a strategic inflection point is when the balance of forces shifts from the old structure, for the old ways of doing business and the old ways of competing, to the new."[3]

- At 19 months old, Helen Keller was considered "deaf, dumb, and blind" as people were known at the time. More soothing words like "visually impaired" were not in vogue in the late 1800s. Many people in such situations would have spent the remainder of their lives lamenting their fate, blaming anything imaginable for their maladies, and wallowing in self-pity. She made a more positive big-picture choice:

  > If I regarded my life from the point of view of a pessimist, I should be undone. I should seek in vain for the light that does not visit my eyes and the music that does not ring in my ears. I should beg night and day and never be satisfied. I should sit apart in awful solitude, a prey to fear and despair. But since I consider it a duty to myself and to others to be happy, I escape a misery worse than any physical deprivation.[4]

It was a choice between optimism and pessimism. And because she made that choice, she became the first deaf-blind person to earn a college degree. She then went on to inspire millions of people.

These three examples are instructive because they highlight several important issues.

First, big-picture choices can be made at a variety of levels. These particular cases underscore that strategy can occur at the national, organizational, and personal levels. Strategic choices can also be made at the divisional level, such as marketing, human resources, and information systems.

Second, big-picture choices can refer to a number of different issues.

- With Roosevelt, the issue was this: "Which enemy should we fight first and which should we hold at bay?" Strategic translation: Which *major priority* should be tackled first?

- With Grove, it was "What should be the company's focus in the future?" Strategic translation: What should be the *strategic direction* of the company?

- With Keller, it was "Do I want to live my life as an optimist or pessimist?" Strategic translation: What should be *my orientation* to the challenges ahead?

Third, big-picture choices are neither clear cut nor inevitable. Making the choices involves weighing both benefits and concerns. In each case, there were reasonable arguments to be made for different choices. Roosevelt could have reasonably argued that retribution against Japan was the first priority instead of the threat of Nazism. Today, few would doubt the wisdom of Roosevelt's strategic choice or even Andy Grove's. However, at the point of decision, there were arguments on both sides. In hindsight, the success of the decisions seems almost inevitable. But at the time, there were no guarantees that these decisions were the right ones. As one theorist noted, "In the nature of things you can never try to escape one danger without encountering another; but prudence consists in knowing how to recognize the nature of the different dangers and in accepting the least bad as good."[5]

What are the big-picture choices for the social media strategist? Here is a preview of the five strategic elements—the **5 Cs**— of a superior social media strategy:

- **Coordinates**: What are your major goals? What are their relationships with one another?

- **Channels**: What social media platforms should you actively manage? Passively manage?

- **Content**: What types of content should you post? What's the right mix of images and words? When should you post?

- **Connections**: How should your social media be connected to one another, to organizational departments, to executives, and to decision-making processes?

- **Corrections**: How will you assess effectiveness and correct missteps?

The 5 Cs—**coordinates, channels, content, connections**, and **corrections**—are all considered big-picture choices because these choices then allow you to drill down to more specific actions and tactics. For example, once you have decided on several interrelated major goals (e.g., coordinates), you can then drill down to more specific objectives. Likewise, after you have decided to highlight images of employees who love their job (e.g., content), you can then select the appropriate pictures or shoot videos.

SUPERIOR STRATEGISTS COORDINATE THE CHOICES

If you make all the right big-picture choices, does that mean you have a good strategy? No. Superior strategy is not just about excellent decision making; it's about design, making your choices work together to achieve victory. Assume you selected a world-class violinist, accordion player, and ukulele player to perform in your trio. Bravo, you made great big-picture choices. But you'd still hear a chorus of boos if you asked them to play a Bach trio sonata or almost any other imaginable tune. The design or structure of your strategic product and your big-picture choices should be mutually reinforcing. That's not likely to happen if you have a violin, accordion, and ukulele playing classical music.

Of all the elements of superior strategy, coordinating the choices is the least appreciated and most often overlooked. It took decades for U.S. military strategists to find the mechanisms to coordinate superior air power (e.g., the Air Force) and ground forces effectively. Embedding air controllers with Special Forces (e.g., Delta Force, Navy SEALS, etc.) proved decisive in military conflicts around the globe. Richard Rumelt, known as the "strategy's strategist," put it this way: "A good strategy doesn't just draw on existing strengths; it creates strength through the coherence of its design. Most organizations of any size don't do this."[6]

The social media cosmos makes coordination of choices even more difficult than the chamber music director's task. Why? We are dealing with many more possible combinations than just three instruments and one piece of music. Moreover, the music director has decades of conventional pairings to use as a reference point for harmonizing the sounds. Unfortunately, for the social media manager, the reference points are not readily available, and even those that may exist tend to shift over time in the dynamic social media cosmos.

Nevertheless, superior social media strategists take on this daunting task. In particular, they seek to synchronize the coordinates, content, channels, connections, and corrections—the 5 Cs—into a coherent and robust structure. We will return to this issue in another chapter. For now, a few examples might start you thinking about this challenging issue:

- Consider a company that wants to encourage social media followers to buy its product or service (e.g., coordinates) but fails to provide a usable link between social media posts and the company website (e.g., connections). This may sound absolutely absurd. It's not. We've done numerous head-to-head social media comparisons between competitors and discovered this happens all too frequently.

- Or consider a situation in which executives want a social media presence to augment their reputation as "thought leaders" (e.g., coordinates) and the social media manager decides to focus resources on Twitter and LinkedIn (e.g., channels). This focus makes a lot of sense because thought leaders often gain credibility through making astute observations about daily events. Likewise, the LinkedIn channel emphasizes a more professional rather than personal orientation. In this case, the choices coordinate well and reinforce one another.

SUPERIOR STRATEGISTS COORDINATE THE CHOICES INTO A COHERENT PATH FORWARD

One major concern that always pops up in conversations about strategy centers on identifying the appropriate level of abstraction. Complaints such as these are heard: "Strategy is too abstract to act on," or "It's all talk and no action." If "strategy" were put on trial for these accusations, here's how it should plead: "guilty" on the abstraction charge but "not guilty" on the no-action charge. Superior strategies are abstract in the sense that they sketch a general framework for moving forward.

Abstraction proves valuable because people can determine where to concentrate their energies without dictating a precise course of action. This general overview, in turn, allows people to address the challenges creatively, and it avoids stifling the innovative spirit that inevitably deflates when weighed down by strict rules, regulations, and protocols.

The path forward emerges from coordinating the choices into a vision of the future. Note that we are not talking about specific tactics at this point but instead about the big-picture direction for the social media effort. In the past, iPhone fans were not able to discern precisely the rhythm of new releases, but they had a general sense of the timetable of Apple's strategy. Apple employees, designers, and suppliers did, as well. This management path fostered just enough predictability to allow the company to make resourcing decisions without creating lock-in. In short, it provided just the right mixture of direction and flexibility. What's the name of the strategy? "Tick-Tock." On the "tick" of the yearly clock, Apple introduced a major phone upgrade, such as a different size of iPhone. On the "tock" of the odd years, Apple enhanced many preexisting features of the version, such as improved pixel density for the camera. In short, one year Apple introduced major innovations, and the next year it enhanced those innovations with more minor tweaks. Note how the strategy, while abstract, guided consumers, suppliers, and software developers.

Let's shift focus to the social media world. Consider actor Rob Lowe, who has a noteworthy social media reputation. What's his personal social media strategy? He asks himself the following questions before posting anything:

- Does it need to be said?

- Does it need to be said by me?

- Does it need to be said now?[7]

After steering his thoughts over these speed bumps, anything goes. In essence, he uses these questions to self-regulate with an eye toward enhancing his personal brand by avoiding posting something stupid or foolish. What's the name of his content strategy? We don't know what he calls it, but it could be neatly summed up as a "test-post" approach.[8] The questions supply the filter, and each post meets the demands of his fans for the "authentic" Rob Lowe. Note that the **test-post content strategy** abstractly outlines an approach while not dictating a precise course of action. And it may explain why Rob Lowe doesn't post too many stupid things, which so many others in his industry seem to do on a regular basis.

SUPERIOR STRATEGISTS CRAFT AN ORCHESTRATED SET OF TACTICS

Superior social media strategy evolves into specific actions because it tells us where to direct our energies in a social media universe of possibilities. In fact, if the social media strategy does not imply actions, then it should be deemed a failure. We call these actions tactics because they are basically ways to implement the strategy. **Social media tactics** shift and change all the time in order to avoid unforeseen perils and exploit emerging opportunities. Yet good tactics still respect the broader and more permanent strategy. In fact, I'd estimate that 95 percent of social media gurus opine in their blogs about tactical issues. Great social media managers routinely monitor these sites for potentially useful tactics that could enhance their strategic mission. Importantly though, a great social media manager always views these tactical suggestions through a particular strategic lens developed for a specific organization or individual.

Table 2.1 presents some of the tactical concerns that every social media manager must grapple with on a regular basis. Note how the answers to these tactical questions usually can be resolved by referring to the strategy. For instance, a strategy based on "providing thought leadership" in a particular domain suggests certain tactics. If you are a health care thought leader, then your audience expects commentary on health crises and widely publicized medical studies. That's an easy timing decision: tweet or post something when these events occur. If there's a Zika virus scare, then the social media team better spring into action and get some commentary posted ASAP. If *USA Today* announces that a miracle cancer drug passes a clinical trial, then the team needs to get its experts lined up for advice. Likewise, such a strategic mandate would imply that the speculations of a snake oil salesman—often in the guise of medical breakthrough commentary—should not be reposted.

TABLE 2.1 Examples of Social Media Tactical Issues

Tactical Categories	Related Questions
Timetables	• How often do we post? • Is it event or schedule driven?
Posts	• What should the post say or visualize? • What content should we avoid?
Reposts	• What kind of material should and should not be reposted from other sites? • How will we curate the right material from all that is available?
Content length	• How long should our content be on different social media?
Link placement	• Where should we place links to other material? • What posts should contain links to our home page?
Tagging	• What posts warrant a hash tag? • What tags will help our search engine optimization (SEO) results?
Word selection	• What words should we use in our posts? • What words should we avoid in our posts?
Image selection	• What images are inbounds? • Which are out-of-bounds?
Testing	• What content deserves testing before posting?
Interaction ratios	• What percentage of our posts should request input from followers?
Political support	• Whose support do you need to implement and sponsor your social media strategy?
Sourcing decisions	• Who creates the content? • Who should post?
Feedback mechanisms	• What tools, methods, and analytics should we use to gather feedback?

Conclusion

Superior social media strategists make deliberate and conscious major decisions about all the elements discussed in this chapter. In other words, they don't just select Facebook as the channel because "everybody else is using it." They don't just assume that business goals and the social media approach align into a coherent design (e.g., coordinates). These are all strategic issues requiring contemplation, discussion, and conscious decision making. This is all hard work requiring deep thought, but it's better than hiring a pricy social media shaman to rid your organization of some ghastly decisions inflicting harm on your brand.

Creating a strategy is not cost free. It takes time, energy, and effort to create a robust strategy. Nevertheless, the benefits outlined in this chapter far outweigh the costs. Social media team members want to know where they should focus their minds, energy, and action. Every organizational leader would like to make wise use of scarce resources. Everyone wants to avoid doing something stupid. A social media strategy provides all those benefits and more as we outline in the next chapter.

Key Terms

5 Cs:
- Coordinates 20
- Channels 20
- Content 20
- Connections 20
- Corrections 20

Social media strategy 15
Social media tactics 23
Test-post content
  strategy 23

Deep Dives

These exercises are designed to enhance your understanding of key ideas, principles, and approaches.

1. Describe three examples of the difference between a strategy and tactic in your personal or professional life.

2. There are five key features of a superior social media strategy (e.g., making big-picture choices, coordinating choices, etc.).

Create a two-column table. In column one, rank order these features in terms of difficulty to accomplish, from most difficult to least difficult. In column two provide your rationale.

3. Reflect on your personal experiences with leaders. Create a list of five signs that they are thinking tactically rather than strategically. Provide examples.

NOTES

1. M. Porter, D. Adriaens, R. Hatton, M. Meyers, and J. McKittrick, "Why the Seahorse Tail is Square," *Science*, July 3, 2015, 46.
2. R. Rumelt, *Good Strategy Bad Strategy: The Difference and Why It Matters* (New York: Crown Publishing, 2011), 276.
3. R. Tedlow, *Andy Grove: The Life and Times of an American* (New York: Portfolio, 2006), 229.
4. H. Keller, *Optimism: An Essay* (New York: Fides, 2012), p. 21 of 30 (e-book).
5. Machiavelli's *The Prince*, quoted in V. Kahn, *Machiavellian Rhetoric: From the Counterreformation to Milton* (Princeton, NJ: Princeton University Press, 1994), 40.
6. Rumelt, *Good Strategy Bad Strategy*, 9.
7. Rob Lowe on *Access Hollywood Live*, July 14, 2015.
8. Ironically, Rob Lowe said in the *Access Hollywood Live* interview that his posts are "unfiltered," July 14, 2015.

CHAPTER 3

What Are the Benefits of a Social Media Strategy?

"Everyone needs a strategy. . . . Despite the problems of finding ways through the uncertainty and confusion of human affairs, a strategic approach is still considered to be preferable to one that is merely tactical, let along random. Having a strategy suggests an ability to look up from the short term and trivial to view the long term and the essential, to address causes rather than symptoms, to see woods rather than trees. Without a strategy, facing up to any problem or striving for any objective would be considered negligent."

—Lawrence Freedman

As a kid, I can remember an epic boxing match between George Foreman and Muhammad Ali. There was no question in my mind who to root for and who was going to win. In youth, it's easy to distinguish the good guys from the bad guys and predict events with absolute certainty. So I was stunned when my hero lost. And then I got angry because Ali announced his winning strategy. He called it "rope-a-dope." Calling my hero a "dope" was the last straw. Over time, broken and angry hearts can lead to open and reflective minds. As my ire subsided and the contemplation began, I soon saw the strategic genius behind the memorable phrase. Ali's strategy made perfect sense for the opponent (e.g., Foreman had superior punching power) and the setting (e.g., the ferocious heat of Zaire, Africa). I soon realized that all battles—physical, psychological, or business—involve not only a clash of skill but also of strategy. This was the dawning of a life-long interest in strategic issues.

To be honest, the emotional impact was as devastating as one of Foreman's right hooks because I had to acknowledge that "good guys"—even good guys with lots of skill and fans—don't always win. Good strategy trumps great skills and lots of fans. But the lessons from this psychological right hook kept emerging over time. These are highlighted below.

THE BENEFITS OF STRATEGY

You and your organization need a strategy because you want to win the fight. You want to be Ali, not Foreman, in the social media jungle. You'll lose a few battles, some people may think you're crazy, but you'll end up winning the contest. Still, in my hero's defense, he must have learned some pretty important strategic lessons; after all, he has sold a lot more grillers than any boxer in history. Regardless of whether you are trying to win in the boxing or home-shopping ring, a good strategy will help you in the following major ways:

First, a sound strategy helps guide your deployment of scarce resources. A bedrock principle of Economics 101 is that all resources are limited, even ones that may appear unlimited, like oxygen. Take a hike up a 10,000-foot mountain anywhere in the world and you'll find that out pretty quickly! In the social media world, the resources include such things as time, personnel, and creativity. A good social media strategy induces you to answer some basic questions:

- On what social media platform (e.g., Facebook, Twitter, Pinterest) should we concentrate our time and attention?

- What kind of people do we need to hire to execute our strategy?

- Where should we place our creative resources?

Answers to questions like these flow directly from your strategy. In other words, a good strategy ensures that you don't fall into the trap of thinking you should do everything. That's a recipe for disaster. To paraphrase the great Chinese military strategist Sun Tzu, attempting to be strong everywhere is the formula for being strong nowhere. Unfortunately, many social media managers work under pressure to be on all platforms, communicating all the time. In fact, if you look at the job postings for social media managers, you'll see the words "master of all social media platforms" prominently featured. That word, "all," sends shivers through the spine of a true strategist.

Second, a sound strategy helps coordinate people and resources. The previous benefit highlighted the *selection* of what resources to employ. This benefit underscores how to *coordinate* those resources. "Getting everybody on the same page" requires effort, which incurs costs to organizations. A good strategy minimizes these coordination costs by using the mental shortcut implied by the strategy. Why? The strategy tells people what to ignore as well as what to pay attention to. The greatest coordination costs are incurred during meetings. How does a good strategy diminish those costs? It should control the agenda by putting particularly beneficial issues on the table and relegating other issues to the sidelines. A social media team that agrees on a core idea and coordinates resources around it should shape other employees' expectations about roles, timing, and performance.

Consider a social media team that decides on an **assess and respond strategy** when it detects negative feedback about a product or a service. Basically, the strategy is to *assess* posts and *respond* in the appropriate manner. The responses could range from directly replying to the post to ignoring it. Compare and contrast how two social media teams might handle the situation: Team A operates with an assess and respond strategy, while Team B doesn't have a specific feedback strategy.

Team A detects a troubling post that maligns the company's reputation. It immediately springs into action by 1) deciding which of their generic responses to launch (e.g., apologize, take corrective action), 2) crafting a few likely retorts, 3) selecting the best one, and 4) posting a response. Meanwhile Team B may or may not spot the potential threat to the company's reputation. After all, members of this team leave it to chance whether such hazards might appear on their radar screen, or worse, on an executive's radar screen. Let's assume, though, that someone on the team comes across it. Now what? The team debates whether to respond or not, which in turn gets tangled up in a discussion about what to say specifically in response, leading to another deliberation about who should respond and when to release the response. Even if those issues are eventually resolved, then another thorny issue crops up: who has final approval on the response? Does it have to be vetted by executives and the legal department? And so on.

Team A's strategy ensured that members paid attention to something important, thoughtfully executed a decision-making process, and responded to a potential threat in a timely manner. Team B's "strategy" accrued none of these benefits and probably made a bad situation worse. And it took a lot of organizational time and energy. Team A minimized the coordination costs because the strategy was already in place. The benefits of a good strategy emerge over time and over many different situations. In contrast, Team B's coordination costs occur every time a potential crisis happens, and the likely benefits are short lived. Worse, those coordination costs often yield only short-term benefits because every potential crisis is treated as a unique event. A strategy provides a workable framework for creating fluid and rapid coordination.

Likewise, systems, procedures, and technology need to work together to advance your strategic goals. The assess and respond strategy suggests that the team needs resources dedicated to detecting potential threats that might appear on almost any social media platform. Those resources might take the form of particular software technologies or tasking specific team members with monitoring designated social media channels.

Systems, protocols, and procedures need to sync with the strategy, as well. For instance, a protocol might designate that certain people in the organization are notified when particular types of posts or a threshold number of similar posts occur. In contrast, the B team must make those coordination decisions on the spot, often under pressure and surely in a haphazard ad hoc manner. This is clearly not the ideal situation for daily tasks and surely not for crises.

Third, a sound strategy provides a powerful message to educate employees in the organization. Social media managers grapple with the age-old question, "How do I get messages across to a wide array of people?"

Entire books have been devoted to answering this question, but one crucial part of the answer lies in selecting the proper level of abstraction. In other words, how much detail do you need to provide? Providing too many details inhibits learning, much less remembering. Providing too few invites confusion and chaotic implementation.

A good strategy positions the message at just the right level of detail or abstraction; it's the **Goldilocks zone**—not too hot, not too cold. Consider two strategies: Ali's "rope-a-dope" and a **tease and seize strategy**. The idea behind "tease and seize" is that you *tease* your target audience with several different kinds of posts, and then you monitor results and *seize* the opportunities implied by the feedback. Some might charge that these catchy phrases 1) leave out a lot of details and 2) don't really tell you what to do.

Guilty on charge one: these strategies *do* leave out a lot of details. That's by design. Instead, they focus attention on the essential elements necessary for success. You assume that the strategist's tactical competencies will fill in the unspoken details. Note that Ali's strategy was almost entirely defensive, and it was assumed in later rounds that he would

TABLE 3.1   Tease and Seize Content Strategy

Steps	Illustration
1. Think about the kind of posts that will work best	
2. Craft the posts	Winnow
3. Narrow down the choices	
4. Post them to various audiences	
5. Monitor results (e.g., winnow)	Exploit
6. Post follow-ups to ones that yielded the most positive results (e.g., exploit)	
7. Repeat	

unleash his natural boxing skills on a weakened opponent. Likewise, the tease and seize strategy says nothing about developing innovative posts; we assumed that ability. One team of strategy experts put it this way in the *Oxford Handbook of Strategy*:

> An organizing framework [strategy] can never be right, or wrong, only helpful or unhelpful. A good organizing framework [strategy] is minimalist—it is as simple as is consistent with illuminating the issues under discussion—and it is memorable.[1]

Innocent on charge two: good strategies *guide* but do *not dictate* actions. They do so by highlighting issues that may not be all that natural for the strategists. Ali certainly didn't defeat other opponents in the way he defeated George Foreman. The rapid experimentation and implementation mindset implied by the tease and seize strategy does not come easily to an engineer who takes a more methodical approach grounded by careful planning conventions. The social media strategist who liberally sprinkles the phrase "tease and seize" in her presentations to the staff and executives signals a need to shift the mindset when dealing with social media efforts.

In addition, "tease and seize" sends a tempering message to highly creative people. Creators of posts often become enamored with their own cleverness. That's both good and bad. The good: they will invest lots of creative energy into the task, which might yield a surprising outcome. The bad: the creators can become overly infatuated with their creations and don't know when to cut their losses and move on. The tease and seize strategy seeks to maximize creative potential while minimizing the downside risks. Plus, it helps everyone "save face" by submitting creative efforts to an impartial jury of followers.

Fourth, a sound strategy provides stability during tumultuous times and crises. People often do really stupid things when emotions run high or when events spin out of control. A good strategy stops you from doing something rash and reckless by providing stability. Why? Your strategy should take into account tumultuous situations you might encounter and help you think through the issues when your mind, not your emotions, rule.

Assume that somebody made an inflammatory comment about you or your organization. You're hot. You're mad. Rightly so! And you want to respond immediately with something even more caustic. That's the natural human response, but it's probably not a good strategy. How could a strategy help you avoid doing something that will escalate the situation that you'll regret later? Simple. Your administrative protocol, which emerges from your strategy, could dictate that at least one other person in the organization reviews the potential retort before posting.

A sound strategy narrows down operational choices into a manageable few during difficult times. It does not dictate precise choices because you want to cultivate flexibility while having a sense of direction. Douglas Feith, former undersecretary of defense for policy, summarized it best:

> The value of having a strategy is that you don't have to wake up every day and ask yourself basic questions about the best course of action. Well-chosen strategic ideas do not require frequent revision. They help fix your course and guide tactical choices, even as events unfold in unanticipated ways—as events always do.[2]

CONCLUSION

Gluttony and laziness yield short-term benefits but exact a heavy long-term toll on the spirit, mind, and body. The strategic benefits of eating properly and exercising emerge in the long term. Likewise, whimsical social media indulgences and indolent thinking may satisfy in the short term but inevitably extract heavy long-term costs. The strategic benefits of completing the requisite homework, thinking through the strategy, and building consensus emerge over time; fiascos are avoided and opportunities seized.

One way to ease the burdens of exercise programs or strategy planning is to make it fun. Think of strategic planning as a mental beach volleyball game that keeps your mind in shape as you indulge in a fun competition. Instead of smashing volleyballs, you are going to be bumping around compelling ideas. There is no better place to start this freewheeling contest than by surveying the social media cosmos. That is the subject of the next chapter.

KEY TERMS

Assess and respond
  strategy 29

Goldilocks zone 31
Tease and seize strategy 31

DEEP DIVES

These exercises are designed to enhance your understanding of the chapter's key ideas, principles, and approaches.

1. The chapter outlines four major benefits of developing social media strategies. Develop a 4 × 3 grid. In column one, list the four benefits. In column two, list a counterargument for each benefit. In column three, indicate your retort to the counterargument.

2. List and illustrate three signs that your social media strategy has moved out of the Goldilocks zone.

3. Draw diagrams of the a) tease and seize strategy and b) assess and respond strategy. Use your diagrams to point out three major advantages and three disadvantages of each strategy.

NOTES

1. J. Kay, P. McKiernan, and D. Faulkner, "The History of Strategy and Some Thoughts About the Future," in *The Oxford Handbook of Strategy: A Strategy Overview and Competitive Strategy*, vol. 1, edited by D. Faulkner and A. Campbell (Oxford: Oxford University Press, 2006), 27–52, 44.
2. D. Feith, *War and Decision: Inside the Pentagon at the Dawn of the War on Terrorism* (New York: Harper, 2008), 89.

CHAPTER 4

The Social Media Cosmos

"Content is king, but context is God. You can put out good content, but if it ignores the context [e.g., dynamics] of the platform on which it appears, it can still fall flat."

—Gary Vaynerchuk

Getting your mind around the social media universe can intimidate even the most intellectually curious and gifted. It should. The social media cosmos is large, complex, dynamic, and as ever changing as the universe surrounding earth. How can you do it?

When you are faced with a knotty, multifaceted issue, it is best to stand back and examine it from different angles. In this case, three different perspectives can enrich our understanding of the social media cosmos: functional, dynamics, and experiential (see Figure 4.1).

FUNCTIONAL PERSPECTIVE

Just like any other tool, social media performs unique functions. For example, the modern-day pencil is an exquisite tool designed to sketch images, draw new contraptions, and record (and erase) our thoughts.

FIGURE 4.1   Understanding the Social Media Cosmos

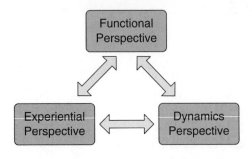

We can also use it to doodle our way through a boring meeting or stir up a can of paint.[1] So we always need to take into account both what our tools are *intended* to do and how they are *actually* used. Approaching social media in terms of the unique functions it performs, taking into account what its tools are intended to do and how they are actually used, means viewing social media from a **functional perspective**.

You can use charcoal to etch an image, but it is not particularly efficient or effective. The pencil replaced instruments ill designed for this purpose. In some sense, tools can be understood by looking back at their ancestors and identifying what features they add and subtract from the original. Consider the technical genealogy of the pencil. The word "pencil" that we use today emerged from the Middle English word "pencil," which literally means "artist's brush."

How would you explain the value of a pencil to an artist who never picked one up? Let's give it try: "A pencil is like a brush that maintains a constant flow of paint minus all the hassles of managing a color palette." To be sure, few artists would have thrown off their smocks and thrown away their brushes based on that pitch. But they would have understood what a pencil does and some would even have imagined all kinds of uses for this novel tool.

We can apply a similar formula for understanding social media platforms:

1. Find a familiar tool or activity that the social media is <u>most like.</u>

2. Identify a key feature that is <u>added</u> to the familiar tool or activity.

3. Pinpoint a feature that is <u>subtracted</u> from the familiar tool or activity.

For simplicity we can call this **ML+- thinking,** or "most like plus minus thinking." Using this kind of thinking you could describe Facebook, Twitter, and LinkedIn as follows:

Facebook is like sending postcards to a bunch of friends and family anytime you want minus the hassle of stamping and addressing each one.

Twitter is like preparing mini-personal press releases minus the media middleman plus the assurance you'll reach your target audience.

LinkedIn is like a giant job fair that never stops minus the hassles of dressing up.

Table 4.1 presents some ideas about how the ML+- thinking could be used to describe the unique functionality of the more popular social media.

Those familiar with the tools described in Table 4.1 might quibble with the descriptions. That's OK. The point is not to be persuasive or comprehensive but informative to a particular audience. Clearly, you can do a lot more than send postcards on Facebook. The table, however, does help the uninitiated understand the basic idea behind an ever-growing array of social media platforms. The larger point is that every social media manager will interact with people who have no understanding of these platforms. ML+- thinking supplies the conversational starting point.

Describing an automobile as a "horseless carriage" would certainly have helped someone in the 1800s understand the newfangled contraption. But it wouldn't be particularly helpful to someone shopping for a new car today. Likewise, the descriptions in Table 4.1 may or may not be helpful for two major reasons. First, *familiarity* shifts over time and with each audience. In other words, column one descriptions should change with the audience and as the platform evolves. If your audience already uses Facebook, then you might describe Snapchat as "Facebook without a permanent record." Second, the *importance* of features shifts over time. In other words, columns two and three can change over time.

TABLE 4.1 ML+- Platform Thinking

Platform	Most Like (ML)	Plus (+)	Minus (-)	"Sexy" Statement
Facebook	Meeting up for coffee Pictures on fridge Journal	Real-time updates Digital interaction Open access	Face-to-face interaction Tangibility Privacy	• Online reunion every day • Catching up without your pants on • Your personal diary for the world to see
Twitter	Newspaper headlines Social media fast food Conversation at convention	Real-time updates Unlimited menu Large audiences	Details Credibility Conversations	• Online corkboard • Modern newspaper without the details • Pageless diary
Pinterest	Scrapbook Mom's coupon book Bulletin board	Unlimited space Unlimited virtual filing drawers Customizing	Paper and albums Filing cabinets Physical presence	• Digital scrapbook with unlimited space • Real-time corkboard • A corkboard in your pocket
Snapchat	Texting Instant messaging Post-it note	Participation Experience sharing Visual updates	Historical record Archives Accountability	• Snapshots that fade away • Peeking around the corner • Self-destructing image messaging

This change can happen because the platform features morph over time. For example, viewership shifted on Facebook as it increased the size of pictures appearing in feeds. Likewise, users may start using platforms or platform features for purposes other than the creators originally intended. YouTube, for instance, looked more like a dating site when it first launched in 2005. Today, of course, for some people it represents a viable alternative to network television.[2]

Despite these caveats, ML+- thinking provides social media managers with a powerful descriptive tool to build buy-in for their strategy. Astronomers need more than a powerful telescope to fathom the cosmos. Likewise, social media managers need other strong tools to understand the social media universe. The next section provides another one.

DYNAMICS PERSPECTIVE

A number of factors influence the effectiveness level of particular social media. Table 4.2 presents an analysis of the factors that most influence the underlying dynamics of popular social media channels. The word "dynamics" was chosen with care. These are not attributes of the platforms. Rather, the ratings represent the underlying *usage patterns* that typically emerge from the platform's attributes. The word "dynamics" focuses attention on how users actually make use of the platform rather than on some inherent characteristic of the platform. Viewing social media through this **dynamics perspective** involves assessing the significance to users of factors such as credibility, geographic location of receivers, images, and much more. The ratings presented in Table 4.2 represent the opinions of hundreds of users and experts with whom we consulted over time. Listed below are the key factors we asked them to evaluate:

- **Time Sensitivity**: How important is the timing of the post?

- **Source Credibility**: How important is the credibility of the source making the post?

- **Receiver Location**: How important is the geographic location of the followers?

- **Category Choice**: How important is it to select the right category within the social media platform?

- **Word Selection**: How important are the words chosen in the post?

- **Image Choice**: How important are images in the post?

- **Information Utility**: How important is the utility of the information provided in the post? Is it something followers can use in their lives? Is it something they are interested in?

- **Emotional Impression**: How important is the emotional impression of the post? Does it make followers laugh? Cry?

- **Audience Size**: How important is audience size for the typical user?

These factors help us comprehend the unique dynamics of particular social media platforms. LinkedIn gurus will not necessarily be Facebook superstars. Why? As Table 4.2 suggests, success on LinkedIn requires offering posts with more informational rather than emotional value.[3] There are other ways to make use of Table 4.2:

First, you can determine how to enhance your social media effectiveness. For example, learning to master the rhythm of Twitter requires paying a lot of attention to your timing. If you tweet at the wrong time or too infrequently, then your message will be as lost as a single chirp in a bird sanctuary. In fact, the life span of most tweets is 18 minutes. If not read in that timeframe, it gets drowned out by a cacophony of other chirps.[4] If you are going to master Instagram or YouTube, you better have your optic nerves tuned to your audience's visual field.

Second, you can hone your strategic sensitivities. As we will see, crafting strategy requires a deep understanding of your target audiences' preferences. That includes knowing which of the factors in Table 4.2 might be most important to them. For example, if your target audience values mobility and is often on the go, then certain platforms such as Instagram should figure prominently in your strategy.

TABLE 4.2 Social Media Platform Dynamics

The chart below rates the importance of various social media factors on a 0 (not important) to 10 (very important) scale. These ratings emerged from discussions with over 100 experts and users.

	Time Sensitivity	Source Credibility	Receiver Location	Category Choice	Word Selection	Image Choice	Emotional Impression	Information Utility	Audience Size
Twitter	9	9	4	5	9	5	7	9	9
Facebook	8	9	5	5	8	8	9	8	8
Instagram	6	7	5	4	4	10	7	3	7
LinkedIn	5	9	3	7	8	4	2	10	7
Pinterest	3	5	2	10	3	9	5	8	7
YouTube	3	5	2	7	3	10	7	7	6
Snapchat	9	6	4	3	4	10	8	3	4

Third, you can better allocate your time and resources. For example, if your strategy involves YouTube videos, then you might want to invest some time into educating yourself on staging, script writing, and story-telling. Or, you could just hire a videographer. If you want to be influential in the Twitter world, then you better allocate resources to honing your pithy writing skills. For example, the editors of the premiere scientific journal, *Science*, asked young scientists to tell about their field in six words. Here are some gems from young scientists: Norman Alvares described his field as "Fire Science: Hot bodies, cool heads," while Carol Alpert described her field of science communication as "Science journalists seek acronym-free story."[5] In fact, researchers have determined that the shorter the tweet, the greater the likelihood it will be read.[6]

EXPERIENTIAL PERSPECTIVE

I've saved the most widely used perspective, the **experiential perspective**, for last. Why? Most people equate experience with competence. But that may not be the case. Almost anyone can name someone who has driven for many years but whom you wouldn't want to put behind your steering wheel. However, sometimes the *only* way to understand something deeply is to experience it directly. You can learn a lot about the moon by peering through a telescope, but the astronauts who set foot on the surface have a far more profound appreciation than the rest of us mere earthlings. In short, experience offers both perils and promise. Knowing how to manage both properly goes to the heart of thoughtful learning.

What's the peril of experience? After all, isn't "experience the best teacher"? Not necessarily. Here's why. First, some experiential mistakes can prove fatal to your career. Just ask former Congressman Anthony Weiner, an experienced tweeter. He mistakenly tweeted out an R-rated image that raised suspicions about his judgment and ultimately cost him his job. Unfortunately, that scenario plays out time and time again. Second, what "works" during one time period may not work particularly well in another. AM radio, for instance, once thrived by playing pop music. Now it survives on talk radio. Likewise, big box retailers such as Sears and Macy's prospered for decades but face enormous challenges today because of online retailers such as Amazon.com. Third, sometimes people learn the wrong lessons from their experiences. Overcoming self-deception is the first hurdle to learning the right lessons. For some people, this barrier proves as daunting as climbing a fire wall in a Tough Mudder race. Why? Protecting their ego and "saving face" are more important to the person than learning something useful. Consequently, these people spend far more time blaming others or doubling down on a bad idea than they do in actual learning. In short, when you engage in experiential learning you want to avoid fatal mistakes, complacent thinking, and learning the wrong lessons.

Social media mistakes are inevitable; learning the right lesson from your mistakes is not. Ditto for social media successes: if you post often enough, you'll have successes but this does not guarantee that you'll glean the right lessons from your victory.

The good news is that learning the right lessons is easy, if—and it's a big *if*—you develop the right mindset. What's the right mindset? It's cultivating your curiosity, thinking experimentally, and building the right habits (see Figure 4.2).

CULTIVATING CURIOSITY

Curious people seek out any and all opportunities to learn. This sensibility proves particularly helpful when learning the mechanics of specific social media platforms. It takes a while to get comfortable with all the options and functions of each tool. For example, many LinkedIn users overlook the key words or gallery functions, which can help them grow their personal brand.[7] How could they find out about it? They could read *LinkedIn for Dummies*. They could read blogs about options. They could ask a friend who is a LinkedIn guru. All these strategies work. Or they might just stumble across a LinkedIn function when they accidentally click on a button. That works, too.

THINKING EXPERIMENTALLY

Curiosity energizes the experimental attitude. Experiments provide a more systematic learning experience, and they help you learn the right lessons. Think of each post and the resulting feedback as an experiment. Did you get the results you wanted? What surprises occurred? What did you learn to do and not to do? You don't need a multimillion

FIGURE 4.2 Generators of Valuable Experiences

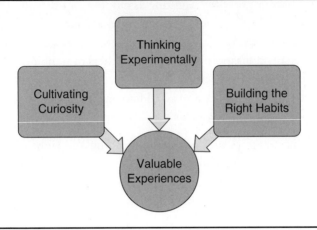

dollar telescope to do these experiments. All you need is a creative spirit and a willingness to contemplate the feedback.

The bottom line is that social media experts operate with this mantra in mind: "I'm curious, and I love experimenting with new tools, ideas, and approaches. I'm going to have some hits and misses. But I vow to learn from both."

BUILDING THE RIGHT HABITS

Anybody can make a vow, like a marriage vow, but your habits are what determine if you'll live happily ever after or end up in divorce court. Good habits have three basic characteristics: 1) they are simple, 2) they can be frequently used, and 3) they yield short- and long-term benefits. Here's a habit that fits the bill: Brush your teeth (simple) everyday (frequent) and you'll have healthy oral hygiene for years to come (beneficial).

What are some good social media habits to honor your social media vow? It's not quite as straightforward as teeth brushing but consider the following:[8]

1. Do a morning scroll of your feeds, lists, and streams.

2. Respond to direct interactions (comments, replays, messages, mentions, etc.).

3. Routinely check what your competition is doing.

4. Search for posts containing hashtags and keywords associated with your organization.

5. Curate content to share.

6. Check your key analytic indicators.

7. Tweak a tactic and evaluate.

8. Monitor news about social media.

9. Share team successes or wins.

10. Record your successes, mistakes, and new opportunities.

The last habit may well be the most important because it cultivates the right kind of learning in a dynamic environment.

Conclusion

The social media cosmos incrementally evolves every day and occasionally explodes with supernova-like force. So what? That means if you want to become a master of the social media universe, you'll need to adjust your understanding of the functions of various social media constantly, even as you seek a deeper knowledge of their underlying dynamics. Most important, you'll need to cultivate the right mindset to learn from your social media experiences. All too often, people assume that experience equates with competence. Don't fall into that trap. Instead, embrace and enjoy the dynamism of the ever-evolving social media cosmos.

Key Terms

Dynamics perspective 39
Experiential perspective 42

Functional perspective 36
ML+- thinking 37

Deep Dives

These exercises are designed to enhance your understanding of the chapter's key ideas, principles, and approaches.

1. Refer to Table 4.2.

   a. Circle three ratings that you believe are inaccurate and three other ratings that you believe are accurate.

   b. Provide justification for your judgments.

2. Using ML+- thinking, create an explanation of a social media platform that is not widely used for a) an audience that has limited social media experience and b) an audience with a lot of social media experience. Provide your rationale.

3. Assume you are limited to only three factors from Table 4.2 to make strategic decisions about social media channels (e.g., platforms). Which three would you pick? Assume you are limited to only three factors from Table 4.2 to make strategic decisions about social media content. Which three would you pick? Provide your rationale and how you went about making the decision.

NOTES

1. H. Petroski, *The Pencil: A History of Design and Circumstance* (New York: Alfred A. Knopf, 1992).
2. Check out the WayBack Machine to see how these sites have changed. See https://archive.org/web/. Thanks to Elizabeth Hintz for this tip.
3. Students of Aristotle might put it this way: On LinkedIn, logos trumps pathos, while on Facebook pathos trumps logos.
4. P. Bray, "When is My Tweets Prime of Life?" *YouMoz* [blog], November 12, 2012, https://moz.com/blog/when-is-my-tweets-prime-of-life. Accessed January 28, 2017.
5. J. Sills, "Science in Brief," *Science*, July 1, 2016, 22–24.
6. A. Malhotra, C. Malhotra, and A. See, "How to Create Brand Engagement on Facebook," *MIT Sloan Management Review*, Winter 2013, 18–20.
7. See A. Brinkman, "11 Incredibly Useful LinkedIn Features You Might Not Be Using," *HubSpot* [blog], April 21, 2014, http://blog.hubspot.com/insiders/linkedin-features. Accessed July 17, 2016.
8. Thanks to Jena Richter and Adam Halfman for sharing many of these ideas.

PART II

Crafting
Your Strategy

This section highlights how to craft your strategy (see the figure entitled "Crafting Your Social Media Strategy"). The model in this figure outlines the seven steps, corresponding to the seven chapters in this section, necessary to form an effective social media strategy and plan.

You start by understanding your competitive environment (Chapter 5). This means taking a deep look *internally* at your organization and *externally* at the competitive environment. Excelling at this stage helps you determine viable options at later stages. Often when we find problems in an organization's social media strategy or complaints from executives about the return on the investment, we can trace it back to some inadequacies at this stage. If you don't understand the climate and soil where you are planting social media strategy, then many of your best ideas will simply wither on the organizational vine due to lack of both support and proper nurturing.

Steps two through six (chapters 6–10) focus on coordinates, channels, content, connections, and corrections. These are the 5 Cs of social media strategy, representing the five core elements of your strategy. The coordinates (Chapter 6) represent a special kind of strategic goal and are influenced by the research you've done in step one. The channels embody the social media platforms and other communication vehicles (e.g., the website) you are selecting to achieve your strategic goals (Chapter 7). The content element refers to the type of images, ideas, and information that you'll post, tweet, or share on your social media platforms (Chapter 8). The connections element focuses on how your platforms are linked to each other and other organizational processes (Chapter 9). The correction element of your strategy highlights how you plan to manage errors and missed opportunities (Chapter 10).

The final step (Chapter 11) may well be the most tricky and challenging. Why? It involves syncing up the 5 Cs into a mutually reinforcing and sustainable structure. That means that superior social media strategists decide to abandon some great ideas because the structural elements won't support them. It's like creating a great design for an additional room in your house but then abandoning the plan because the foundation won't support it. We do not want that to happen! So, we examine how to double-check and sync all your strategic thinking. Let's dive in!

Crafting Your Social Media Strategy

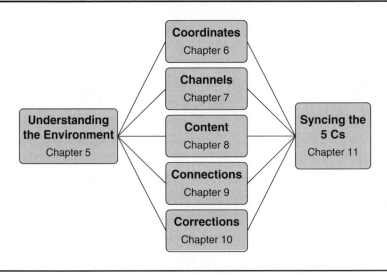

CHAPTER 5

Understanding the Competitive Environment

"In summary, the idea is to try to give all *of the information to help others to judge the value of your contribution; not just the information that leads to judgment in one particular direction or another."*

—Richard P. Feynman

Warning: Most people don't read warning labels, particularly when they are familiar with the issue. But please read this one: crafting your social media strategy is far more fluid and organic than what is implied by the steps we will discuss. Strategic planners often get trapped in the presumed linearity of their process. We don't want to get caught in that snare, which robs the process of its creativity, dynamism, and fun.

Effectively assessing the competitive environment requires exceptional research skills, analytical abilities, and a temperament comfortable with uncertainty. The approach outlined below is designed to be fact based and to ground your professional judgments thoughtfully. Having this outline allows you to shift your judgments deliberately but quickly when the facts change. The process has four essential stages that ideally should be followed in order:

Facts—Collect relevant *facts*

Anchors—Isolate the essential *analytical anchors* implied by the facts

Judgments—Make *judgments* based on the analytical anchors

Validation—*Validate* your judgments

The **FAJV** acronym reminds all the participants in the process of how important it is to let the facts drive judgments rather than the other way around. It's the antidote to a potent thinking virus—the **confirmation bias**—that inflicts every human being. This bias can be defined as a tendency to seek out evidence to support preexisting opinions or ideas—rather than allowing our judgments to emerge from the facts.

STAGE 1: FACTS— COLLECT RELEVANT FACTS

Collecting *relevant* facts is not like collecting seashells from the beach. Why? Some of the most significant shells lie hidden offshore while others reside on distant beaches. Complicating your fact hunting adventure is the challenge of determining the relevancy of the facts you've collected. What may seem insignificant at one point in time may turn out to be a treasure trove of relevancy at another. You just don't know. That's why you collect as many facts as possible and do the relevancy sifting later.

What beaches should you search? Start with these three: 1) your own organization, 2) your competitors, and 3) the social media cosmos. As any treasure hunter knows, the search could go on forever. So you need to set a limit: say 100 facts for each beach. What kinds of treasures should your team seek? See Table 5.1 as a starting point for some questions to answer. Learning about the business goals, for example, is essential for crafting the strategy elements discussed in the following chapters. Ditto for questions about your competitors' social media presence.

TABLE 5.1 What Types of Facts Should You Seek?

Category	Questions
Your Organization	• What are your top business goals? • What external agencies exert significant influence on your organization? • Who are your organizational leaders? What is their social media presence? • What are the major historical milestones for your organization? • What is the mission of your organization? What are its core values?
Your Competitors	• Who are your major competitors? • How do your competitors compete against your organization (e.g., price, quality, convenience)? • What social media platforms do your competitors use? • What channels other than social media do your competitors typically use? • What kinds of content do your competitors typically post? • Who are your competitors' organizational leaders? • How does your organization stack up against the competition on key business and social media metrics?
Social Media Cosmos	• What new social media platforms have been launched in the last 12 months? • What are the primary social media platforms used in your industry? • What changes have the major social media platform providers instituted in the last 12 months? • What have been the issues most frequently discussed by social media experts in the last 12 months?

(Continued)

TABLE 5.1   (Continued)

Category	Questions
Stakeholders	• Who are your stakeholders (e.g., customers, shareholders, suppliers, government agencies)? • What are the typical social media usage patterns of your stakeholders? • What are the major concerns of your stakeholders? • For what purposes would your stakeholders never use social media? • When do your stakeholders most typically use social media platforms? • Where do your stakeholders make use of social media platforms (e.g., in the office, at home, off-site)? • Why do your stakeholders make use of social media?

All facts are not created equal. Some, such as your business goals, you can assert with 99.9 percent confidence. Others, such as your competitors' posting strategy, may be more speculative. That's OK as long as you indicate your level of confidence in the various facts you've collected. The other factual twist you'll encounter involves their level of relevancy. Clearly, some facts, such as your level of available resources, are significant. Others may not be, at least initially.

Table 5.2 provides a handy tool to capture these factual dynamics. The tool, particularly when used by a team of professionals, provides a starting point for an in-depth strategic discussion. Why? It often encourages useful disagreements about the credibility and utility of certain facts, which can prompt intriguing insights. Finally, it encourages strategic thinking because it underscores the fluid nature of anything we call a "fact." After all, business goals change all the time and what we can assert with nearly 100 percent confidence today may change in a competitive blink of the eye.

TABLE 5.2 Judging the Credibility and Utility of Your Facts

Facts	Credibility H, M, L	Utility H, M, L
Category 1		
Category 2		
Category 3		

NOTE: H = high, M = medium, L = low

STAGE 2: ANCHORS—ISOLATE THE ESSENTIAL ANALYTICAL ANCHORS IMPLIED BY THE FACTS

Analytical anchors represent descriptive convergence points linking many facts together. They are objective statements about fundamentally important patterns about the competitive environment. In other words, these are the key insights you've extracted from the facts collected in the first stage, discussed previously. Analytical anchors are neither good nor bad; they are by design descriptive not evaluative. They do, however, represent a point of view about what is deemed to be important.

Isolating the key analytical anchors of the competitive environment often proves tricky, but the following steps can be useful: First, review all of the "100 facts" gathered about the organization, the firm's competitors, and the social media cosmos. Discuss the facts in each category by clarifying odd statements and noting surprises. Second, look for facts that appear to coalesce into a pattern or appear related to a similar theme. These will be your analytical anchors. Drawing diagrams connecting the facts or isolating pods of numbered facts often proves extremely helpful; the more visual you make this enumeration the better. Third, decide on an appropriate descriptive statement or label to put on the key insight pods. Here are some examples in each of the categories:

- We have a small but loyal group of social media followers.

- Competitor X frequently touts low-cost products on its website.

- Our target customers are more likely to use Twitter than Facebook.

Remember, you are looking for a few key analytically based anchors that can be used to make actionable insights in the next step. Avoid making evaluations such as this: "We are *better* than our competitors at promoting events." Instead, be descriptive, by stating something such as, "We post about *more* promotional events than our competitors do." Describing rather than evaluating inoculates you against stealthy cognitive biases that often silently undermine clear thinking. It also gives you detail about why or in what way your promotional efforts are effective. (The word "better" is a tip-off to an evaluation while the word "more" signals a descriptive statement.)

Disconnecting the anchors from evaluative critiques proves extraordinarily useful for a number of reasons. First, this process inhibits you from rushing to judgment. Anything that slows down our natural tendency to make lightning quick assessments enhances the probability that we will think strategically about the issue. That's why juries hear all the facts of the case before rendering a verdict. Second, the process helps you discern the upside and downside of any situation. Let's assume your competitor has a more established social media presence than you do. This fact is neither good nor bad. It is just a key observation or analytical anchor about the environment. It is a reality you will have to deal with. It creates some challenges but also some unique opportunities. Finally, separating the analytical anchors from your evaluative judgments cultivates fact-based discussions. If we can agree on some of the basic observations about the situation, then it should enhance the odds of moving forward together on other strategic tasks. The power of this kind of thinking is revealed in the following story.

In a relatively obscure 1965 journal, *Electronics*, Gordon Moore articulated the kind of platinum-level insight we seek at this stage. Today, it has become almost prosaic to make mention of the famous Moore's Law that accurately prognosticated the "doubling of (electronic) circuit complexity every year or so."[1] At the time, however, it was a brilliant insight about the state of the electronics industry, an insight that would turn out to have profound consequences for every person on the planet. As his biographers noted, "Moore's Law is the product of human imagination. The phrase Moore's Law is known around the world as a technical observation, the one that describes the development of digital electronics and computing. It is that, but it is also far more. It is an astonishing story of imagination, zeal, and world revolution."[2] This one insight amalgamates many key facts about the competitive environment, including manufacturing costs, consumer demand, and technical know-how. This key insight, among others, led eventually to the formation of a legendary Silicon Valley company that Moore help found and led for many years. Of course, a critical insight alone—even one as profound as Moore's Law—does not guarantee you'll create and grow into a company like Intel. This kind of success also requires an ability to see the implications of your insights. That is the issue addressed in the next stage.

STAGE 3: JUDGMENTS—MAKE JUDGMENTS BASED ON THE ANALYTICAL ANCHORS

Stronger is better than weaker, right? More is better than less, right? Many people would agree with both statements. That would be a mistake. First, consider adhesives. Is stronger really better than weaker? If you were trying to repair a water hose, you would want a strong adhesive that would withstand corrosive elements. But if you wanted a visual reminder of an important passage in your favorite social media book, you'd want a weak adhesive, such as a Post-it® note. Likewise, are more choices always better than fewer? Not necessarily. In fact, researchers coined the phrase "paradox of choice" to indicate that having too many choices often leads to the paralysis of indecision. In other words, the number of choices becomes so overwhelming that you just can't make a choice.[3] People looking to make a major purchase often run headlong into this paradox.

Traditionally, strategic planners often work with teams to identify strengths, weaknesses, opportunities, and threats (e.g., a **SWOT** analysis). This process can be revealing but also misleading if not tempered with the perspective offered in the fact-gathering and anchor-seeking stages already described. For example, is a strong adhesive a strength or weakness? It's both. It's a strength for your garden hose but a weakness for your favorite social media book. Likewise, are more choices in the big-box store an opportunity or threat? They're both. They're an opportunity for shoppers to select the best product for their circumstances, but also a threat if they feel intimated to even walk into the store.

Strong-weak and more-less conundrums illustrate an essential feature of the strategist's mindset. Namely, thinking strategically is not some kind of mechanical exercise about designating strengths, weaknesses, opportunities, and threats. Depending on how you look at it, an analytical anchor of the competitive situation might turn out to be all of the above—a strength, a weakness, an opportunity, as well as a threat.

Table 5.3 provides a tool to help you abide by this principle. In column one, you record the analytical anchors you've previously identified. In the other columns, you identify how each anchor could translate into a strength, weakness, opportunity, or threat for your organization and your social media team. Consider, for example, a university's goal to expand outreach to alumni and prospective students:

Analytical anchor: The vast majority (over 90 percent) of our social media followers are students who live on campus

Strength: Students living on campus have a tightly knit social media network that appears to be meeting their needs (we can reasonably infer this from facts gathered about social media usage patterns)

Weakness: Students living on campus have different social media preferences than the community at large, student commuters, and government officials

TABLE 5.3 Anchor-Based SWOT				

Analytical Anchors	Strengths	Weaknesses	Opportunities	Threats

Opportunity: Students residing on campus could be potential advocates in expanding the network

Threat: Campus-based content might be misunderstood or even inflammatory to outsiders

This is exactly the kind of "it cuts both ways" thinking that will eventually lead to a superior social media strategy.

We need to add one more tweak to this step. After a strategist ascertains the SWOTs for each anchor, it can be useful to highlight the predominant evaluation exposed by the critique. Which anchors are primarily strengths? Weaknesses? Opportunities? Threats? Simply circling the proper column or columns can do the trick. If I'm a researcher tasked with developing a strong adhesive but I inadvertently create a weak one, then I'd circle the weakness cell in Table 5.3. Then the central strategic question would be this: "How do we transform this *weakness* into an *opportunity*?" That's almost exactly what happened at 3M when they developed Post-it® notes.

In the university example described earlier, your team might make the counterintuitive determination that this analytical anchor is primarily a weakness or a threat. This insight, in turn, might suggest a strategic decision to establish a distinct social media presence for the community and another for prospective students.

STAGE 4: VALIDATION—VALIDATE YOUR JUDGMENTS

Facts, anchors, and judgments are laden with uncertainties. You'll never get rid of all the uncertainties but you can increase your confidence by asking the right questions and validating your conclusions.

Your validation tests can range from the informal to the more rigorous (see Figure 5.1). Verifying a fact with a quick Google search, checking out an insight with a trusted colleague, or quizzing a group of friends about your critique would be considered more informal tests. Conducting focus groups, administering surveys, and setting up an experimental study provide more rigorous forms of testing. Any of these approaches might work for your social media team.

Usually organizations do not have the inclination or resources to devote to the more formal techniques. In the social media cosmos, that's usually a good decision because by the time the results of a formal study become available, some new social media asteroid blazes on the horizon. In short, most formal social media studies barely have a half-life longer than a Snapchat photo.

Therefore, most social media managers discover that informal testing techniques, when properly used, usually provide the most utility and value. Responsible use of informal testing helps you resist the lure of the confirmation bias. Humans fool themselves all the time. As noted, one of the primary ways we do so is by seeking confirming rather than conflicting information. Such practices protect our egos and fuel our hopes at the expense of us acquiring accurate information and achieving our goals. Resisting this natural urge can be relatively easy:

> **Novice's natural tendency**: I'll just ask a colleague, "Don't you think I'm right about X, Y, or Z?"
>
> **Expert's thoughtful alternative**: I'll ask, "How might the X, Y, or Z conclusion be wrong?"
>
> **Novice's natural tendency**: I'll look for only the facts that support my insight.
>
> **Expert's thoughtful alternative**: I'll search for all the facts related to the insight.

FIGURE 5.1   Validation Options

Call a Friend Google Search Interviews Focus Groups Surveys Experiments

⟵───⟶

Informal   **Rigorous**

> **Novice's natural tendency**: My social media expert says this is what we should do.
>
> **Expert's thoughtful alternative**: I'll ask, "What do other professionals advise?"

Note the tendency of the novice's informal tests to personalize and seek supportive commentary. The expert's approach de-personalizes the testing process and seeks out contradictory information. In short, the novice's approach pushes the confirmation bias button; the expert seeks to disconnect it.

Using informal testing techniques might not honor traditional social scientific standards, but the advantage is that it will speed up the process. Sometimes, it makes sense to slow down and use more formal techniques for particular facts, insights, or critiques, especially ones that are either doubtful or pivotal to your emerging social media strategy. In the doubtful category you might question the legitimacy of an insight about a competitor's social media message mix. A quick study might confirm your team's impression. In the pivotal category, you might test a perceived strength about your customer service team's responsiveness to social media complaints.

Let's assume you've completed all the stages already outlined and perhaps even iterated through the process several times. Now it's time to summarize those insights into a short document that will serve as a staging point for selecting your coordinates, channels, content, connections, and correction processes (i.e., the 5 Cs).

Some words of caution about this stage: on the surface, this final document may appear rather prosaic and uninspiring to those not involved in its creation. This simple appearance is, of course, a mirage. The exact opposite reflects the reality. In fact, this document synthesizes all the hard work poured into the FAJV stages. That's why it often makes sense to note the key facts used to reach each major insight. This step may be necessary to garner support from those not involved in the process.

One final note: It's OK to backtrack on the steps described in this chapter because significant issues can emerge with the twitch of your cursor. A strategic insight might occur in the deep recesses of your mind during your REM cycle as you're sleeping, tucked away in your cozy bed. Bottom line: move forward but don't be afraid to backtrack and reexamine. In retrospect, getting to the staging point for selecting your 5 Cs may appear far more linear than it really was. Or at least, you can tell people that.

Conclusion

A former, highly admired U.S. senator, Patrick Moynihan, once quipped, "You're entitled to your own opinion. You're not entitled to your own facts."[4] As he knew all too well from debates in the U.S. Senate, opinions drove fact finding rather than the other way around all too often. That's a recipe for strategic dysfunction. In contrast, the FAJV process outlined in the chapter provides most of the ingredients for cooking up a great social media strategy.

Key Terms

Analytical anchors 53

Confirmation bias 50

FAJV 50

SWOT 56

Deep Dives

These exercises are designed to enhance your understanding of the chapter's key ideas, principles, and approaches.

1. Rank order the FAJV elements, from most difficult to do to least difficult to do. Provide at least three arguments for your ranking. Suggest three ways to overcome the challenges you will face when tackling the most difficult item on your list.

2. Develop three arguments for the value of adding "analytical anchors" to the traditional SWOT analysis.

3. Create a two-column chart. Label column one, "Informal" and column two "Rigorous." In column one, provide three typical situations for which it makes the most sense to use more informal validation methods. In column two, provide three typical situations for which it makes the most sense to use more formal validation methods. Provide a justification for the selections in your chart. (Hint: see Figure 5.1 for a list of validation options.)

NOTES

1. A. Thackray, D. Brock, and R. Jones, *Moore's Law: The Life of Gordon Moore, Silicon Valley's Quiet Revolutionary* (New York: Basic Books, 2015), 261.
2. Thackray, *Moore's Law*, xix.
3. B. Schwartz, *The Paradox of Choice: Why More is Less* (New York: HarperCollins, 2009).
4. E. Hume, *Tabloids, Talk Radio, and the Future of News: Technology's Impact on Journalism* (Washington, DC: The Annenberg Washington Program in Communications Policy Studies of Northwestern University, 1995). Paper available at http://ellenhume.com/wp-content/uploads/2016/12/tabloids_printable.pdf. This quotation has also been attributed to Bernard M. Baruch and James R. Schlesinger.

CHAPTER 6

Coordinates

*"To think strategically is difficult and unnatural. You may imagine
you are being strategic, but in all likelihood you are merely being
tactical. To have the power that only strategy can bring, you must
be able to elevate yourself above the battlefield, to focus on your
long-term objectives, to craft an entire campaign, to get out of the
reactive mode that so many battles in life lock you into. Keeping
your overall goals in mind, it becomes much easier to decide when
to fight and when to walk away. That makes the tactical decisions
of daily life much simpler and more rational. Tactical people are
heavy and stuck in the ground; strategists are light on their feet
and can see far and wide."*

—Robert Greene

We often forget to marvel at everyday events that require amazing
feats of ingenuity, special skill, and sheer courage. Consider the
thousands of successful airplane landings executed every minute across
the globe. Sure it is commonplace, but that should not diminish our
awe at the imaginative powers of airplane designers, the engineering
skills of runway builders, and the bravery of the pilots to hurl thousands
of tangled pounds of steel, aluminum, wires, computers, and passengers
into thin air. It's a daily marvel we rarely find awe inspiring. That's
unfortunate but perhaps understandable, as the extraordinary becomes
commonplace with each successful flight.

A superior social media strategy is infused with similar qualities. The special efforts exerted in crafting it are soon forgotten as daily successes accumulate. In this chapter, we take a hard look at the underlying factors that can lead to this kind of success story.

What does it take to land a plane successfully? The air speed has to be right. The pitch of the plane has to be just perfect. To get the speed right and the pitch perfect, the pilot must know with precision the exact coordinates of the runway—longitude, latitude, and altitude. If the pilot doesn't get every one of the coordinates correct, then the plane crashes.

Likewise, if the social media strategist fails to get all the coordinates correct, then the entire enterprise is put in jeopardy. Strategic planners often focus attention on goals. Fair enough. The pilot's longitude goal is vitally important but the plane still crashes if he or she misses on the latitude and altitude. That's why I prefer to use the term *coordinates* because it emphasizes the imperative of achieving success in multiple dimensions.

Characteristics of Superior Coordinates

Geometry teachers love talking about coordinates, even if they find them challenging to explain. In simple terms, a *coordinate* defines a position or point in space. A triangle has three coordinates or points of connection. Social media strategists should, at a minimum, think in terms of triangles. That is, they should select three interconnected and mutually reinforcing goals. Selecting and reaching one goal will not allow you to dominate the social media space. Three strongly linked goals help you define and dominate the space. Your social media triangle of goals creates order and provides an orienting structure in an otherwise bewildering galaxy of possibilities and ambiguity. Superior coordinates have three features.

First, superior coordinates represent tough, "big-picture" choices about what to do and what not to do. You can do almost anything in the social media world, but you can't do everything. Why? Resources are limited. That means we must make wise choices about what to do and what *not* to do. In fact, the late Steve Jobs of Apple once said, "I'm as proud of what we don't do as I am of what we do."[1] Superior social media strategists, like visionary tech pioneers, select the coordinates engendering the most benefits while limiting the downside. They don't try to do everything. The "difficult and unnatural" part of strategy, referred to in the introductory quotation, surfaces during discussion of the coordinates because it often means setting aside some *worthy* goals in favor of *coordinated* goals. It means not pursuing some enticing goals for something even more valuable that leverages your strengths and provides more long-term benefits.

Second, superior coordinates enrich one another. Disconnected points do not form a triangle. Likewise unconnected social media goals do not form a wedge against the competitive forces. Instead, great strategic goals strengthen one another. Consider these three goals:

- Build a more interactive website that highlights our social media presence.

- Make better use of social media platforms to draw attention to our website.

- Partner with key organizational members to garner support and content ideas for our digital strategy.

This simple example shows how the goals or coordinates augment one another by intertwining elements of one goal into another.

Third, superior coordinates robustly define the operating space. Novice social media managers often fall into the trap of defining their job by the social media platforms they oversee. To be sure, managing social media platforms represents one dimension of their job, but that's an overly narrow view of their operating space. This is like airline pilots who think only in terms of altitude. They will certainly crash if they don't consider longitude and latitude. Robustly defining the operating space means establishing goals for your content decisions, channel selections, connection choices, and correction mechanisms, as well. And there is one more important dimension, organizational goals, discussed in the next section.

PRINCIPLES FOR
FORMULATING COORDINATES

Transforming typical goal statements into coordinates requires a special mindset. Conventionally, people have been taught to formulate SMART goals (i.e., specific, measurable, actionable, realistic, and time bound). That's fine. But, establishing coordinates requires a higher level of thinking, one that has been honed by military strategists and thinkers. In fact, the concept of strategic thinking emerged from military campaigns dating back to the dawn of civilization. Generals needed a way to deploy limited resources and make lightning quick decisions while staying above the fray of the bloody day-to-day business of war. Strategic ideas emerged from that necessity. Over time, those ideas have been honed, debated, and applied to many other ventures, such as business and even our everyday lives. With that rich history in mind, consider the following three important classic strategic notions.

First, respect the "unequal dialogue" in your organization. Senior military officers in the United States and Europe abide by the doctrine of the **"unequal dialogue"** when interfacing with civilian leaders. Professor Eliot Cohen, a former strategy expert for the U.S. military, explains how the conversation was both a dialogue and unequal: "a dialogue, in that both sides [military and civilian leaders] expressed their views bluntly, indeed, sometimes offensively, and not once but repeatedly—and unequal, in that the final authority of the civilian leader was unambiguous and unquestioned."[2]

Ideally social media managers would have similar debates with their own organizational leaders. Sadly, that may not happen because many leaders fail to grasp the significance of social media in achieving their organizational goals. So it may be a while before we see leaders in charge of social media listed as members of most organizations' senior leadership teams. One hopeful sign, though: some more progressive companies have a chief digital officer (CDO) or a chief digital information officer (CDIO).

That said, social media managers could promote this level of influence by honoring the fundamental sentiment behind the "unequal dialogue." This means recognizing that the organization's goals should guide the social media goals. If your business is seeking to drive down costs, then you had better develop social media goals that do just that. If your organization wants to grow its customer or donor base, then you had better find strategic ways for using social media to help achieve this goal. In short, if you can't demonstrate a strong and tight link between your organization's goals and your social media goals, then you don't deserve to be included in any dialogue with senior leaders, equal or unequal.

Second, "don't fight the last war." This is one of the great strategic maxims, frequently invoked but often ignored. It is far easier to envision lessons learned from previous wars than it is to imagine the lessons needed for the future. The first is based on relative certainties, the latter on uncertainties. That's why the military routinely falls into the easy and understandable habit of designing weapon systems to deal with known and conventional threats. That's why the 9/11 commission reviewing the attack cited "lack of imagination" as one of the major reasons for the strategic failure to anticipate such an event. The commission noted that, "Imagination is not a gift usually associated with bureaucracies. . . . It is therefore crucial to find a way of routinizing, even bureaucratizing, the exercise of imagination."[3]

Avoiding the "last war" mindset in the social media cosmos requires a nimble mind attentive to the fluid dynamics of current trends as well as the more stable elements of the industry. These sensibilities are as rare as they are valuable. Consider how many organizations originally responded to social media. They posted nearly the identical content they had been using for years in their flyers, direct-mail pieces, and TV advertisements. This "cut and paste" strategy was simple and easy. And it was a strategy for the "last war" and soon proved feeble and inadequate.

Third, know when to play offense, defense, and use special teams. Offensive campaigns seek competitive gains while defensive measures focus on holding existing ground. Military leaders know that mounting an effective offensive campaign generally requires more resources than maintaining a defensive one. That's why successful military commanders avoid attacking everywhere all at once. The often invoked "pick and choose your battles" maxim neatly sums up the sentiment. Unfortunately, it does not sum up the pressures on most social media managers. The reason? Organizational leaders often tell social media managers what battles to fight. One common request is to be robustly present on *all* social media platforms while serving all the diverse stakeholders' needs. Social media managers, like generals, often do not have the resources to do all that is asked of them.

Knowing when to play offense, defense, and use special teams provides a way out of this conundrum. Consider the pressures to have a presence on all social media platforms (i.e., all channels). A thoughtful social media manager selects the platforms that are most likely to be used by the firm's target audiences and that best suit its core messages.

Offensive campaigns work in tandem with defensive ones. On some platforms, it's best to invest lots of resources and lean forward. On others, it's best to play defense by proactively securing relevant domain names, monitoring posts, and linking to more robust platforms. Occasionally, you must mount a special teams' effort designed to deal with a peculiar problem or unexpected challenge. This campaign might be focused on a platform previously relegated to the sideline or on resolving a content issue presenting a potential threat to your organization.

These three principles—respecting the unequal dialogue, being imaginative about future challenges, and matching resources and strategies to particular aims—are essential for beginning to formulate coordinates. However, translating these principles into coordinated goals requires a discussion protocol that maximizes and reconciles the inherent tensions between analysis and imagination. The next section outlines such a process.

A DISCUSSION PROTOCOL FOR CRAFTING COORDINATES

Coordinates are essentially synchronized macro-level goals. Establishing useful coordinates tends to be rather organic and a bit messy. That's OK. Good strategic discussions are rarely linear, but they need to move forward. They tend to loop back as your thinking clarifies and new issues emerge. A simple structure facilitates robust but forward-thinking discussion.

There are many possible protocols that can infuse the discussion with just the right amount of structure and robustness. The distinguishing feature is that they start out with relatively general and disconnected insights but conclude with more specific and coordinated goals. In essence, it is a winnowing process that seeks to cull out the best strategic insights. The quality and utility of your final set of coordinates hinges on the quality of the competitive analysis, and your ability to glean the right lessons from it and imagine a path forward. Try some variant of the following protocol to achieve these challenging standards.

First, review your competitive analysis and seek out hidden connections. Your competitive analysis contains hints about possible sources of strategic advantage. Some are readily apparent; others are not. Think of yourself as a quarterback reviewing the game films of your team's next opponent, seeking out critical insights of opportunities to exploit and dangers to be avoided. Just imagine the insights that could be gleaned from the "game films" of your social media campaign matched up against those of a competitor.

A single insight gleaned from the competitive analysis can be helpful, but connecting multiple insights into **insight pods** totally tilts the playing field in your direction. A simple way to move the discussion in that direction is to group together pods of insights on a whiteboard. Then challenge the group to draw lines and arrows between the pods. If this sounds a little like diagramming a football play, you are right because you are literally trying to envision the hidden connections. Drawing your insights gives you a better picture of what you need to do and what you need to avoid.

Second, construct a "brain-prodding" chart like the one in Table 6.1. This chart equips you with a tool to honor the unequal dialogue principle. Listing the business goals in column one guides your creative brainstorming in column two. Table 6.1 provides some possible starting points, but it is not meant to be comprehensive.

Your competitive analysis naturally leads to speculation about possible strategic goals to pursue. Write down possible communication goals to pursue. No need to be linear or logical at this point. Imagination and audacity trump reasonableness and consistency.

Third, discover clusters of goals or pods of insights. If you completed step two successfully, then you have assembled an unruly hodgepodge list of goals with various levels of specificity pointing in several different directions. It should be like a child's toy chest—a tangled joyful mess

TABLE 6.1   Brainstorming Business and Communication Goals

Business Goals	Possible Communication Goals
Improve Sales of Product or Service	• Drive people to website • Respond to concerns • Encourage positive reviews • Create teasers for new offerings • Provide demonstrations • Share company experts with public • Provide prepackaged content to opinion leaders • Launch a "share-with-a-friend" program • Ask for user-generated content • Provide incentives
Decrease Costs	• Create cost-cutting idea contest • Highlight cost-saving stories • Demonstrate benefits of cost savings • Shift employee recruitment to online platforms • Conduct consumer research with online platforms
Increase Event Attendance	• Promote activities • Provide reminders • Give prompt feedback • Answer questions • Share event content • Provide exclusive benefits • Create a contest

with insights tossed in of various value. Now it's time for the adults to come in and sort things out, tossing out the less valuable items and selecting the treasured ones. Drawing pod-like clustering lines between the assorted goals from column two often proves illuminating.

Clustering the goals usually requires clarifying the more abstract ones. Some goals may not easily fall into a cluster and may stand alone.

Fourth, label and evaluate the pods. For example, in Table 6.1 one cluster of insights emerges around increasing engagement (e.g., respond to concerns, encourage positive reviews). However, the pods are not equal. Separating the truly significant ones from the others often proves challenging. But it must be done if you want to craft a truly superior strategy. A note of caution: some of the least exciting insight pods can prove exceedingly valuable when linked with other, more ambitious goals. For example, reimagining your website when coupled with reorienting your social media content to stimulate more interaction could prove to be a winning strategy.

Fifth, determine how the goals could be linked together to accomplish something unique and spectacular. Recall that goals are not coordinates until they link to one another. Think geometrically. Drawing diagrams helps. Sketching lines with arrows of various thickness helps indicate how tightly the goals align. Thicker lines indicate a more synergistic relationship between the pods. Arrows point to the potential sequences implicit in the constellation of goals; what needs to happen first, second, and so forth. You might even put numbers on the arrows to indicate steps necessary for the strategy to be realized fully.

Some of the pods in your diagram might be "link-less" or "relationship free." Drop them, modify them, or, at least, put them in the "things to think about in the future" bin. Generally, you seek pods with multiple lines connecting points; triangles beat single lines every time. Why? The connections between pods show that you are carving out a unique space in the competitive environment that is not easily reproduced. And often the results are spectacular. The bonus: you've transformed mere goals into coordinates.

CONCLUSION

Great strategic coordinates provide the conceptual scaffolding for all your other major decisions. The coordinates frame and consequently constrain all your other strategic decisions about channels, content, connections, and corrections. If the coordinates represent the strategic blueprint and framework, then the channels you select symbolize the roofing, paneling, and flooring of your strategy. These are things we all see but don't think about very often. The social media strategist, like a good designer, does. That's the issue we turn to in the next chapter.

Key Terms

Insight pods 69   Unequal dialogue 66

Deep Dives

These exercises are designed to enhance your understanding of the chapter's key ideas, principles, and approaches.

1. Forget about social media for a moment. List three of your personal or professional goals that enrich one another. Explain how these goals act as coordinates, enriching each other and your life.

2. Describe three potential dangers associated with taking the unequal dialogue principle too far. Provide examples.

3. The opening quotation for the chapter argues that thinking strategically is difficult and unnatural. Create a two-column chart. In the first column, identify three reasons that strategy is "difficult and unnatural." In column two, identify action steps to counter each reason.

Notes

1. Steve Jobs quoted in, J. Elliot, *The Steve Jobs Way: iLeadership for a New Generation* (Philadelphia, PA: Vanguard Press, 2011), 157.
2. E. Cohen, *Supreme Command: Soldiers, Statesmen, and Leadership in Wartime* (New York: Free Press, 2002), 209.
3. *The 9/11 Commission Report: The Final Report of the National Commission on Terrorist Attacks Upon the United States* (New York: W.W. Norton and Company, 2004), 344.

CHAPTER 7

Channels

"Choose your social media channels just like divas select their wardrobe, with an eye on comfort, function, and just the right amount of drama."

—Dr. So What

People disclose things on their Facebook page that they might never mention in a face-to-face chat. They post pictures they would never show you in person. So what? Channels influence people in subtle ways beyond their awareness. Channels also shape messages in unrecognized ways. Sarcastic jokes, teasing remarks, or tongue-in-cheek comments usually require facial expressions or vocal inflections to communicate the underlying jocular intent. Channels such as email or Twitter strip away these signals from your intended message. As a result, most people overestimate the likelihood that others, including friends, will accurately interpret their intended message.[1] Emojis might help, but not much. Bottom line: channel selections influence stakeholder impressions. Superior social media strategists account for these basic channel dynamics, which are discussed in the next section.

CHANNEL DYNAMICS

Channels are the mediums through which our messages pass to reach others. Face-to-face communication is often considered the richest channel because so many different types of signals—verbal, nonverbal, and visual cues—can be transmitted through it. Telephones, memos, and emails are more lean channels because they suppress certain signals easily relayed in a face-to-face channel. But these channels have a broader reach because they facilitate communication to people separated by space and time.

Social media channels, such as Facebook, Twitter, and YouTube, share some of the same advantages and disadvantages of the more traditional channels. Understanding these costs and benefits helps social media managers both select the right channels for their organizations and make the best use of ones selected. The costs and benefits emerge from a deeper understanding of three underlying dynamics at work.

First, channels connect senders and receivers. Waterways provide a connection between two points (think of the Panama Canal). Likewise, Facebook, Twitter, and other platforms act like canals connecting you with family, friends, colleagues, acquaintances, and organizations. This raises an important question for social media managers. Namely, to which audience or stakeholder group does the channel primarily connect? Under what circumstances? For example, most people agree with comedian Jerry Seinfeld and find telemarketers annoying.[2] Yet if those same people had a customer service problem with the company that the telemarketers represented, they would often seek to resolve the issue over the telephone. These are exactly the situational dynamics you take into account when crafting your social media strategy.

Second, each channel has a unique capacity to transmit particular types of signals. Social media platforms resemble canals in another sense. You can't sail the Queen Mary through every canal or waterway on the planet. Likewise, you can't expect to ship robust, complicated messages through every social media channel. You have to know if the channel can carry the message effectively between points A and B. Michael Dubin instinctively knew this when he used an amusing YouTube video to launch the Dollar Shave Club. A message on this platform, unlike a word-laden tweet, could demonstrate visually and cleverly the superiority of his blades and the convenience of his service. His simple but provocative tag line, "Our blades are f****ing great," worked well in this channel. Indeed, four years after establishing the company, he sold it for one billion dollars.[3]

A mismatch between the channel and the message can be devastating. Highly emotional conflicts, for instance, are not well managed in email or Twitter. Instead, these should be managed face to face or on the phone. The feedback quality and the ability of the sender and receiver to detect tone, emotions, and intensity of opinions decrease the likelihood that the interactions will spin out of control. On the phone, for example, misunderstandings can be detected and corrected more quickly than they would be with dueling tweets.

Third, channels cultivate unique conventions, customs, and norms. Each social media platform restricts distinct types of interactions while encouraging other types of interactions. The opportunities emerge from the constraints, which, in turn, influence audience composition and conventions about the types of messages exchanged. For example, LinkedIn set up incentives that "opened up a communication channel between recruiters and people in long-term employment relationships who may be looking for jobs" but who want to keep their job search "under wraps."[4] Facebook's relative transparency would not be a wise choice for users with these distinctive desires. Clearly, the customs and norms in the social media cosmos are evolving at a faster rate than those for traditional communication channels. So what? It is even more important for social media managers to monitor them.

PRINCIPLES FOR SELECTING CHANNELS

The dynamics discussed in the last section suggest that effective social media managers should abide by several key principles reviewed. These are as follows.

First, select platforms that sync with your coordinates and your target audiences' preferences. Assume that you, your friends, and business colleagues live in New York City. Even though you have a driver's license, you've never owned a car, despite your life-long fascination with automobiles. Further, assume that it's your lucky day and you've just inherited a tidy sum of money. Question: What vehicle should you purchase? It's a trick question, of course. The logical answer is that purchasing a car will probably not advance any of your personal or professional goals. And a new car, even the sleekest, fastest, and most fashionable, is unlikely to enhance your friendships or business liaisons. In fact, your new car might undermine those relationships because you would be spending so much time driving and maintaining it. A better question would be, "In light of my personal and professional goals, how can I best use these new funds?" Unless you defined your lifelong ambition as becoming a luxury car owner, buying a car would be a poor use of this unexpected financial windfall.

You, as a social media strategist, face similar decisions. Namely, which communication vehicles or channels should you select? Answer: It depends on a number of factors reviewed in this chapter. But the discussion should center on the coordinates you've established and the social media platform preferences of your target audiences. Bottom line: Strongly consider selecting the channel if it will advance your strategic goals *and* if your target audiences use the social media platform. If you live in Knoxville, Tennessee, which has limited public transportation, buy the sports car of your dreams.[5]

Too often leaders take the naïve position that because everybody uses the platform, it's the right platform for them. Maybe. Maybe not. The hype-masters love talking about the number of people using particular platforms. Fair enough. The number of Facebook users, for example, staggers the mind. That may *or* may not be relevant to you because the really important factor is whether or not *your* target audiences make regular use of the platform to access the kind of content you provide. For example, one thought leader who relies on Twitter maintains a Facebook account for primarily defensive purposes. Why? So no one else will claim the platform account name and post material. He found that his followers respond far more frequently to tweets than to Facebook posts.

Second, consider niche social media platforms that may serve your needs. Almost all the buzz in the mainstream and business press goes to the big social media hitters like Facebook, Twitter, Snapchat, and Pinterest. But there are plenty more **niche platforms** that might best serve you and your audiences' social media needs. Many academics, for instance, use ResearchGate to chat, request conference papers, post their latest research ideas, and query their followers about potential research ideas. Likewise, many professional administrators of Apple networks turn to Slack for professional support on pesky and quirky system issues. This by-invitation-only social media network boasts more about its exclusivity and relatively small size than any of the social media big hitters.[6] The site's code of conduct, "Don't be a dick," might explain why avid users freely share tools, best practices, and job postings.[7]

Other less publicized platforms, but with larger user bases, might also be worth considering. Your author has a particular affinity for Waze, which has saved him a few dollars on those rare occasions when the foot gets a little heavy on the accelerator. Waze describes itself as the "world's largest community-based traffic and navigation app." It's a real-time social media network, helping drivers save time on the road by alerting them to potential hazards and radar traps. Some marketers for fast-food restaurants might find that this lower-profile platform, whose tagline is "Outsmarting traffic, together," also helps its customers "Outsmart hunger, together."

Third, select platforms that you can master on a tactical level. Another factor in the platform selection calculus involves your ability and desire to master the channel. Frankly, your ability presents less of a challenge than your desire or motivation. Google any of the social media platforms for basic advice. Masters of any type never stop learning, experimenting, and innovating.

On the motivational level, it comes down to a basic question: Do you want to embrace and commit to mastery of the tactical skills needed for particular platforms? Those skills shift depending on the channel. Twitter masters post often, for instance. LinkedIn masters may not post as often but they create provocative content in a number of different ways. If you have the desire and skill set to excel on the platform, go for it; if not, then consider more passive management strategies even if your target audience makes use of the channel. Why? Your audience will soon discover your shortcomings if you are not prepared to invest in mastery.

STRATEGIC CHANNEL SELECTION

Principles guide us, but how do we use them to make strategic decisions about channels? That's the issue we turn to next.

SYSTEMATICALLY STUDY A WIDE VARIETY OF POTENTIAL SOCIAL MEDIA PLATFORMS

Here's how to conduct the study in three easy steps.

Step 1: Craft an investigative agenda designed to interrogate each platform. There are some standard questions you will want to answer about each potential channel. Think of it as putting the channel through a tough cross-examination. Just thinking about the queries forces you to go beyond the hype and creates a framework for making insightful comparisons. Listed in Table 7.1 are some of the questions the social media manager should be able to answer.

As a starting point, consult the fact sheets in Appendix 1 for answers to some of the big-hitter questions. A note of emphasis: It's enticing to think that social media is free. A more discerning individual might be tempted to say, "Well, it's not free; the advertisers pay for it." That may be closer to the truth, but it tells only part of the story. Every click, like, or repost generates data that can be sold to marketers, governments, and even less savory entities. One of my favorite platforms, Waze, sells my location data in the aggregate. I understand that, but I'm OK with it. Some people may not be. The bottom line: if you don't have a rudimentary understanding of the platform's business model, then you may be exposing your company to potential threats.

Step 2: Cast a wide net of inquiry. One of the cardinal mistakes of rookie detectives is to narrow their search prematurely. It's easy to get caught up in the hype of the major players such as Facebook, Twitter, and Pinterest. Two problems emerge from prematurely narrowing your choices. First, we often assume that familiarity with the hype breeds true understanding and appreciation. You could be quite familiar with your smiling next-door neighbor whom you see on the street every day. But that doesn't mean you really know what goes on in her home behind closed doors. The social media strategist wants a peek behind the doors. Second, social media strategists commit malpractice by confining their

TABLE 7.1 Investigative Questions for Social Media Platforms

Key Questions
• What are the historical milestones of the platform?
• How does the platform make money?
• What types of content do users typically post?
• Who are the typical users (e.g., demographics, lifestyle, income level)?
• What types of organizations make the most use of the platform?
• What are the linkage opportunities to other social sites and our website, etc.?
• What are the benefits versus the risks of using the platform?
• What kinds of free analytics are available?
• What are the notable success stories associated with the platform? Horror stories?

selection process to the big hitters. After all, you might be ignoring niche players that deliver some speculator value. As a starting point, you might consider the platforms in Table 7.2.

Step 3: Know when to move on to the next strategic step. You could study platforms forever and never make a selection. Your author has some academic colleagues caught in this loop. How do you know when you've investigated enough platforms in enough depth to move on? Fortunately, there is a semiempirical answer to this question. On the depth question, you can rely on your investigative agenda (see Table 7.1). Have you answered the majority of those questions with a sufficient level of specificity to feel comfortable about using the platform?

On the breadth question, we have computer scientists to thank for a useful guideline, or heuristic, to use. They call it the "optimal stopping problem" where the "crucial dilemma is not which option to pick, but how many options to even consider."[8] If you have one month to craft your social media strategy, how much investigative time should you devote to searching for the best channels before making the decision? The answer is 37 percent of your time or about 11 days. This optimizes

TABLE 7.2   Primary Functions of Social Media Platforms

Functions	Platform	
Social Sharing	• Facebook* • Google+ • Myspace	• Ning • Bebo • Snapchat
Personal or Professional News	• Twitter • Tumblr • reddit • Slack	• Hacker News • Quora • digg • ResearchGate
Location Oriented	• Waze • Foursquare • Yelp	• Meetup • Nextdoor • MapMyRide
Music and Art	• Spotify • Vimeo • DeviantArt	• Pandora • YouTube • SoundCloud
Professional	• LinkedIn • SlideShare • Yammer	• Xing • Slack
Image Sharing	• YouTube • Flickr • Instagram	• Snapchat • Vimeo • Periscope
Shopping	• Yelp • UserVoice • Venmo	• Pinterest • Facebook • letgo
Messaging	• Messenger • Snapchat • WhatsApp • Skype	• WeChat • Google Hangouts

*NOTE: Some platforms may have several primary functions.

the probability that you'll make a very good decision because you've nearly exhausted the possibilities of learning about the scope of your choices. If you waited until the 30th of the month, you might have learned a little bit more, but it is unlikely that you'd have turned up something that would significantly influence the decision.

EVALUATE AND SELECT THE PLATFORMS FOR ACTIVE AND PASSIVE MANAGEMENT

Criteria should drive your decision-making process when you label a channel as an **actively managed platform** or a **passively managed platform**. Listed below are the mechanics of the process.

Step 1: Establish a list of evaluative criteria. You might consider the following as a starting point:

- Is the platform aligned with our coordinates and goals?
  - o Business goals
  - o Communication goals
- Do our target audiences use the platform?
  - o Primary audiences
  - o Secondary audiences
- Can we master the use of the platform?
  - o Desire
  - o Ability
- Do we have the resources to support the platform?
  - o Equipment
  - o Personnel
  - o Budget

Step 2: Craft a channel evaluation grid (see Table 7.3). The rows list all the channels you've investigated, including the usual suspects such as Facebook, Twitter, and Instagram. The columns contain the evaluative criteria you've established. There's a little twist though. Note the double line separating the final column from the others. This column represents the goal line because it's the place to note your final judgment about the projected status of the channel. How are you going to manage it? Actively, passively, or are you going to simply ignore it?

Step 3: Judge each channel against the criteria. If the channel helps you meet your primary business goal, place a check in the space. If not, leave that space blank. If your first target audience uses the channel, check it. And so on. If you want to be more sophisticated, you can assign scores to each space.

Teams use different methods to complete the grid. Some prefer an open discussion on all items. Others ask participants to complete the exercise privately and then compile the results. Both approaches have merit and drawbacks. An open debate can provide useful insights from a variety of perspectives, but dominant individuals can also monopolize the conversation. Individually rating the items avoids this drawback and is more efficient. The major drawback of the individual ranking process is that, as in any private voting system, we are not privy to the thinking processes that went into the rating. That's why I prefer a hybrid approach in which each team member privately completes the grid (except the final column) and then the team comes together to discuss the results.

Step 4: Decide about the status of each channel. Because your reputation or brand can be promoted—or sullied—on almost any social media platform, you should be managing every one of them, right? Partially correct. It's true that the trolls, pirates, and mischief makers could attack your company or brand from any platform. But that does not mean you need to manage all the possible social media platforms actively. The task is too daunting, even for a Fortune 100 company. In fact, throwing resources at every platform, even if it were possible, sabotages the strategic architecture.

Every general knows that it takes more energy and resources to be on the offensive as opposed to the defensive. In fact, according to some military theorists, mounting an offensive campaign as opposed to a defensive campaign requires about an 8/1 ratio of resources. Let's translate those sentiments to the mission of the social media "general." Being on the offensive, or active on every platform, squanders resources and

TABLE 7.3   Channel Evaluation Grid

Channel	Coordinate Alignment		Audiences' Use of Platform		Potential to Master Platform		Resource Availability			A or P or I*
	Business	Comm.	Primary	Secondary	Desire	Ability	Equip.	Personnel	Budget	
Facebook										
Twitter										
Pinterest										
Snapchat										

*A = actively managed, P = passively managed, I = ignored

undermines your effectiveness. Designating the few platforms you'll manage actively and relegating the rest to more passive management is the smart choice.

So how do you determine which ones to manage actively and which ones to manage passively? You can simply add up the check marks (or ratings) from the "Channel Evaluation Grid" of Table 7.3 and you'll have a pretty good idea about which platforms should be managed actively or passively. However, debating whether to place an A (active) or P (passive) or I (ignore) in the final column can be amazingly illuminating. Why? These check marks and totals reveal nothing about how much each team member values a specific criterion. One team member, for instance, might prize audience X over audience Y. Another might reverse the judgment. Revealing and reconciling these underlying, and often hidden, insights can be beneficial when deciding about placing an A or P or I in the final column. After all, strategists see the intrinsic value of making tough choices with limited resources.

CRAFT A "JOB DESCRIPTION" FOR EACH CHANNEL

Clayton Christensen of Harvard Business School developed the notion of disruptive innovation. He argues that the best way to sustain innovation is to think in terms of the jobs your customers want their products and services to perform. We can use similar logic when designing a job for each channel. To paraphrase Christensen: A social media platform's job is the aspiration that the channel is seeking to fulfill in a specific circumstance.[9] In other words, we want the channel to work for us, not the other way around. And we want it to perform a particular role in a specific situation. So we craft a **platform job description** to determine how we want a particular social media channel to work for us.

We can start by designating the primary and secondary "duties" of each platform in certain circumstances. In other words, what are the channels' primary functions? Look to the coordinates and the communication goals for insights. For example, Twitter's primary job function could be "providing real-time updates of live events." Think about the two critical aspects of this "job description": "Providing real-time updates" fulfills followers' aspirations, and "live events" specifies the circumstance. Or consider what the editor in chief of one of the top social media brands, National Geographic, noted: "We approach each [social media platform] differently, customizing content to meet the unique expectations and desires of each site's users. For example, our Snapchat audience—mostly younger people—wants a more kinetic, high-energy approach to information than our audience on Facebook." *National Geographic* boasts 2.6 billion social engagements, right up there with Victoria's Secret and the NFL.[10]

You also need to develop a scorecard for each platform. Great managers coach and develop their employees. But they can only do that if they are clear about their evaluative criteria or their scorecard. How many "real-time updates" should our Twitter "employee" post a month? How will the quality of those updates be judged? How are we going to measure the influence of the channel on the organizational goals? These are the kinds of questions worth contemplating.

BUNDLE THE CHANNEL "DUTIES" INTO MANAGEABLE JOBS FOR YOUR SOCIAL MEDIA TEAM

So far we've been looking at each channel individually. Do you know anyone with only one job duty or responsibility? Instead, various duties are bundled into meaningful units that should synergistically reinforce one another. This approach makes sense for the channel duties, as well. It can be particularly beneficial to bundle an actively managed platform with a passively managed one. Your actively managed channels might more aggressively push out content while the passively managed ones serve as a safety valve in case you pushed a little too hard. Additionally, you invest more time and energy in the actively managed channels, so the passively managed ones help balance out your workload.

Just a note about passive management: at a minimum, it means securing the platform names that some audience members might access or stumble across. Protecting your name or related names—even misspelled ones—costs you almost nothing and involves a minimum investment of time and energy. Even securing the name for your website across all the possible domains (e.g., .com, .org, .net, .us, or .eu) is a bargain for most large companies. Beyond securing the name and related variant of the name, the social media general could link the passively managed social media platforms to the actively managed ones or even to the website.

It would, of course, also make sense to regularly monitor the passively managed platforms. After all, a good general always checks on where to send a limited number of reinforcements.

ASSIGN THE RIGHT PERSON OR TEAM TO THE TASKS

Obviously, some person or team needs to perform the functions. Less obviously, making sure this work gets done well means selecting and training the right people with the right skill sets and the right motivation to do the job. This management piece may sound easy, but it's not necessarily so. Too often, the default assumption of more seasoned managers is that "if you're young and you regularly use social media, then you'll do a good job." That may or may not be the case.

CONCLUSION

Selecting the right channels resembles selecting the appropriate utensils, plates, and bowls for a meal. You don't serve a gourmet meal on paper plates with plastic spoons. And what exactly does the gourmet meal consist of? That's the content question, which has been silently simmering on the back burner in this chapter. And it's the question that we answer in the next chapter. Enjoy the feast!

KEY TERMS

Actively managed platforms 81

Niche platforms 76

Passively managed platforms 81

Platform job description 84

DEEP DIVES

These exercises are designed to enhance your understanding of the chapter's key ideas, principles, and approaches.

1. List three objections you might encounter when asking a team to discuss and complete the Channel Evaluation Grid (see Table 7.3). How would you counter each objection?

2. List three other important questions that should be added to the "Investigative Questions for Social Media Platforms" list proposed in Table 7.1. Discuss why you think these are important questions to add.

3. Select three platforms you frequently use. Craft a job description for each of them. Develop a scorecard for each based on your "job description."

NOTES

1. M. Riordan and L. Trichtinger, "Overconfidence at the Keyboard: Confidence and Accuracy in Interpreting Affect in E-mail Exchanges," *Human Communication Research* 43 (2017): 1–24.
2. Many Seinfeld fans will recall Jerry's clever response to one telemarketing call during his TV series. See https://m.youtube.com/watch?v=hllDWSbuDsQ.
3. P. Ziobro, "Funny Video Led to $1 Billion Deal," *Wall Street Journal*, July 21, 2016, B2.
4. M. Piskorski, *A Social Strategy: How We Profit From Social Media* (Oxford: Princeton University Press, 2014), 16.
5. Knoxville, Tennessee, was ranked as one of the nation's worst cities for public transport in 2011 by the Brookings Institution; see A. Tomer, E. Kneebone, R. Puentes, and A. Berube, *Missed Opportunity: Transit and Jobs in Metropolitan America* (Washington, DC: Brookings, May 2011), https://www.brookings.edu/wp-content/uploads/2016/06/0512_jobs_transit.pdf.
6. See macadmins.slack.com.
7. Thanks to Bryce Carlson for making me aware of this community.
8. B. Christian and T. Griffiths, *Algorithms to Live By: The Computer Science of Human Decisions* (New York; Henry Holt, 2016), p. 22 of 712 (e-book).
9. C. Christensen, Karen Dillon, and David Duncan, *Competing Against Luck: The Story of Innovation and Customer Choice* (New York: Harper Business, 2016), p. 53 of 392 (e-book).
10. S. Goldberg, "Where Social Media Fits in National Geographic's Mission," *National Geographic*, April 2017, http://www.nationalgeographic.com/magazine/2017/04/editors-note-social-media/.

CHAPTER 8

Content

"This postcard from the edge of reason came to feel like a developmental milestone, an instant of self-consciousness in which it became clear that I was undergoing a transformation. I was being freshly coded with certain expectations of the world, one of which seemed to be an unflagging belief in the responsiveness of others and which never seemed to learn from its disappointments. Digital technology was reshaping my responses, collaborating with my instincts, creating in me, its subject, all kinds of new sensitivities."

—Laurence Scott

Your audiences rarely know about your goals (i.e., coordinates), channel decision-making process, connection choices, or your corrective mechanisms. But they will directly respond to your content. If your content fails to resonate, then your entire social media strategy will collapse in a heap of good intentions. Content represents the words, images, and videos you choose to post. These are tactical concerns, but they should be guided by a laser-like content strategy. This chapter outlines how to develop this kind of strategy.

Content decisions boil down to three connected questions:

- What are my content options?
- Who generates my content?
- How do I select the right content?

What Are my Content Options?

This question reminds me of when a young child asked a librarian, "What kind of stuff is in your library?" The librarian, like a skilled social media expert, was tempted to say, "Well almost anything and everything." Of course, that's not the intent of the question. Rather, the inquiry highlights the challenge of getting your mind around an almost limitless array of options. Lurking around the edges of the clumsy question lies several hidden concerns: 1) How can I be sure I don't inadvertently rule out some potentially useful opportunities? and 2) How can I think about a universe of possibilities this large? Here's where the librarian's familiarity with different genres of books, types of journals, and categories of artifacts can be useful. Likewise, social media specialists need some kind of organizing framework to answer these core questions.[1]

Content options fall basically into two major options (see Table 8.1). The most obvious option is **form**: Is the content primarily in the form of a picture, text, video, audio clip, or graphic? Social media platforms vary in their ability to transmit different forms of content effectively. We discussed this issue in depth in the channels chapter, but it is worth noting the choices at this point, as well.

A less obvious option involves the **type** of content, regardless of form. Based on numerous grassroots examinations of what actually gets posted on social media sites, my students and I arrived at the following generic categories:

- **News and Information**: Content that highlights new information, breaking stories, or trending topics of interest

- **People**: Content that features customers, employees, partners, celebrities, or even proud parents with cuddly animals

- **Events**: Content that emphasizes time-sensitive information, happenings, or occasions

- **Calls to Action**: Content that asks readers, fans, or followers to do something

- **Amusements**: Content that entertains, distracts, or provides joy
- **How-To**: Content that features processes, procedures, or demonstrations
- **Inspiration**: Content designed to uplift the spirit of others or encourage people
- **Commentaries and Opinions**: Content that highlights benefits, motivations, rationales, or how to make sense of events
- **Indices**: Content that provides an indicator or metadata about the substance of the post and often builds a sense of virtual community

Table 8.2 provides more detailed examples of each area.

This category system helps the social media strategist think about the type of content categories that are most likely to yield positive results. And even if you cannot determine what content will yield the most

TABLE 8.1 Content Options: Type and Form

Form → Type ↓	Pictures	Text	Videos	Graphics
News and Information				
People				
Events				
Calls to Action				
Amusements				
How-To				
Inspiration				
Commentaries and Opinions				
Indices				

TABLE 8.2   Examples of Various Types of Content

Type of Content	Examples
News and Information	• Provide updates • Post breaking news • Discuss a trending topic, news, or hashtag • Share a compelling statistic • Share a testimonial about your organization • Answer frequently asked questions • Link to an interesting infographic • Correct a common misperception • Create a fact-myth list • Craft a compare-contrast document • Create a "top 10" list • Update customers on new products, services, or major projects
People	• Chat with customers • Share pictures of customers • Interview a celebrity or thought leader • Recognize an employee or good deed • Thank a fan • Introduce a new employee • Post images of executives with employees • Highlight everyday heroic acts of your employees • Present images of your employees as volunteers serving the community • Celebrate birthdays or milestones
Events	• Stream an event live • Mark organizational milestones • Post image or thought with a seasonal theme • Create posts that count down to a major organizational event • Post reminders

Type of Content	Examples
Calls to Action	• Prompt attendance at an event • Encourage voting on a preference • Cross-promote another organization • Encourage sign up for an email, a mailing, or a follow-up phone call • Promote signing a petition on an issue • Request that followers "like," retweet, bookmark, download, or add to favorites • Offer downloadable coupons • Start a contest • Invite subscribers to share something with colleagues, add content, upload a video, review a product, request a product sample, or reserve a spot now
Amusements	• Share a behind-the-scenes story • Direct followers to a valuable free resource • Post images of compelling or unusual places that feature your product or service • Share a funny picture of your workspace • Create a quiz • Sing a song • Share a tasteful joke • Develop puzzles • Share optical illusions • Juxtapose unusual images • Share a fun fact
How-To	• Share a valuable tip • Develop a tip sheet • Outline a process • Provide advice on how to approach a problem • Create and share a decision flow chart • Develop a how-to video • Post instructions for completing a task

(Continued)

TABLE 8.2   (Continued)

Type of Content	Examples
	• Share recipes • Highlight how to join a mailing list • Provide tutorials • Create checklists for completing a task
Inspiration	• Share an inspirational quotation • Craft images that provide a perspective on life • Post stories about helping others • Share thoughts from successful people • Share links to motivational blog posts • Tell compelling stories about persistence, integrity, courage, compassion, self-discipline, or loyalty
Commentaries and Opinions	• Provide commentary on major events • Create blog posts that help followers make sense of confusing issues • Explain the rationale of a major decision
Indices	• Use hashtags to mark your content • Include links to relevant websites and blogs

positive results before posting, the categories suggest ways to think about analyzing reactions to the posts. For example, are we getting more "likes" by posting pictures or text? Are we getting greater reach with "amusements" or "how-to" content?

Of course, the challenge with this category system, as with all others, occurs when something falls into multiple categories. For instance, a post that features your picture with a celebrity at the Super Bowl falls into both the *people* and *event* categories. Despite these kinds of categorical overlaps, it can be useful to consider the groupings. For example, you might find that certain kinds of *people* AND *event* posts generate the most buzz. This type of trial and error approach may be the only way to truly optimize your content strategy. Thinking about these content issues at the right level (e.g., thinking about form categories and type categories) rather than at the specific post level (e.g., thinking about a Super Bowl picture) separates thoughtful strategists from the mindless tinkerers who occasionally stumble on success.

Who Generates the Content?

Short answer: writers, photographers, videographers, and sound and graphic artists. Long answer: in the ideal universe, a cadre of these professionals would be orbiting around the social media manager, meeting every need. In the real world, though, most organizations will not devote those kinds of resources to the social media department. Instead, the social media manager needs to be resourceful and strategic when responding to this question.

The social media manager's options range on a continuum from internally produced to user generated. The organization exerts more control with internally produced content and less control at the other end of the continuum (see Figure 8.1). Each approach has benefits and drawbacks associated with it that are reviewed in Table 8.3.

INTERNALLY PRODUCED CONTENT

If you have the talent and time, then creating your own content may be the best option. Doing so allows you to maximize control and align your content with your strategic goals. The potential drawbacks include the amount of time needed to create the content and the limitations of your team's expertise and creativity.

CURATED CONTENT

This content is drawn from other sources that you repurpose. One of the main jobs of a museum director is to curate or select the pieces that will be showcased in an exhibit or in the permanent collection. That's almost exactly the job the social media manager has when selecting **curated content**. Thought leaders who pass on insightful blogs to their followers would fall in this category, as would politicians who retweet supportive comments.

FIGURE 8.1   The Continuum of Content Generation

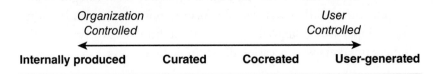

	Internally Produced	Curated	Cocreated	User- Generated
Potential Benefits	• Alignment with organization's goals • Consistent messaging • Protection of the brand image • Coordination with other organizational initiatives and communication tools • Opportunity to customize, modify, and tweak posts		• Organic appeal • Resonates with target audience • Lower cost to produce and manage • Wider access to talented content producers • Loyalty fostered through participation	
Potential Drawbacks	• Inability to attract talent with sufficient breadth and expertise • Recruiting and training costs for talent • Appearance of "cookie-cutter" or programmatic posts		• Lack of interested content providers • Posts that are not aligned with organizational goals • Conflicts of interest	

TABLE 8.3   Considerations in Selecting Approaches to Deriving Content

If the content resonates with your audiences, then you may well have hit a home run. Of course that depends on whether the audiences encountered the content in other venues first. There are other potential dangers. Overreliance on curated content, for instance, may undermine your brand, particularly if you are positioned as a thought leader. Some fans might reason, "What original thought has this 'thought leader' ever provided?" Or just ask President Donald Trump about the dangers of repurposing content. During the 2016 primary campaign, he occasionally retweeted questionable content and photos, some of which were linked to white supremacists. In a rare moment of introspective regret, he opined, "The tweets are fine. The retweets get a little bit shaky."[2]

COCREATED CONTENT

Content created with your followers' or customers' input can infuse creativity into the mix and cultivate greater audience loyalty. To launch the Lenovo Vibe X2 phone in India, the phone maker commissioned artwork from 10 artists. Social media team members challenged their Twitter and Facebook followers to "vibe up" the original art by adding a visual layer or new words. These were then featured on a microsite (#VibeUpMyLife).[3] It was a huge success. Likewise, contests to suggest a new potato chip flavor or beverage would fall into this category.

Great **cocreated content** often increases brand loyalty by providing minor celebrity status to the featured users, who in turn act as brand evangelists. On the flip side, great cocreated content requires a lot of energy and resources to manage effectively. Inevitably, someone will seek to hijack the opportunity for more nefarious causes. Controls need to be in place for such an eventuality. If you don't want that hassle, then you might consider curated content.

USER-GENERATED CONTENT

Purely **user-generated content** marks the other end of the continuum. Fans develop this content without any prompting. Content may include a clever or funny use of a product that catches the eye of social media managers. Wise social media managers jump on these unexpected opportunities. The difference between purely user-generated content and curated content is simply a matter of degree. With curated content, the social media manager actively scans certain predetermined channels looking for potential material. With purely user-generated content, the social media manager stumbles onto something potentially useful. It's like the difference between switching between your programmed favorite channels versus channel surfing for anything that might be of potential value.

These are the benefits of purely user-generated content: innovative ideas, pleasant surprises, and the recruitment of new loyalists. These are the costs: it takes a lot of energy and time to sift through all the potential content, and you might never find exactly what you require. Consequently, many social media managers save valuable resources by only curating content from trusted sources.

How Do I Select the Right Content?

Your content strategy defines the target zone for your posts. Five principles should guide your selection of messages, images, and videos. These principles can also help you determine the timing and sources of your posts, tweets, and updates (see Figure 8.2).

COORDINATE ALIGNED

The fundamental question content creators or curators should ask is, "Will this content help us advance our business and communication goals?" If so, then consider it. If not, drop it. It's really that simple. You may find a satirical political cartoon fiendishly clever, but if it doesn't advance your business goals, don't repost it or even "like" it. This is message discipline at its most basic. You can still have fun but be thoughtful about what you post.

Complexities emerge when the goals (i.e., coordinates) push you in slightly different directions. For example, one business had two primary goals of 1) maintaining its current customer loyalty and 2) expanding its customer base. On the surface, those coordinates appear to be perfectly compatible. The business decided to email a provocative marketing piece that appeared to be a personalized condolence card, stating, "Sorry for your loss." If the recipient clicked on the image, the following message appeared: "Sorry you missed out on our sale. . . ." It worked. This marketing piece generated more responses and sales than any piece in the business's history. How can you argue with results like that? Well, it also offended a number of customers who had recently experienced a death in the family. Those customers decided to take their

FIGURE 8.2 Principles of Great Content

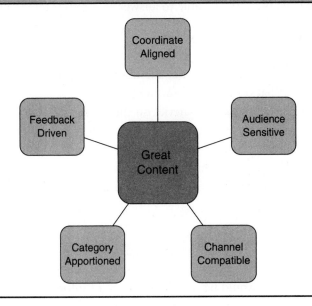

business elsewhere. The law of large numbers dictates that this was almost inevitable. If you send the material to a large enough group, then it is highly probable that some of the recipients will have recently lost a loved one. On balance, the company gained some new customers but also lost some loyal ones. Was it worth it? You can be the judge, but the company decided never to repeat the gimmick. And the executive team learned how difficult it was to balance seemingly compatible goals.

AUDIENCE SENSITIVE

Your coordinates determine your target audiences. If you are primarily trying to reach other businesses (B2B), then by default you've selected the target audience. It doesn't much matter if Kim Kardashian likes your posts in most B2B worlds. On the other hand, if you are trying to reach young people with your product (B2C), Kim flashing her support could help a great deal.

Bottom line: Crown your audiences "kings," and go from there. What do they want? What types of people do they listen to? Where do they want to receive their content? Listed below are some questions social media managers should be able to answer about their target audiences:

What

- What keeps audience members up at night?
- What do they find funny?
- What kinds of material do they post?
- What are their underlying motivations for monitoring social media?
- What would they find surprising?
- What would they find intriguing or useful?

Who

- Who would be thought credible and/or funny?
- Who are the opinion leaders in the audience?
- Who would be the worst source of information?
- Do they prefer pictures, text, videos, or graphics?

Where

- Where do they use social media (e.g., at work, at home, at a restaurant)?
- When do they consume social media on particular platforms?
- How do they access social media (e.g., phone, computer, portable device like an iPad)?

Thoughtful answers to these questions reveal audience preferences, which in turn provide rocket fuel to your content strategy decision-making process.

CHANNEL COMPATIBLE

Why not use the same material across all your social media platforms? After all, it's quick, simple, and efficient to implement. It's also totally off base. It undermines your effectiveness. Why? What works well in one channel often will not work well in another. For example, an advertisement that works well on television will often fall totally flat on radio. Or a TV ad that works well during the Super Bowl will fall flat on the

Home Shopping Network. Different social media channels resemble the differences between radio and TV channels in many cases. Instead of using the same material across all platforms, use the following as your guide for determining channel-content compatibility:

Craft content that resonates across platforms while respecting the unique dynamics of each platform. This operative principle allows you to build synergy across platforms while advancing the same goals. It's like advertising the same product or promoting the same idea but using different approaches when using radio and television. Selecting the right image matters much more on the Pinterest platform than it does on Twitter. Words matter more on some platforms; pictures matter more on others. We can be even more specific based on the nuances of how typical users make use of the platform. For example, the singer Rihanna uses Instagram for glamour shots—poses in a jeweled bikini with feathers and the like. Yet she uses Snapchat for postings showing the more everyday sides of her personality, such as a video clip of her killing a bug in a hotel room. Both images work for the respective platforms and reveal her underlying sophistication in exploiting the nuances of each platform.[4]

Master details. Each social media channel exhibits peculiarities that you need to take into consideration when creating content. You need to detect the ambient unstated rules that silently guide each platform. For instance, followers' psychological clocks tick far faster on the Twitter platform than they do on the LinkedIn platform. In fact, researchers discovered that the faster Twitter pages were updated, the "stronger the perceptions of organizational goodwill" and the perceptions of trustworthiness.[5] The speed of posts presents one timing challenge to social media managers, but another one involves the best days and times to post. Why is this so critical? Well, we all live in a tsunami of social media messages. Consequently, we prioritize our consumption based on the rhythm of our professional and personal lives. Detecting the rhythm of most of your followers enhances the likelihood of success.

Timing issues are only one of the details that matter. Others include the length of the post, the words used, the size of the images, and the types of images. Many useful heuristics have emerged from research by scholars and others:

- Shorter posts tend to garner more "likes" and sharing than longer ones.[6]

- Using VIPs in your videos boosts appeal.[7]

- Compelling content can be produced by professionals or amateurs. It doesn't really matter as long as it is surprising, funny, or joy inducing.[8]

- Content that emphasizes authenticity, community pride, identity with common values, and fun tends to build stronger engagement.[9]

Caution: use these heuristics as a starting point rather than an end point because, like all generalizations, they may or may not apply to your specific target audiences. And if you do discover a trend that varies from the norms, don't share it! That's your secret sauce.

CATEGORY APPORTIONED

What category system makes the most sense? That depends on your goals, audiences, and platforms. The category system we've been discussing throughout the chapter—*form and type*—provides the most comprehensive overview of the possibilities. However, many organizations will hone that list down into a more workable category system.

Over the years, we've directed our research teams to detect the category systems used by a wide variety of organizations, products, and people. For example, one team found that the posts promoting the energy drink Red Bull could be classified into the categories of humor, motivation, sponsored events, information, and calls to action.[10] Another team analyzed two prominent politicians' posts during a campaign and found that the posts fell into the categories of personal attacks, political opinions, poll results, issues, humor, and personal information.[11]

What's the payoff for looking at your posts through a categorical lens? Think of it as if you're measuring ingredients for your favorite dish. You don't want one flavor to overpower another; instead, you want to get the right proportions to maximize the taste. Likewise, your categories need to be properly proportioned to maximize your users' experience. If 50 percent of your posts are sales pitches (or "calls to action"), then you are adding way too much salt to the mixture—your users may taste it once, but they aren't coming back for more. *New York Times* bestselling author and storytelling entrepreneur Gary Vaynerchuk advocates a "jab, jab, jab, right hook" content strategy. In his delightful book, he explains:

> Jabs are lightweight pieces of content that benefit your customers by making them laugh, snicker, ponder, play a game, feel appreciated, or escape; right hooks are calls to action that benefit your businesses.[12]

His ratio of three customer-focused posts to one sales-focused post might work well in the marketing arena. In other arenas, such as public relations or human resources, you will want to work out a ratio that best achieves your business goals.

What's the proper category mix? Iron Chef Bobby Flay would laugh you out of the kitchen for asking what's the proper amount of sugar for every dish he prepares. He doesn't know until he tastes it; it all depends on what dish he's preparing. Likewise, the proper amount of ranting, commenting, and selling depends on for whom you're cooking up your posts, the platforms on which they will be viewed, and when they will be posted (i.e., audience, platform, and timing).

Two opposing forces tug on a social media manager's posting patterns. One force pulls in the direction of random inspirations—posting almost anything that seems to vaguely fit your objectives. The other force yanks you in the direction of predictable prototypes—posting the same type of material over and over again. Neither is advisable. If your posts are too random, you fail to cultivate a trustworthy identity. If your posts are too predictable, you risk boring your audiences. Thinking of posts in categories or genres reconciles the tension between the two opposing forces. If you pick the right categories, then you will earn your followers' attention while cultivating a dependable identity.

Categorical thinking breeds strategic thinking about your posts. It makes your trade-offs visible and encourages the social media strategist to ask, "Is this the right mix for this audience on this platform at this time?" It also imposes a kind of editorial discipline on the entire social media enterprise. Having a target percentage of posts in a given category prods you to seek out content in those areas. If you have too many possibilities in one content category, this category-apportioned approach forces you to choose only the best ones. It's like an Iron Chef who knows that the new dish needs a certain zing to it.

FEEDBACK DRIVEN

No matter how thoughtfully you prepare your content, you can always tweak it. Listening to the feedback from your assessment processes provides two types of signals: strong and weak. Strong signaling starts the nanosecond your network senses you've committed a major gaffe. If you routinely monitor the feedback, you will know almost instantly when a mistake occurs. The good news: if you have the right social media trauma skills, you can almost immediately respond and stop the hemorrhaging. More on that issue in another chapter.

Sensing weak signals requires the acute hearing that only teenagers possess. As we age, our hearing at the very high end of the sound spectrum fades. That may be why young people often seize on trends long before they become mainstream; they literally and figuratively hear things that other people can't. Similarly, the wise social media manager seeks out signals that others may not hear in their networks. One of the best ways to seek out weak signals is to regularly ask questions such as these:

1. What surprised us this week?

2. What emerging trends do we see outside of our networks?

3. What data trends from our platforms' metrics do we notice that suggest we need to tweak our approach?

Sensing weak signals requires that we use both ears—one tuned to numerical data, the other to the peculiarities in the stream of user feedback.

For many people the word "corrective" only signals addressing problems. We are taking a more robust view by including seizing new opportunities, as well. Wise social media managers look at both sides of the corrective equation in a never-ending quest to fine-tune the content to achieve the goals.

CONCLUSION

The principles presented in this chapter can help you make great content decisions. Even though your content decisions are the most visible and sexy part of the social media game, great content does not ensure a great social media strategy. That can only be accomplished by paying close attention to perhaps the least noticeable part of your strategy. This relatively hidden strategic element—the subject addressed in the next chapter—will determine if the right people receive your content or if you're broadcasting to ghosts.

KEY TERMS

Cocreated content 97

Curated content 95

Form (category of content) 90

Type (category of content) 90

User-generated content 97

DEEP DIVES

These exercises are designed to enhance your understanding of the chapter's key ideas, principles, and approaches.

1. Rank order the principles in Figure 8.2 from least difficult to follow consistently (1) to most difficult (5). Provide your rationale.

2. Find three recent examples of poor social media content decisions. Discuss which principles of great content each decision violated.

3. Construct a grid. On the horizontal axis, list the five social media platforms you are most familiar with. On the vertical axis, insert the content categories from Table 8.2.

   a. Using the grid, place a check by the social media platforms that seem most compatible with the content category.

   b. Place an X by those channels that are least compatible with the content category.

   c. Provide your rationale.

NOTES

1. I consulted with two librarians at the University of Wisconsin–Green Bay on the ideas in this section. Thanks to Paula Ganyard and Debra Strelka.

2. N. Andrews, "Trump's Edge on Twitter Cuts Both Ways," *Wall Street Journal*, April 18, 2016, A7.

3. See Vinaya, "The 11 Best Content Co-Creation Campaigns of 2014," *Lighthouse Insights,* December 19, 2014, http://lighthouseinsights.in/content-co-creation-campaigns-2014.html/.

4. D. Seetharaman, "The Answer is in the Stars," *Wall Street Journal*, October 14, 2015, R1–R2.

5. P. Spence, K. Lahlan, A. Edwards, and C. Edwards, "Tweeting Fast Matters, But Only If I Think About It: Information Updates on Social Media," *Communication Quarterly* 64, no. 1 (2016): 55–71, 64.

6. A. Malhotra, C. Malhotra, and A. See, "How to Create Brand Engagement on Facebook," *MIT Sloan Management Review*, Winter 2013, 18–20.

7. "Social Media: Making Clickbait Videos For the C-Suite," *Harvard Business Review*, September 2016, 22.

8. D. Pirouz, A. Johnson, M. Thomson, and R. Pirouz, "Creating Online Videos That Engage Viewers," *MIT Sloan Management Review*, Summer 2015, 83–88.

9. Q. Huy and A. Shipilov, "The Key to Social Media Success Within Organizations," *MIT Sloan Management Review*, Fall 2012, 73–81.

10. Thanks to Professor Daniella Bina's students: Nicole, Pete, Sirah, Rhonda, and Henry.

11. Thanks to Sarah Alexander, Sandra Graybill, Karli Peterson, Taylor Thomson, and Ashley Vickney.

12. G. Vaynerchuk, *Jab, Jab, Jab, Right Hook: How to Tell Your Story in a Noisy Social World* (New York: Harper Collins, 2013), 7.

CHAPTER 9

Connections

"*Pathways act as an essential guiding force on this planet: on every scale of life, from microscopic cells to herds of elephants, creatures can be found relying on trails to reduce an overwhelming array of options to a single expeditious route. Without trails, we would be lost. The soul of a trail—its* trail-ness*—is not bound up in dirt and rocks; it is immaterial, evanescent, as fluid as air. The essence lies in its function: how it continuously evolves to serve the needs of its users.*"

—Robert Moor

Historians often label significant periods of time with illuminating names such as the Dark Ages, the Enlightenment, the Industrial Revolution, the Great Depression, or the atomic, space, or information age. The monikers shine a bright light on the central issue of the age while almost magically describing the underlying forces shaping government policies, commerce activities, and the average person's day-to-day experiences and cultural sensibilities. For instance, the Great Depression ushered in unemployment lines, soup kitchens, the New Deal, penny-pinching business practices, and federally funded artists depicting economic hope. In short, to understand a particular era profoundly, you need to appreciate, investigate, and contemplate the central issue of the day.

Years from now, some historians will label the current age. What will it be? No one can know for sure, but I suspect the "Connectivity Age" will be in the running.[1] Email and social media can connect people across the globe. Our mobile devices can connect us to our real-time bio-physiological data, to our heartbeats or the number of steps we take, as well as to the thermostats in our homes. And our "things" can be connected to one another in wondrous ways. For example, our smart refrigerator can take pictures of the food we have in stock and send these to our phones or other devices; some fridges can even order a food item on Amazon.com.

The bottom line: deeply understanding connectivity helps us to better appreciate the forces that shape both our world and great social media strategies. This may sound simple. After all, what could be easier than drawing a line between two channels, such as Facebook and a website? But in theory and in practice, it's not so simple and straightforward. In fact, the connectivity issue may well be the least appreciated and discussed feature of great social media strategies. We often value the people close to us more after we take time to peel back the layers of their persona, revealing deeper complexities of their character. That's exactly what we are going to do with "connectivity."

UNDERSTANDING CONNECTIVITY

A single line between two nodes masks a great deal of complexity. It's like trying to understand traffic flow by mapping only the location of stoplights. To gain even a rudimentary understanding of connectivity, you need to understand 1) nodes, 2) links, and 3) networks.

NODES

Nodes are points of reference. Cities are the nodes on the airline destination map. People are the nodes on your family tree. Faucets, dishwashers, toilets, and showerheads are nodes in your plumbing system. Mobile phones, cell towers, and electronic switching stations are the nodes allowing us to connect to each other while driving down the road.

The obvious nodes in the social media world would include social media sites, websites, and the email system. The less obvious nodes play an equally important role in the success of your social media strategy. These include

- Traditional media (e.g., print, kiosks, menus, advertisements)

- Decision-making practices (e.g., resolving customer service complaints, researching markets)

- Partner advertisements (e.g., website of a company selling your products or services)

Thinking outside the traditional social media platform box resembles creating networks that connect our lawn sprinklers to our cell phones.

Certain nodes, like certain connections, generate more value than others. The **bull's-eye node** is the *target* node that you designate for your network. It could be the "buy" button or "apply here" button on your website. Or it could be "Tap to view products" or "Shop now" on a social media platform.[2] Designating bull's-eye nodes often starts the strategic conversation about connections. (See Figure 9.1.)

LINKS

Knowing what nodes are linked and what nodes are not linked proves illuminating. It's as simple as drawing a line between two nodes. The pipes are a plumber's links. The airline routes are the pilot's link. The roads are the driver's links. The social media manager's **links** are many and diverse. Consider the following questions:

- Is the company website linked to its Twitter account?

- Is the Twitter account connected to Facebook?

- Are Pinterest posts linked to customer service representatives?

- Does the menu at your favorite diner publicize its website and social media venues?

- Does the research and development department review social media posts to find new product or service opportunities?

FIGURE 9.1 Examples of Bull's-Eye Nodes

Answers to questions like these often reveal missed opportunities. Even deeper layers of insight emerge from understanding the concepts of direction, capacity, and volume.

Direction

Simply placing an arrow on a line between two nodes greatly enhances our understanding of the connective tissue in the system. An arrow captures the direction of the flow, helping us anticipate likely breakdowns and bottlenecks. Do two-way connections trump one-way connections?

Not necessarily. After all, you want the water flowing through your toilet to go in one direction.

Capacity

Understanding direction helps explain toilet or traffic backups, but we also need to understand the capacity of the pipe or road to manage the flow. The greater the capacity, the smoother the flow; the bigger the pipes, the fewer the backups. Yet enhancing capacity, whether for a pipe, a road, or a reporting line in an organization, incurs startup and maintenance costs.

Volume

Volume answers the question about the typical amount of traffic that flows through the link. Clearly, volume depends on capacity; if your heart pumps too hard through a blood vessel, you'll burst the blood vessel. Capacity sets the *upper* limit, but it doesn't say much about the *typical* amount of traffic carried through the channel. Is it 2 percent of capacity or 95 percent of capacity? Identifying the volume answers that question.

NETWORKS

Networks emerge from how the nodes and links are connected on a macro-level. Even a rudimentary scan of almost any network reveals that some nodes in the network are much more important than others. A fogged in O'Hare International Airport (the Chicago node) disrupts air traffic around the globe. A foggy Green Bay Austin Straubel International Airport (Green Bay, Wisconsin, node) would barely register on the global scene, unless, of course, the Green Bay Packers were in a playoff game at Lambeau Field that day.

Scholars devote entire books and journals to understanding networks. Although we cannot discuss all the fascinating ideas related to this topic, we can highlight some basic concepts that can greatly enhance your social media strategy:

Hubs

Hubs are nodes that play a role in more than one network. O'Hare International Airport connects to cities all across the world and serves as a major hub for numerous airlines. Austin Straubel International Airport would not be considered a hub, in spite of its official name. Although it is important for the residents, it really represents an endpoint in the commercial airline system.

Hinges

These are nodes that connect otherwise separate groups in the network.[3] **Hinges** are the linchpins of the network. If this node goes down, then two groups will not be able to connect.

Path length

This represents the number of links that separate any two nodes in the system. This distance of separation reminds us of the kids' game of telephone: The more links in the chain, the greater the **path length**, and the stronger the likelihood of distortion.

These basic ideas supply the thinking tools we need to understand connectivity. We will put these tools to work in the next section.

CONNECTION PRINCIPLES

A number of fascinating properties and principles emerge from understanding the concepts of nodes, links, and networks. We highlight a few below.

The pattern of connections (network) is more important than the strength of individual components (nodes). A company with a fantastic website (a node) that lacks the right network connections is functionally useless. This does not mean, though, that the higher the number of connections, the better the network. Rather, it means that we have to think about what function we want our network of connections to perform. Sometimes, the goal is to access as many people as possible, which is exactly the philosophy of companies advertising during the Super Bowl. Sometimes, it is to restrict access to a limited number of exclusive relationships. ISIS, for example, wants to fish for potential jihadist recruits and publicize their horrific acts, but its network does not seek the attention of intelligence agencies such as the CIA. So ISIS is very clever about setting up exclusive relationships with its members and potential recruits. That's why journalist Rukmini Callimachi, a *New York Times* correspondent covering terrorism, needs to spend hours a day trying to find a way to join encrypted or hidden social media channels and chat rooms.[4]

Three archetype networks emerge from the various combinations of hubs, hinges, and path length:

- **Centralized**: A most extreme form of a **centralized network** of connections has one hub, zero hinge points, and a path link of two—between point A and B. (See Figure 9.2)

- **Decentralized**: An extreme form of a **decentralized network** of connections has many hubs and hinge points as well as a potentially large number of path links. In Figure 9.3, a message going from node A to B must pass through four hubs and hinge points. The path link is five.

- **Distributed**: An extreme form of a **distributed network** directly connects every node with every other node. This sort of network rarely happens, even in our brain's deeply connected neural structure—it is much too unwieldy. Rather, most distributed networks take on the character of the one in Figure 9.4. In this case, connecting point A to point B requires zero hubs and hinge points, but the path length can range from one to many depending on how a message is routed. The beauty of a distributed network is that there are so many ways to connect A to B. For instance, you could wind your way through multiple hinge points to reach node C and then arrive back at your neighboring node B.[5] This is not possible in either the centralized or decentralized network.

If you carefully examine the different types of basic networks in Figure 9.2 through Figure 9.4, you'll discover that each contains the same number of nodes. This means that anyone who justifies the quality of their social media strategy by emphasizing the number of platforms is most likely missing the boat. How the nodes are *connected* trumps the *number* of nodes in the network almost every time.

FIGURE 9.2   Centralized Network

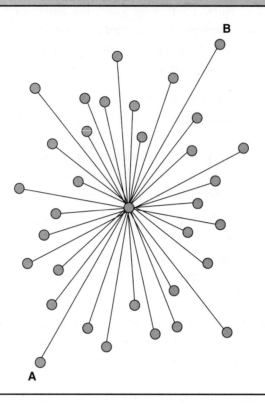

Likewise, it's not the number of connections that is crucial. You may want some "dead" links because these serve your purpose. Consider this unfortunate example: for centuries, pig farms in Malaysia were geographically separated from bat habitats. As the farms grew in size, the two habitats came in closer and closer contact. What happened? The bats transmitted their viruses to the pigs, and through the pigs, these viruses worked their way into the human food chain. That's not a good link between species because the Nipah virus ends up killing up to 70 percent of the people afflicted with it.[6] Therefore, the key question is this: Does the network of connections help you meet your business and communication goals? To answer this question, you have to understand the next principle.

FIGURE 9.3   Decentralized Network

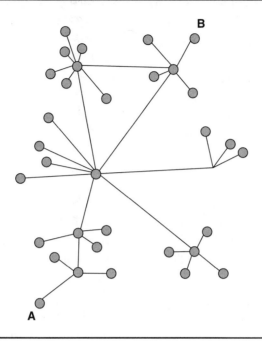

FIGURE 9.4   Distributed Network

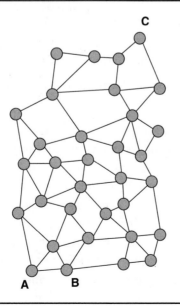

There are trade-offs associated with every type of network. Table 9.1 summarizes insights gleaned from years of testing different types of networks. The table also implies that asking, "What's the best type of network?" resembles the question, "What's the best mode of transportation?" The best network, like the best mode of transportation, depends on what you are trying to accomplish. Selecting the right network configuration involves making trade-offs between potential benefits and costs. Bicycling provides many health benefits, but it is a rather slow way to make a cross-country trek.

For example, a centralized network structure or some related variation, such as a hierarchical structure, makes perfect sense if you want to maximize "command and control" by a "five-star general," authority figure. The trade-off: if the enemy kills the general, the network might collapse. Indeed, President Eisenhower recognized the threat posed by nuclear weapons to a centralized network and subsequently changed the entire thinking behind the traditional command and control structure. Under his leadership, a highly distributed type of communication network emerged for command and control called ARPANET (Advanced Research Projects Agency Network). This network, in turn, became the impetus for the structure of the current Internet.[7] The Eisenhower story should be instructive on at least two levels: first, the structures that worked well in one circumstance may not work at all in a different situation. Recall that General Eisenhower was the Supreme Allied Commander during World War II.[8] Second, it requires the intellectual dexterity of leaders like Eisenhower to recognize the need to shift approaches as the situation changes. It is far too easy for most people to rely on previous "best practices," which are often no longer relevant.

Likewise, it might make sense to build one type of social media network for one audience segment and adopt another form for a different audience segment. For example, you might determine that your social media platforms and websites should be connected in a highly distributed network. That way consumers can easily move from one platform to another. Yet the company's internal nodes (marketing, publicity, administration) need to be more decentralized. Why? You don't want to create an internal situation where "everybody is responsible for everything," which devolves into nobody taking responsibility for anything. In essence, the internal network performs a routing function, making sure that the *right people* are informed about the *right issues* at the *right time.*

TABLE 9.1 Potential Upsides and Downsides of Basic Networks

Network	Potential Upside	Potential Downside
Centralized	• Maximizes command and control • Encourages quick decision making • Fosters quick implementation of central node decision	• Collapses if command node goes down • Central node may experience overload • Noncentralized nodes may experience information deficits
Decentralized	• Encourages specialized expertise • Promotes diversity of thought • Balances consensus development and decision speed	• Fosters clique formation • Distributes information unevenly • Network suffers if hinge goes down
Distributed	• Spreads locus of control • Protects communication network if one or more nodes go down • Cultivates many ideas	• Hinders forming consensus • Slows decision making • Variations may occur in quality of implementation

Networks have both structural and emergent properties. Thus far, we have highlighted the physical structure of networks. In other words, where are the roads on the map? What nodes are theoretically linked to one another? Answers to these questions allow us to determine how the network structure constrains as well as facilitates certain types of connections. But that only tells us about the flow *possibilities*, not about the *actual* flow of messages and information through the network. Indeed, the existence of a link does not tell us if the link is used as intended or if it has morphed into something else. Trying to understand a network by only looking at its structure would be like only examining a road map to understand traffic flows. Sure, it's helpful, but it only tells part of the story.

You can add a deeper layer of understanding by looking beyond the purely structural features of the network and examining its emergent properties. The emergent properties explain how the network is actually used versus its potential use, as in recognizing that traffic flows into the city during the morning rush hour and out in the afternoon. Adding this level of precision allows us to make greater use of the link properties (e.g., capacity and direction). And it provides a natural gateway into our strategic thinking tool, the connections matrix.

CONNECTIONS MATRIX

The **connections matrix** synthesizes the most useful elements from our discussion above by underscoring the key decision points for social media strategists (see Figure 9.5). Think of it this way: the horizontal axis—number of links—looks at the number of roads in the network,

FIGURE 9.5 Connections Matrix

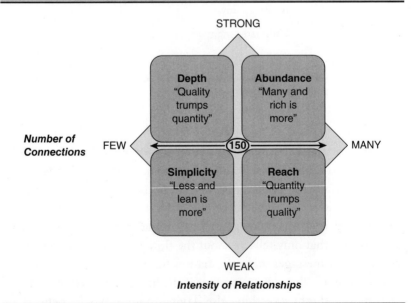

STRONG

Depth
"Quality trumps quantity"

Abundance
"Many and rich is more"

Number of Connections FEW ◄———(150)———► MANY

Simplicity
"Less and lean is more"

Reach
"Quantity trumps quality"

WEAK

Intensity of Relationships

TABLE 9.2 Tendencies of Strong and Weak Connections

Intensity	Tendencies	Examples
Strong	• Frequent • Two way • Highly varied content	• Significant others • Close friends and family • Work team
Weak	• Occasional • One way • Limited content variety	• Pop star or movie star • Thought guru • Politician

while the vertical axis—the intensity of connections—focuses on the flow of the cars.

The horizontal axis of the matrix represents the raw number of links in the network. Pop star Justin Bieber, with millions of Twitter followers, would be at one end of the continuum. Someone who uses Facebook only to stay in touch with immediate family members would be at the other end of the continuum. Note the number 150 in the middle of the horizontal axis of the matrix. This is the Dunbar number, named after Robin Dunbar, who discovered that the average person has the capacity to maintain meaningful relationships with only 150 people.[9] So that number is a nice marker on the axis, reminding us when the dynamics start shifting.

But the raw number of links tells only part of the story. You also need to know about the intensity of the connections that emerge from those links. Note that intensity is primarily a function of the emergent properties of the network. In particular, connections with a strong intensity tend to be frequent, two way, and diverse, containing a high variety of different types of messages. This connection would be like the one between you and a close friend or parent. In a word, these connections are strong and rich (see Table 9.2).

On the other hand, connections of weak intensity tend to be less frequent and one way and to contain limited or generic content. This would be like a relationship you have with a distant relative, who connects with you solely through her annual happy holiday form letter. You would also have a weak link if you were a follower of some pop icon, politician, or TV personality. The link is still weak even if contact is more frequent because it is primarily one way; chances are the pop star won't read any of your posts.

Strong or weak links do *not* equate with good and bad. Strong ties are familiar, fast, rich, and stress resistant. If you post something stupid to people to whom you are strongly tied (e.g., close friends), they are likely to be more understanding than those with whom you have weak ties. Strong ties require a lot of maintenance and caring to work. Weak ties have lower maintenance costs, but they could be potentially useful for discovering new information. The president of the United States has a lot of weak ties with citizens via Twitter feeds but is unlikely to come to your aid if you need something.

Combining these two dimensions (intensity and number) yields a matrix that highlights the underlying strategy implied by network choices (see Figure 9.5):

Simplicity: The strategy of "less and lean is more" makes perfect sense for someone immersed in preparing for a final exam or a grueling medical school rotation. After all, maintaining those links takes time away from a highly demanding task.

Depth: The **depth strategy** is characterized by the "quality trumps quantity" philosophy. People in the late stages of their careers tend to limit the number of relationships they maintain, seeking out very rich interactions with those with whom they connect.

Reach: The **reach strategy** embodies a "quantity trumps quality" approach. It makes a lot of sense for someone who aspires to be a public figure, for example, a pop star, thought guru, or politician. These people desire wide exposure, but not deep connections.

Abundance: This strategy combines the richness of the depth and the wide breadth of the reach strategy. The "many and rich is more" mantra would work well for some CEOs seeking to lead large complex organizations with many varied stakeholders.

Each strategy has upsides and downsides. For example, at first glance, it might appear that the **abundance strategy** trumps all the others. But if you take a deeper look into what's required to execute the strategy successfully, you'd see that it requires a lot of time and energy to manage. In contrast, the **simplicity strategy** requires much less time and energy but there is a cost: a limited ability to enlist the help of others quickly. Figures 9.6 and 9.7 summarize other potential strategic costs and benefits. Because all strategies involve trade-offs, successful strategists reach their goals by maximizing the benefits while minimizing costs. With a good strategy, you take the good while enduring the bad.

We can extend this line of thinking by examining the inherent tendencies of various social media and other communication channels. For example, Twitter naturally leans toward the reach strategy because it emphasizes more one-way than two-way interactions. It's no wonder that we see so many politicians and pop stars fully embracing it. On the flip side, micro-social media sites such as The League (for "hot successful people"), lean toward depth strategies because of the exclusivity of

FIGURE 9.6   Connections Matrix: Potential Benefits

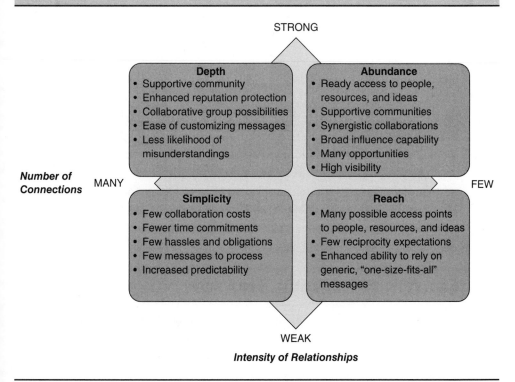

FIGURE 9.7 Connections Matrix: Potential Costs

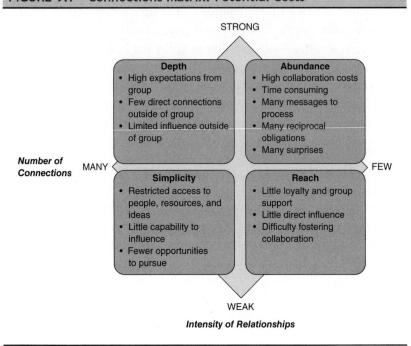

STRONG

Depth
- High expectations from group
- Few direct connections outside of group
- Limited influence outside of group

Abundance
- High collaboration costs
- Time consuming
- Many messages to process
- Many reciprocal obligations
- Many surprises

Number of Connections MANY / FEW

Simplicity
- Restricted access to people, resources, and ideas
- Little capability to influence
- Fewer opportunities to pursue

Reach
- Little loyalty and group support
- Little direct influence
- Difficulty fostering collaboration

WEAK

Intensity of Relationships

membership and the emphasis on two-way communication.[10] Ditto for a more pedestrian social media site, Nextdoor.com, devoted to neighbors sharing updates with those in their immediate neighborhood.[11] Note that we are only talking about tendencies because all the major social media platforms could conceivably be used to execute the reach, depth, or abundance strategies. Twitter, for example, has a tool to facilitate one-on-one, two-way communications. Ditto for Facebook. However, because many users often fail to embrace these features, the actual usage may differ from what the platform providers intended.

CRAFTING NETWORK STRATEGY

Our discussion in the previous sections about networks and the connection matrix should shape the contours of your social media strategy. Molding the strategy into something more solid requires further thought and artistry that starts by considering the following actionable ideas:

Identify a broad range of nodes and links. It's tempting to think only of nodes in terms of your social media platforms and websites. It's also enticing to limit your concept of links to only electronic pathways. Resist these temptations! A robust view of nodes includes the billboards, table kiosks, newsletters, other printed matter, and TV/radio ads that may or may not display links to social media platforms. In addition, nodes include the people, departments, and decision-making processes connected to social media sites. Likewise, the links may be electronic, but they also include face-to-face discussions, meetings, and written reports.

Viewing nodes more robustly, as opposed to considering them as simple dots in a network, also means taking into account the unique sensory mechanisms operating in the node. Neuroscientists discovered that "each type of neuron [or network node] has its own characteristic input-output connectivity profile, connecting with other constituent neuronal types [or types of nodes] with varying degrees of specificity."[12] In essence the nodes in our brains (neurons) often behave in slightly different ways because they display different degrees of sensitivity depending on the type and amount of stimuli. That's almost exactly what happens when you choose to communicate the same message using two particular nodes from the broad array of connections associated with your social media platforms. A single graphic tweet, for instance, might not cause much excitement in your Twitter network, but the exact same image on Pinterest might ignite a wave of interest. A good social media strategist therefore considers carefully the "connectivity profiles" of various nodes. In short, thinking robustly about links and nodes unlocks a world of possibilities and opportunities.

Map out and evaluate your existing network structure. Simply brainstorming all the nodes in your system and then diagramming what nodes are linked can prove enormously revealing. Add another layer of depth to your diagram by noting the typical direction of the flow through the links and volume of the flow. Using arrows and the thickness of lines can neatly illustrate these features of the network.

This graphic illuminates issues that are only dimly hinted at with a line. A critical examination of the diagram may expose underlying strategic connections mistakes as well as new opportunities. We will explore this idea in more depth in the assessment chapter.

For now, let me note the following: We've conducted dozens of connection audits for a wide range of enterprises and brands, including *The Ellen DeGeneres Show*, Donald Trump's political campaign, Snickers, Nike, and numerous small businesses. One of the more astonishing findings to emerge from these audits was the incredible number of broken links and one-way links in the networks. For example, one company's website was not hyperlinked to its Facebook account, Twitter feeds, or Pinterest postings. In another case, a company's Facebook account was not linked to its website. We had no way to determine if these were strategic decisions or not. However, it was curious that sometimes there was no way for potential consumers to make a one-click link to a site to purchase a product or service or to volunteer for a campaign. It's hard to imagine this circumstance resulted from an optimal connection strategy.

Mix and match your connection strategies. As we've emphasized, there is no utopian or one-size-fits-all connection strategy. Instead the strategy must match the competitive landscape, your goals, and the audiences' desires. The depth strategy, for instance, makes a lot of sense for business-to-business relationships (B2B) or business to employee (B2E) types of relationships. A reach strategy works well for pop stars, thought gurus, politicians, and most business to consumer (B2C) types of relationships.

However, there is no need to adopt just one strategy. You might, for instance, adopt a depth strategy for one of your target audiences and a reach strategy for another target audience. In fact, that's exactly the strategy pursued by Red Dress Boutique, a business that sells women's dresses, clothing, accessories, and shoes by creating a "place that would bring color and confidence and happiness to a woman's day." Diana, the founder, shared this thought about her business vision: "You cannot walk in my store [or visit the website] without seeing me in it. From the way Red Dress looks to the clothes that are picked . . . my soul is on display. XOXO."[13] Her soul must also think strategically because her company pursues both the depth and reach strategies in the social media world through Instagram and other platforms. One relatively select group of customers acts as market researchers, passing judgment on styles, pricing, and offerings that make sense for the target audience. The connections within this group are intense but with relatively few people. This classic depth strategy provides the advice needed to execute a reach strategy aimed at the masses of customers. This enormously successful company skillfully matches its social media strategy with its business goals. Note how Red Dress Boutique turns the traditional approach firms have taken to marketing research and purchasing on its head; the "experts" are the actual consumers.

Develop the skills and commitments to match your connection strategies. Anyone with a passing interest in social media can't help but notice the daily flood of "free" advice about how to market your products via social media. The majority of the advice givers hype reach strategies, telling you how to reach more followers or create more pseudo-engagement by garnering more "likes." The problem: the same skills designed to garner more followers or visibility may well undermine a simplicity, depth, or abundance strategy. A shocking visual or a racist comment might attract a lot of new social media followers, but it will undermine a depth strategy based on mutual respect for your followers. Consider Megan Phelps-Roper who had 87 twitter followers prior to releasing an outrageously offensive tweet on World AIDS Day in 2009. After she tweeted a sentiment grounded in a belief structure cultivated at the Westboro Baptist Church in Topeka, Kansas, she increased her number of followers by more than a thousand. Over time, the young woman came to regret and recant such activities.[14]

Let's assume you are aware of the potential risks of offending people but still decide to pursue a reach strategy. If so, then you should read Ben Parr's book, *Captivology*. He advocates using one of the following triggers to seize people's attention:

Automaticity: Selecting images, colors, or sounds designed to capture our attention automatically. Whether you want to or not, you'll pay attention to a loud sound or the image of a tiger rushing toward you.

Framing: Shifting the way we normally view a subject. Think of juxtaposing images that aren't normally seen together.

Disruption: Violating our expectations in some unusual way. For example, imagine creating a headline that violates all the previously reported polling results about a major election.

Mystery: Creating suspense or uncertainty that begs to be resolved. You don't have to be Agatha Christie, but it might help to adopt her persona.

Reward: Promising an external or internal reward. You could offer a discount or the answer to a quiz that provides a personal insight, for example.

Reputation: Using the credibility of experts, celebrities, or historical figures to seize attention. Think about the endorsements your communications could include.[15]

You'll have to discover which approaches will attract the most attention for your audiences.

In contrast, if you select depth and abundance strategies, then you'll find that your audiences value reciprocation over attention-garnering stunts. That requires vigilance and meaningful engagement (see Figure 9.8). It requires a greater ability to personalize and target messages than you need in a breath strategy. In short, just because you or your team skillfully executes one strategy, it will not guarantee success with another strategy. You are playing games as different as baseball and basketball. Sure, great athleticism helps in all sports, but as Michael Jordan knows from personal experience, a championship ring in one sport won't guarantee one in another.

Judge effectiveness based on the strategy employed and the ease of reaching "bull's-eye nodes." If you employ the reach strategy, you are playing a numbers game. This "more-the-merrier" strategy seeks to enlist and engage as many people as possible. You want to increase the number of followers, click-throughs to a target site, or "likes" on a Facebook page. In contrast, if you employ a depth strategy, then the raw numbers matter less than the quality of the relationships, the richness of the interactions, and the types of insights garnered. These effectiveness criteria are far harder to assess than those for the reach strategy. And the effectiveness judgment on the simplicity strategy boils down to how many social media and other entanglements you want to avoid.

Some nodes are more important than others. The bull's-eye node clearly must be the centerpiece of the connection strategy. The general guideline should be this: *the fewer the links needed to get to the bull's-eye node, the better.* The reason: every link separating your target audience from your bull's-eye decreases the probability that the right people will reach it. Making the target easy to reach increases the probability that people

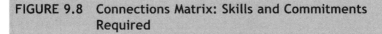

FIGURE 9.8   Connections Matrix: Skills and Commitments Required

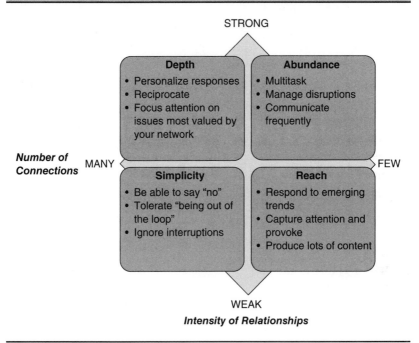

STRONG

Depth
- Personalize responses
- Reciprocate
- Focus attention on issues most valued by your network

Abundance
- Multitask
- Manage disruptions
- Communicate frequently

Number of Connections   MANY

FEW

Simplicity
- Be able to say "no"
- Tolerate "being out of the loop"
- Ignore interruptions

Reach
- Respond to emerging trends
- Capture attention and provoke
- Produce lots of content

WEAK

Intensity of Relationships

hit the bull's-eye node. In short, judging the effectiveness of your connection strategy cannot be reduced to a simple number. Rather, it must also be based on qualitative judgments about whether your connection strategy serves your strategic purpose.

CONCLUSION

When most people discuss social media strategies, the connections component frequently recedes into the background. That's unfortunate. To be sure, nobody but the plumber gets very excited about the network of pipes in your home or apartment. But the moment that a pipe bursts or the sewage flows the wrong way, all that changes. Likewise, when the social media strategy fails to achieve expected results or a social media–induced crisis hits the Internet, it's time to reexamine the connection strategy as well as other elements, such as your content. However, clearly the best time to look at the connection strategy is early in the building process, so it can function like great plumbing—silent and hidden in the background.

KEY TERMS

Abundance strategy 120	Hinges 112
Bull's-eye node 109	Hubs 111
Centralized network 113	Nodes 108
Connections matrix 118	Links 109
Decentralized network 113	Path length 112
Depth strategy 120	Reach strategy 120
Distributed network 113	Simplicity strategy 121

DEEP DIVES

These exercises are designed to enhance your understanding of the chapter's key ideas, principles, and approaches.

1. Figures 9.2 through 9.4 describe three different types of networks. Select two you've personally participated in at work, school, or in your social life.

   a. Create a chart with two columns and two rows. Label the first column, "Network 1," and the second column, "Network 2." Label the first row, "Advantages," and the second row, "Disadvantages."

   b. Reflect on your experiences with each network. Based on your experiences, complete the chart by indicating the advantages and disadvantages of each type of network.

   c. Based on your chart, summarize when it makes the most (and least) sense to use these two networks.

2. Construct a matrix like the one in Figure 9.5.

   a. In each quadrant, indicate three keys to executing the particular strategy successfully.

   b. Provide your rationale.

3. List five social media platforms you are most familiar with.

    a. Identify the bull's-eye node(s) for each platform.

    b. Describe your challenges in locating the bull's-eye node(s) for each platform.

    c. Based on this exercise, describe three lessons learned about the proper use of bull's-eye nodes. Provide your rationale.

NOTES

1. After writing this section, I discovered a widely popular book that made a similar argument in a more extended form. See J. Ramo, *The Seventh Sense: Power, Fortune, and Survival in the Age of Networks* (New York: Little, Brown, and Company, 2016).

2. N. Olivarez-Giles, "A 'Shop Now' Button on Instagram for Buying," *Wall Street Journal*, November 3, 2016, D4.

3. C. Levine, *Forms: Whole, Rhythm, Hierarchy, Network* (Princeton, NJ: Princeton University Press, 2015), 113.

4. C. Roper, "Illuminating ISIS: How One Journalist Uses Social Media to Get Inside the Minds of ISIS," *Wired*, August 3, 2016, 93–95.

5. This feature creates an enormous amount of variety and complexity in a distributed network. We may all end up at point B but through very different paths. For more information see N. Przulj and N. Maloud-Dognin, "Network Analytics in the Age of Big Data," *Science*, July 8, 2016, 123–4.

6. S. Shah, *Pandemic: Tracking Contagions From Cholera to Ebola and Beyond* (New York: Farrar, Straus, Giroux, 2016), 55.

7. S. Malcomson, *Splinternet: How Geopolitics and Commerce Are Fragmenting the World Wide Web* (New York: OR Books, 2016).

8. Note that ARPANET not only involved a structural change in the network configuration but also revolutionized how messages were sent in network structure through packet switching.

9. R. Dunbar, *How Many Friends Does One Person Need?* (Cambridge, MA: Harvard University Press, 2010).

10. You have to submit a profile and then a group of judges decides whether or not you're worthy. See http://www.theleague.com/#are-you-in.

11. Note: With over 111,000 registered neighbors, this site embodies the decentralized network approach.

12. X. Jiang, S. Sheen, C. Cadwell, P. Berens, F. Sinz, A. Ecker, S. Patel, and A. Tolias, "Principles of Connectivity among Morphologically Defined Cell Types in Adult Neocortex," *Science*, November 27, 2015, 1055.

13. "Our Red Dress Boutique Story," Red Dress Boutique website, http://www.reddressboutique.com/our-story. Accessed March 25, 2017.

14. A. Chen, "Unfollow," *The New Yorker*, November 23, 2015, 80–93.

15. B. Parr, *Captivology: The Science of Capturing People's Attention* (New York: HarperOne, 2015), p. 16 of 230 (e-book).

CHAPTER 10

Corrections

"Errors that are obvious to others can be invisible to us, no matter how hard we try to spot them."

—Joseph T. Hallinan

Acknowledging the inevitability of human error does not equate with accepting responsibility for systematically responding to it. This chapter puts that responsibility front and center in your social media strategy. We start by reviewing some more common error sources, which leads to the centerpiece of the chapter about the **corrections matrix**. The concluding section focuses on the implications of the matrix and how to craft the corrections component of your strategy.

SOURCES OF ERRORS

A tangled array of psychological forces and organizational routines produce errors. We discuss the primary ones below.

ATTENTION

Our attention wanders out of necessity. We simply can't pay attention to everything, evn in a wel riten sentence lke this won. We can, however, extract meaning from a sentence—as readers could in spite of the errors in the previous one—without "painstakingly attending to every letter of every word."[1] That's a blessing and a curse. We are blessed with the cognitive ability to chunk large amounts of input to quickly form a response. We are cursed by the same ability and often overlook obvious spelling errors. That's why authors need good copy editors, even if they are horrified by the second sentence in this paragraph. Likewise, social media managers often need someone looking over their shoulders to find spelling errors, missing words, inappropriate images, and potentially offensive posts.

SPEED

Speed dazzles most people, particularly when they participate in activities such as driving, running, cycling, or playing chess. Speed also produces accidents. Just ask anyone who drives a car on a snowy road. Organizations that produce speedy results can dazzle us as well, but at times they miss "a little something," like the extra pickles you ordered with your hamburger. And they often miss out on opportunities, such as pitching a new menu item that might be a bit healthier.

This particular pickle may influence social media managers in major ways because most platforms thrive on speed. Almost every week, celebrities or politicians tweet something they come to regret because they react emotionally to some real or imagined offense. Likewise, celebrities may send the wrong message because, in their haste, they fail to think about potential misunderstandings. Often, mistakes involve pictures that the sender thought were highlighting one message but that unintentionally drew attention to another. Olympic gold medal skier Lindsey Vonn stumbled into this trap when she posted a video of herself angrily destroying the bindings of her skis after one of them detached during a race. Her ski sponsor, Head, thought her displays of frustration reflected poorly on the company. She soon offered profuse apologies to the sponsor and fans while clarifying that she wasn't blaming her skis for the mishap.[2]

A skillful strategist recognizes the value of speed but takes precautions against potential threats. In sum, we all know that "haste makes waste," but we should also recognize that speed could impede thoughtful postings.

HABITS

During which month of the year do you think bank tellers find the most dating errors on checks? If you said, "January," you'd be right.[3] And the answer should be no surprise because most of us put that kind of task on cognitive remote control. Habits, like exercising, can be quite beneficial, but they can also be debilitating when conditions change. Even avid exercisers need to take a day off when they are injured or they risk compounding the problem.

And a social media mistake caused by a habit can even happen to Facebook founder Mark Zuckerberg, whose Twitter and Pinterest accounts were hacked because he did something many of us do. He reused his password, "dadada," from another account that had also been hacked.[4] If it can happen to him, it can happen to anyone and wreak havoc on his or her personal brand.

Likewise, effective social media managers should acquire some healthy habits, such as those discussed in Chapter 4, but there's a flip side. For example, one social media manager had the admirable habit of responding to every post, regardless of the content. He even responded to one particularly vitriolic post. It might have been better just to ignore that post and not set in motion a tirade of other posts that eventually had to be resolved out of the public sphere.

Similarly, organizations develop habits or **thinking routines** that can be potentially problematic. Thought-stopping clichés—"We've always done it that way!"—often stand like giant boulders on the trail leading to new opportunities. These errors of omission simply cannot become the modus operandi in the social media world. It's evolving too quickly.

THINKING BIASES

Mental habits or heuristics help us out most of time. In recent years, one of the richest veins of psychological research involves teasing out these heuristics and crafting countermeasures. The "availability bias," for example, means that we often use the information most available to us to decide. If you use the original retail price to gauge whether an item "on sale" is a "good deal," then you are relying on the available information and will perhaps fall prey to the availability bias. Is it a good deal? Maybe. But if the seller never sold the item at the original

TABLE 10.1   Breaking the Spell of Common Thinking Biases

Bias	Description	Corrective Question
Confirmation	Seeking out information, insights, and arguments that endorse your preexisting views (e.g., only watching TV networks that support your political views)	What contradictory evidence is there?
Sunk Cost	Continuing on a path because so much time or money has been invested on the endeavor, despite the fact that the costs cannot be recovered	If your costs (time, energy, and money) were zero at this point, would you continue on the current path?
Loss Aversion	A tendency to prefer avoiding losses rather than attaining gains (e.g., fear of losing something you already possess)	Are you being overly concerned about potential losses as opposed to potential gains?
Anchoring	Making judgments based on the comparison points provided to you (e.g., comparing the listed price to the "discounted price" on a store shelf)	Is there some other comparison point you should be using?
Framing	A tendency to react to a decision based on how it is presented (e.g., the new procedure will save money for 80 percent of customers versus the new procedure will cost more for 20 percent of customers)	Is there another way to present the problem or decision?
Relational	A predisposition to support positions that your friends adopt	If you took friendships out of the equation, how would you decide?

Bias	Description	Corrective Question
Availability	A tendency to rely on information that is readily available (e.g., relying on what comes up first on a Google search)	Is there any other information that you would like to have to make this decision (e.g., less accessible but more credible information that you should consult)?
Control	Overestimating the amount of power you have over events (e.g., assuming that your safe-driving habits protect you from harm)	What role does chance play in this situation? How will you manage it?
Role	A tendency to make judgments from the perspective of your current role or job duty (e.g., as a manager of department Z versus as a CEO)	If you put on a different hat, how would you view this decision?
Narrative	A tendency to fit the facts to preexisting story lines	Could you use the same facts to tell a different story?

retail price, it might not be. The problem is that we rarely think about this possibility. In Table 10.1, we've identified some common **thinking biases** and some questions that might help you break out of their mystical power.

Social media managers should be particularly attentive to these biases during strategic planning and assessment. The availability bias looms large when assessing the effectiveness of your social media approach. For instance, there are numerous readily available statistics about your social media posts. They may *or* may not be relevant to your business goals. For example, it's helpful to know how many people "like" your posts, but does a particular kind of post drive people to purchase your products or respond to your call to action? That's the key question and one that is not as readily answerable. For example, consider a public service announcement that was launched in Melbourne, Australia, to promote safety on the metro. The tool? A clever and funny video demonstrating "Dumb Ways to Die." The video concluded with "the dumbest way," which was being hit by a train. It was so entertaining that it garnered over 100 million views. It was an advertising "super star," but did it actually improve safety? That's debatable because the number of safety incidents remained almost the same during the year the video went viral.[5]

ORGANIZATIONAL STRUCTURES, PROCEDURES, AND PROTOCOLS

Departments, job descriptions, and meeting protocols are all organizational structures that produce enormous benefits in terms of efficiency, expertise, and effectiveness. It was Henry Ford, for example, who discovered that establishing different "departments" or specialties on an assembly line was far superior to a jack-of-all-trades approach to building automobiles. His successful idea has been replicated and refined in countless organizations.

However, Mr. Ford's structures mass-produce communication challenges as routinely as they do any assembly-line-built automobile. At the top of the list are interdepartmental communication problems. Anyone who has tried to redeem a coupon at a store where the clerks were totally unaware of the promotion has experienced the frustration stemming from an interdepartmental communication problem. Namely, the marketing department may have done a better job communicating with customers than with the company's own frontline employees.[6]

Similar challenges confront social media managers who must coordinate organizational communication across a wide range of departments. Not only do they need to know marketing plans, but they also need to know about products, services, public relations issues, and executive machinations. And they need to know these things almost immediately. That's just one issue that doesn't get factored into most organizational structures. And it's something that can produce unintended errors and missed opportunities.

FIGURE 10.1   The Corrections Matrix

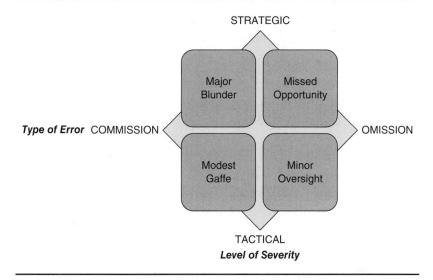

Years ago, Ernst Mach noted that "Knowledge and error flow from the same mental sources, only success can tell the one from the other."[7] He highlighted a profoundly significant idea that serves as a backdrop for this entire discussion. Namely, each of the concerns discussed above—attention, speed, habits, thinking routines, and organizational structures—produce both benefits and costs. We've tried to underscore both while drawing attention to the special challenges they create for social media managers committed not only to acknowledging the occasional error but also to building a strategy to manage the correction process actively. The corrections matrix discussed next provides the intellectual foundation for the strategy.

CORRECTIONS MATRIX

Despite the inherent psychology and organizational barriers, there are some errors that are easier to detect and correct than others. The corrections matrix explains why (see Figure 10.1). It all boils down to understanding the different types of errors. Two basic dimensions define the matrix. The vertical axis identifies the severity of the error: Is it strategic or tactical? The horizontal axis identifies the type of error: Is it an error of omission or commission? The labels in the quadrants describe the type of mistake and hint at the relative severity. To illustrate, let's assume you are running a coffee bar with a social media presence.

The four quadrants illustrate mistakes of various sorts and of different levels of severity: the **minor oversight**, the **modest gaffe**, the **missed opportunity**, and the **major blunder**.

Minor oversight: This quadrant highlights tactical errors of omission. If the barista forgets to add cream to your coffee, then this minor oversight could be corrected easily with the flick of a spoon. Likewise, the social media manager who announces a new coffee blend but neglects to post the related picture could quickly rectify the situation with the click of a mouse.

Modest gaffe: This quadrant spotlights tactical errors of commission. The customer who requests a cup of Irish cream but is served a brew of crème brûlée isn't particularly happy. Nor would customers who respond to a Facebook post announcing a sale on coffee filters only to discover they aren't marked down in the café. Even though these incidents moderately annoy customers, both errors can be corrected easily.

Missed opportunity: This quadrant draws attention to strategic errors of omission. A café, overly influenced by traditional sensibilities, may not recognize the opportunities to market iced coffee. An equally myopic view of social media could lead the same café to ignore the possibilities of lower-profile platforms such as Tinder or Nextdoor. In both instances, nobody did something "wrong," per se. Rather, the café missed out on some innovative idea that could enhance its profitability.

Major blunder: This quadrant sheds light on strategic errors of commission. The café that routinely mixes up its decaffeinated and caffeinated blends because of confusing labeling has stumbled onto a major mess. The social media manager who "aw shucks" it all off on overwhelmed employees, even when evidence mounts of a brewing crisis, compounds the blunder. After all, someone's racing heart might lead to a severe health crisis because he unwittingly consumed too much of a caffeinated blend. Bottom line: the image of the café suffers and this hit has the potential to harm the business's long-term viability.

Or consider the effects of a misspelled or missing word, which can happen with the tap of the mouse. Even spellcheck might not catch the glitch. That's exactly what happened when Adidas had to apologize for misspelling the South American country "Colombia" in ads for the Copa America soccer tournament. It used the famous university spelling, "Columbia," and the Twitter sphere went wild in mocking the company.[8]

The corrections matrix provides social media managers with a robust perspective on error correction challenges. It implies, for instance, that we should use diverse approaches to detect and correct different types of mistakes. More implications are explored in the next section.

So What?

So why is a correction strategy important? And what action steps does the corrections matrix imply? This section directly addresses these questions.

First, detect patterns of errors. Are you consistently making the same kinds of mistakes? This sounds like an easy question to answer, but it may not be. For example, we often discount random errors as mere chance occurrences, shaking them off as we would some minor, annoying bug at a picnic. We fail to detect that we routinely set up the picnic near a swamp with lots of bugs. Because these errors are easy to correct, we hardly give them a second thought.

Keeping a log of errors, large and small, provides the data points necessary for pattern detection. You must have the "dots" to "connect the dots." The log provides the dots, and the analysis allows you to connect them. To be sure, some of the dots will just be random, but what you are really looking for are the ones that are more systematic. In all likelihood, the dots will be tactical in nature, but that does not mean that the underlying source of the errors is tactical in nature. In fact, the source may be something more strategic. For instance, several scattered instances of posting the wrong picture with the text may be an unrelated string of unfortunate miscues. Or this kind of mistake may be an indication of a strategic mistake involving your connection strategy. Perhaps the people or departments providing the images are not properly connected with the social media department.

Second, build an eagle-eyed radar screen. If you're not searching for errors and exploring possibilities, then you won't find them. That's why you need to create a radar screen to detect both. You need to keep real-time tabs on the platform traffic as well as your performance. A good radar screen puts those numbers at your fingertips through a host of analytics. These are discussed in more depth later in the book.

It is also helpful to monitor your competitors' posting behaviors and patterns. Doing so might help you discover your own errors of omission. The corrections matrix spotlights errors of omission. People are far more attentive and upset by errors of commission than by errors of omission. You are far more likely to notice a large slash in a Rembrandt than you are to detect missing artwork. The destroyed painting violates your aesthetic expectation regarding art, but missing artwork represents a forgone opportunity that you might never have thought about. Errors of omission are usually not debilitating in the short term, but they may be in the long term. One forgone opportunity probably will not derail a business or a social media plan. However, if neglecting opportunities becomes a habit, deeper problems start to emerge.

Third, augment your radar screen by recruiting and maintaining your own friendly spy network. As we all have blind spots and anybody can inadvertently push the wrong button, it's helpful to have a **friendly spy network** watching over your posts and your competitors' posts. The role of these friendly spies is to alert you quickly to possible miscues and missed opportunities. In one case, a thought leader inadvertently "liked" some questionable Instagram photos. Let's just say the photos were not appealing to the intellectual interests of his followers. Why did this occur? It could have been that he was just learning how to use his new iPhone or that someone else used his phone. It really doesn't matter. The thought leader was completely unaware of the post, and thus, the error. But his friendly spies saved him and alerted him to the problem before it had much time to do damage to his reputation.

What kind of friendly spies do you want to recruit? Good spies are über-attentive to sensory cues and deeply knowledgeable about platform sensibilities. And they must know what you are trying to achieve. They don't need to be particularly sneaky or have any secret gadgets; they just need to be monitoring, watching, and evaluating posts constantly.

Fourth, build an experimental lab. Bloggers and self–anointed social media gurus offer a lot of advice about the kind of content and the proper timing of posts. Some of it is useful; most is not. And there is a simple reason: Often the database from which they draw their inferences is a) narrowly restricted to their personal experiences or b) based on global trends across the entire platform. In both cases, you just don't know if these same trends apply to *your* core audiences. It's the paradox of best practices. To be sure, we want to study the best practices of others, but we want to ensure that they apply to our own situation.

The alternative? Build an experimental lab where you are constantly testing and improving your posts. You could test different images, words, calls to action, and even the timing of the posts. Testing two versions of the same post—performing what's known as an **A/B test**—is the gold standard. This is one best practice that most social media strategists should embrace. It's relatively simple if you've built the right radar screen (See Table 10.2).

TABLE 10.2 A/B Testing Protocol

Steps
1. Craft a compelling message
2. Select two *different* test images—image A and image B
3. Create a message A by combining it with Step 1 wording and image A
4. Create a message B by combining it with Step 1 wording and image B
5. Randomly assign one portion of your audience to Group A and the other to Group B
6. Simultaneously post message A to Group A and message B to Group B
7. Monitor results over 24 hours and see which one has the most traffic
8. Declare a winner
9. Continue to refine with new wording and images as necessary

This is precisely how former president Obama determined what to post in social media requests for donations to his presidential campaign. The social media analytics wizards determined, for instance, that a black-and-white photo of the president's family generated more donations than a video. Likewise, the words, "Donate and Get a Gift" worked better with first-time donors while the words "Please Donate" worked better with more seasoned newsletter subscribers.[9] Once the social media managers determined these facts, they used them in all subsequent requests for donations.

Fifth, determine what type of corrective action to take. You don't want to overreact and treat all glitches like major strategic errors. Nor do you want to underreact or downplay a major gaffe. A persistent cough could be the lingering effects of a cold or indicate something far more serious. Likewise, a few negative reactions to a post might be a minor annoyance or indicate some significant strategic error. If you frequently misread your audience by posting material they deem offensive, then you should do some soul-searching about your strategy. The key is to match the response with the type of error. And that's where the corrections matrix proves especially valuable.

- *Minor Oversight*: Tweaking your existing approach best suits errors that fall in this category. No need for deep soul-searching or innovative self-examination; just make the adjustment and move on. Experiment and see if it works.

- *Modest Gaffe*: Quickly fixing the problem is your best bet when operating in the modest gaffe territory. Arguing about who is right or wrong is often counterproductive. Even if you win the argument, you might permanently damage important relationships. That's why it's important to anticipate likely errors and challenges. For example, if you operate in the social media space, you will inevitably encounter some angry posts from time to time. You should have a plan in place to triage and deal with these issues. In Appendix 2, Professor Ryan Martin identifies some useful approaches for dealing with angry online posts.

- *Missed Opportunities*: Strategic adaptation best corrects challenges that arise with missed opportunities. You are not completely throwing out your strategy; rather you are making midcourse corrections based on new insights or problems. In one sense, every strategy requires routine adaptation and adjustment. However, if you are constantly making major adjustments to your strategy, then it probably indicates some deep flaw in your strategic planning process.

- *Major Blunders*: Rethinking your entire strategy might be the best response to a major blunder. Something significant is amiss, and it has the potential to greatly influence the viability of the enterprise. Therefore, it makes a lot of sense to go back to the strategic drawing board, diagramming both the underlying cause of a particular blunder and the flaws in your thought process. Asking, "How could we have missed this huge risk?" can go a long way toward reenergizing your strategy.

The bottom line: errors are inevitable; learning from them is not. Two professors may have best summed up the idea in their *Harvard Business Review* article:

> Failure is less painful when you extract the maximum value from it. If you learn from each mistake, large and small, share those lessons, and periodically check that these processes are helping your organization move more efficiently in the right direction, your return on failure will skyrocket.[10]

Sixth, set up a regular assessment process. Logging daily errors is helpful on the tactical side. So is having a robust radar screen. Both tools tend to be focused on the more immediate and short-term situation. But skilled strategists are not content with a log and a radar screen. Instead, they seek out a more comprehensive strategic review of the 5 Cs on a quarterly or semiannual basis. This is such an important process that we devote a chapter of the book to it.

Conclusion

Thoughtful readers probably noticed that this chapter almost brings us full circle. That is, your corrective processes will often indicate the need to a) shift your assessment of the competitive environment, b) tweak your coordinates, c) reexamine your channel choices, d) adjust your content, and e) modify your connection strategy. That's perfectly appropriate. Why? The price of sustained excellence is unrelenting dissatisfaction with the status quo.

Note that we said that a sound correction strategy "almost" completes the circle. There is one more final test, though, which we highlight in the next chapter.

KEY TERMS

A/B test 141

Corrections matrix 131

Friendly spy network 140

Major blunder 138

Minor oversight 138

Missed opportunity 138

Modest gaffe 138

Thinking biases 135

Thinking routines 133

DEEP DIVES

These exercises are designed to enhance your understanding of the chapter's key ideas, principles, and approaches.

1. Recreate Figure 10.1. Identify a social media error that falls into each of the quadrants. Provide your rationale.

2. Conduct an A/B test with your own social media network.

    a. Discuss your rationale for conducting this particular test.

    b. Describe the test and the results.

    c. Discuss three lessons learned from conducting the test.

3. Describe five characteristics of a world-class "radar screen."

    a. Discuss your reasons for selecting these characteristics.

    b. Describe the procedures necessary to launch and maintain the radar screen.

    c. Craft an "elevator talk" about how you'd sell your radar screen to a company's executive team.

NOTES

1. M. Van Hecke, *Blind Spots: Why Smart People Do Dumb Things* (New York: Prometheus Books, 2007), 21.
2. "Vonn's Title Overshadowed by Gaffe," *Green Bay Press-Gazette*, February 21, 2016, 8c.
3. J. Reason, *Human Error* (New York: Cambridge University Press, 1990).
4. See R. McMillan, "Mark Zuckerberg's Twitter and Pinterest Accounts Hacked," *The Wall Street Journal*, June 7, 2016, http://www.wsj.com/articles/mark-zuckerbergs-twitter-and-pinterest-accounts-hacked-1465251954. Accessed June 8, 2016.
5. S. Atchison and J. Burby, *Does it Work? 10 Principles For Delivering True Business Value in Digital Marketing* (New York: McGraw Hill, 2015).
6. P. Clampitt, *Communicating for Managerial Effectiveness*, 6th ed. (Los Angeles: Sage Publications, 2017), chap. 8.
7. E. Mach, *Knowledge and Error: Sketches on the Psychology of Enquiry* (Dordrecht, Holland: Reidel Publishing, 1905), 84.
8. See J. Billington, "Adidas Advertising Campaign Mocked on Twitter for Embarrassing Colombia Spelling Mistake," *International Business Times*, June 8, 2016, http://www.ibtimes.co.uk/adidas-advertising-campaign-mocked-twitter-embarrassing-colombia-spelling-mistake-1564364. Accessed June 9, 2016.
9. B. Christian and T. Griffiths, *Algorithms to Live By* (New York: Henry Holt, 2016), p. 125 of 949 (e-book).
10. J. Birkinshaw and M. Haas, "Increase Your Return on Failure." *Harvard Business Review* 94, no. 5 (May 2016): 89–93, p. 93.

CHAPTER 11

Syncing the Strategy Dots and Crafting Action Plans

"Effective strategy also demands constant management, reassessment, and adaptation largely because war is interactive—the enemy gets a vote."

—Andrew Wilson

A sports team can assemble a great cast of All-Stars, but unless they work together they won't deliver on their promise. That's exactly what happened to the Los Angeles Lakers in the 2003–2004 season. The team assembled a group of perennial All-Stars, including Kobe Bryant, Shaquille O'Neal, Karl Malone, and Gary Payton, to take another shot at a championship. They ultimately did not deliver on the promise; in fact, much of the blame went to the constant infighting and bickering among the superstars. This happened despite the team having a world-class Zen master coach in Phil Jackson.[1]

The same logic applies to the 5 Cs. You can have great coordinates, the right channels, all-star content, great connections, and a stellar correction plan, but your strategy can still fail unless they all sync with one another. This chapter discusses three tests that enhance the likelihood of a social media championship season.

TEST 1: THE COORDINATES TEST

Throughout the preceding chapters we've suggested that the coordinates should sync with the other four Cs. This test, though, brings the issue into an even sharper focus (see Figure 11.1). It's like asking your team, "Are we committed to a championship?" The championship represents the ultimate "business" goal, and the players represent the channels, content, connections, and corrections part of the strategy.

To illustrate the **coordinates test**, we'll assume that one of your goals is to "increase your target audience's attendance at your event." To pass this test, you need to confidently "green light" or answer "yes" to the following questions:

1. *Will the selected channels increase your target audience's attendance at your event (i.e., Coordinates >>> Channels test)?* Pinterest would be a poor choice because you can't provide links for further information or forms to sign up. Facebook or Twitter would be a better choice.

2. *Will your content choices increase your target audience's attendance at your event (i.e., Coordinates >>> Content test)?* Even if you get the platform right, poor content choices can undermine your strategy. Overly wordy messages or lackluster images, for example, rarely inspire action. On the other hand, messages that make use of classic persuasion techniques enhance the probability that you'll inspire others to attend the event. For example, Facebook messages highlighting that group opinion leaders will be attending can be particularly useful.

3. *Will your connection choices increase your target audience's attendance at your event (i.e., Coordinates >>> Connections test)?* Even if your channel and content choices are aligned with the goals, you won't be assured of success without a thoughtful connection strategy component. For example, if the links to the event sign-up are cumbersome or broken, you will undermine all the other good work you've done. A simple trial run of the sign up procedure from the initial alert to the end of the process can often prevent headaches. There are not only technical

FIGURE 11.1   The Coordinates Test

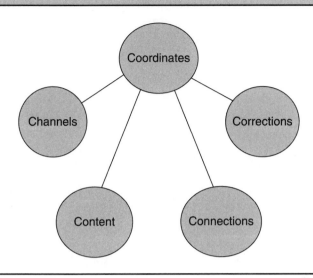

connections to test; you also want to check out connections with key departments and people.

4. ***Will your correction plan increase your target audience's attendance at your event (i.e., Coordinates >>> Corrections test)?*** This test should raise a number of questions. Here are some: 1) Do you have in place a radar screen to monitor results in real time? 2) Are you doing any A/B tests to check out your messaging? 3) Do you have a plan for quickly correcting glitches that will inevitably surface?

These tests are vital, but they do not guarantee success. That's the focus of the second test.

TEST 2: THE SYNERGY TEST

Although Figure 11.1 visualizes the most basic test of your strategy, Figure 11.2 visualizes something more profound—the **synergy test**. It highlights the need for all the elements to strengthen and reinforce

FIGURE 11.2   The Synergy Test

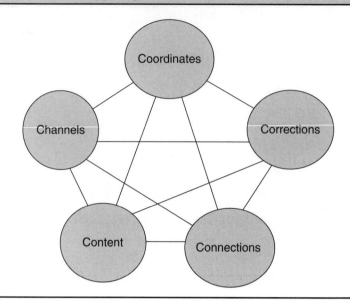

one another. The strategic magic occurs when all the lines buzz with vitality, figuratively and literally.

Table 11.1 outlines a simple way to cultivate these sensibilities by testing for the level of compatibility between the 5 C strategy elements. A "green light" signals a strong, vibrant, and even reinforcing relationship between the strategy elements. The "yellow light" signals a more cautionary relationship between the elements, while the "red light" indicates an incongruent or nonexistent relationship. If your strategy passed Test 1, then you should be able to "green light" all the cells in column one of Table 11.1. This means that your channel selections, message approach, connection decisions, and correction plan match up with all your coordinates. The other cells waiting to be checked suggest six other, even more challenging questions:

1. *Are the channels aligned with your message choices (i.e., Channels >>> Content test)?* On June 23, 2016, the Democrats in the U.S. House of Representatives staged a sit-in to protest the lack of movement on the gun legislation they were trying to pass.

TABLE 11.1 "Green Light, Yellow Light, and Red Light" Compatibility Tests (Synergy Grid)

	Coordinates	Channels	Content	Connections
Channels				
Content				
Connections				
Corrections				

Speaker of the House Paul Ryan invoked House rules and shut down the normal C-Span TV cameras. Democratic representatives soon realized that, without TV coverage, their protest would fail to raise much public attention. They soon switched to Facebook and Twitter feeds to share their protest message. C-Span, in an unprecedented move, broadcast the representatives' live Facebook and Twitter feeds, as well. This innovation borne out of necessity passes the channel-content test with rebel-like flying colors. This commando-like channel choice had a grainy, rebellious, haphazard feel that perfectly suited the protest message. In essence, the channel choice—even though born out of necessity—strengthened the message. In fact, viewership soared into the millions, far surpassing what it would have been through the traditional C-Span feed.[2]

You might not stumble on this kind of alignment between message and channel, but you can think about how well they are aligned. This is where your deep understanding of the channel becomes particularly useful. For instance, LinkedIn would be a superior choice over Facebook for sharing information about a professional job search.

2. *Are the channels aligned with your connection decisions (i.e., Channels >>> Connections test)?* One of the most common yet least apparent sources of strategic failure can be traced back to the particular misalignment highlighted by this question. Consider, for example, one philanthropic organization dedicated to supporting youth musical education. The organization hired

a young person to direct outreach efforts to the community. The young person's social media messages clicked with young people, but they failed to keep the major (and older) donors informed about outreach efforts. Why? The older donors relied on other networks to communicate with one another, such as "old style" email and phone calls. In other words, the connection approaches that worked well with one group did not work well with another group. So this cell would have received a "yellow" or perhaps a "red" light, meriting further inquiry.

3. *Are the channels aligned with your correction plan (i.e., Channels* >>> *Corrections test)?* This may appear to be an unnecessary question. After all, can't you quickly correct errors on every social media platform? Isn't one of the great benefits of social media over traditional print media the speed at which errors can be corrected? All true. But these questions only address part of the correction equation. Both queries assume that the errors have already been detected. Additionally, even if the errors are detected, the questions focus more on tactical rather than strategic issues. Before you give this test the "green light," make sure you can confidently answer the following:

   • Do you have a protocol in place to determine if you are making strategic errors and missing strategic opportunities in your use of selected platforms?

   • Do you have processes in place to detect tactical platform errors and opportunities quickly?

   • Do you have protocols in place to shift your platform strategy as the platform evolves?

   If you can answer "yes" to these questions, then you are ready to go.

4. *Are the message choices aligned with your connection decisions (i.e., Content* >>> *Connections test)?* We've all been with a group of people when someone tells what she considers to be a wickedly funny joke but nobody laughs. Does she lack Amy Schumer's comedic talent? Or is the joke really not that funny? It's hard to judge. Every comedian knows that a joke that works for one audience can utterly fail for another. Likewise, social media managers must determine which messages and images best suit their particular networks.

Note the pluralization of the word "network" in the sentence above. It is all too easy to treat all your social media followers the same, as in a singular "network." Consider again the task of using social media to promote attendance at an upcoming event. Your more casual followers will need messages designed to garner attention and interest. You don't need much of that kind of messaging for your core supporters. You can count on them; they will be there. They need messages with more details and ones telling them how they can help promote the event.

Likewise, internal and external connections should be managed and messaged in different ways. Poorly managed internal organizational connections have undermined countless social media programs. For example, the external marketing team needs to be well connected to the social media team, so both teams can reinforce various messages and campaigns. A direct mail campaign launched by the marketing team could be strengthened by a parallel social media effort. Coordinating those strategies requires messaging designed to promote collaborative relationships between the departments, which doesn't mean merely cc'ing others about the promotional material.

5. *Are the message choices aligned with your correction decisions (i.e., Content >>> Corrections test)?* Every social media manager makes messaging mistakes and misses messaging opportunities. It's inevitable because of the speed of decision making. To "green light" this box in the grid confidently, you need to consider whether your strategy has envisioned several common worst-case scenarios. For instance, how would you detect and correct a surge in angry rants by your followers? On the flip side, how does your strategy detect and respond to emerging cultural trends or political events? The Oreo cookie brand passed this test with flying colors during Super Bowl XLVII, when there was a 34-minute power outage and the game had to be stopped. Oreo tweeted, "You can still dunk in the dark," accompanied by the perfect image. That's precisely the kind of messaging response that a great corrections strategy produces.

6. *Are the connection decisions aligned with your correction plan (i.e., Connections >>> Corrections test)?* In the "Corrections" chapter, we discussed the benefits of recruiting friendly spies to help you detect

errors of commission and maybe even errors of omission (things your competitors are doing that you are not). If you have that semi-clandestine network of connections in place, then you are well on the way to green-lighting this box. The alignment of the connection and correction strategic components spurs other inquiries, as well. For instance, in your organization, do you have the kind of access to senior leadership that will allow you to address quickly erroneous reports that might surface in the print or televised media?

TEST 3: THE TRANSLATION TEST

The final test, the **translation test**, directs attention to how you translate your strategy into action plans and tactics. After your strategy has passed Tests 1 and 2, you are ready to act. Table 11.2 illustrates in an abbreviated form what you need to get down in concrete terms on paper. Simply, in column one, note the various coordinates of your strategy. In column two, indicate the associated channel, content, connection, and correction strategic elements. In column three, specify the related tactics including what needs to be done, who will do it, and when it will be done. A downloadable version of Table 11.2 is available at www.amazingsmstrategy.com.

TEST-TAKING ADVICE

Some words of advice about conducting these tests.

First, don't assume that because you passed Test 1 that you will ace Test 2. The tests suggest a degree of conceptual fluidity between the various

TABLE 11.2 The Translation Test

Coordinates	Other Strategic Elements				Tactics
	Channels	Content	Connections	Corrections	

strategic components. Some people might reason, for example, if all the strategic components align with the coordinates, then the strategic components will align with one another. Maybe. Maybe not. Think of it this way: Assume that you and your partner have agreed to decorate your new apartment in the art deco style. Each of you descends on your favorite shopping spots and purchases furniture, artwork, and curiosities in that style. Both of you are aligned with the strategic coordinate or goal. But there is no guarantee that the purchased items will work well with each other in the available space. In the same way, the coordinates test (Test 1) represents an important vital screen, but it will not guarantee the vibrancy of a social media strategy that passes the synergy test (Test 2).

Second, solicit the opinions and insights of others. No individual person, no matter how smart, can craft a superior social media strategy. Discussions and debates bring out perspectives, challenges, and issues that will not surface from the lone social media genius. Moreover, green-lighting a cell in the synergy grid (see Table 11.1) always translates into making judgment calls, and that requires debate. Even though metrics can be helpful, there is not a simple formula for computing answers to these synergistic questions. The answers summarize a narrative essay in the form of green-, yellow-, or red-light judgments.

Third, expect imperfections. Thoughtfully completing the synergy grid usually results in a number of yellow lights. A chart with all green lights usually signals some level of self-deception. After all, no one has ever crafted the perfect strategy in war or peacetime. Plus, the primary reason for conducting synergy tests is to identify potential opportunities and problems. The yellow and red lights call attention to adjustment possibilities. Maybe the coordinates should be adjusted. Maybe the message strategy needs work, and so on. The entire idea is that the strategic components strengthen and invigorate one another.

In short, treat the tactical approach that emerges from your discussion on green, yellow, and red lights (see Table 11.2) as a living document that needs to be updated regularly.

CONCLUSION

Nestled in the resort town of Fish Creek, Wisconsin, is Julie's Café, a favorite of locals and many tourists to the Door County peninsula. The restaurant has a *business* goal of increasing its repeat business and a *social media* goal of cultivating a friendly atmosphere. You might get a flavor of the café's business approach when you are greeted with the sign "Enter as strangers, leave as friends." And Julie's does a remarkable job of living up to the slogan with its engaging, long-term core staff that trains seasonal servers from all over the world.

The café's social media strategy augments its business strategy. For example, establishing and maintaining a Facebook presence makes perfect sense for a café promoting a casual, friendly waitstaff. The content of much of the business's social media features a healthy dose of crazy, behind-the-scenes action, highlighting both staff and customers. One clever video titled "A Spot on Table 25" focuses on a spot on a table that stubbornly resists all efforts at removal. The creator, Debra Hadraba, who is also a restaurant manager, tells a story as wildly colorful as her signature leggings. The clip begins with customers noticing a spot on the table and thinking that the table needs cleaning. The customers make various frustrating attempts to remove it, until the climactic moment when an unusual solution appears in the form of a green crayon. It wasn't a spot, at all—it was a natural blemish in the wood of the table that could be covered up with the crayon. Video clips and messages such as these creatively put into motion the content strategy. The "spot" also highlights the connection part of the café's social media strategy because it features the friendly staff as well as frequent customers.

Another piece of the café's connection strategy is something customers never see—a special Facebook group the café set up for its seasonal international workers to consult prior to their arrival in the United States. The purpose of that group is to familiarize workers with the menu, each other, and local restaurant peculiarities that they would never learn in their English classes, such as the definition of "bumbleberry pie." That's a delicious example of how the strategic synergy emerges from choices about connections, channels, and content. Julie's owners, Shane and Sande, as well as a "friendly spy network" of regular customers, serve as the corrective mechanism in case something goes awry.

Your inner finance persona might be asking, does this social media strategy really yield results? This question is fair, difficult to answer, and important. In fact, it is so significant that the entire next section of the book is devoted to it. As far as Julie's owners are concerned, they are thrilled with the results because the social media strategy lowers advertising expenses and generates buzz from the patrons, who often request to sit at Table 25. One diner even offered Debra a green crayon to solve the problem of the "spot" on Table 25. Other customers say that the Facebook posts make them feel as if they "already know the staff." That's the gold standard for an establishment that wants to be known for creating virtual and personal friends.

KEY TERMS

Coordinates test 148
Synergy test 149

Translation test 154

DEEP DIVES

These exercises are designed to enhance your understanding of the chapter's key ideas, principles, and approaches.

1. Rank order the three tests outlined in this chapter based on difficulty. Provide your rationale.

2. Find three examples of social media decisions that pass one coordinates test but fail another one. Provide your rationale.

3. One of the challenges in constructing a social media strategy is distinguishing between strategies and tactics. Create a series of five tests that can be used to make the distinction. These tests may take the form of a sentence, such as "We've created a tactic when. . . ." Provide your rationale for the tests.

NOTES

1. Thanks to Michael Sadoff for this example. See R. Bucher, "An Oral History of the 2003–04 Los Angeles Lakers, the 1st Super Team," *The Bleacher Report*, May 26, 2015, http://m.bleacherreport.com/articles/2468658-an-oral-history-of-the-2003-2004-los-angeles-lakers-the-first-super-teams. Accessed June 22, 2016.
2. N. Andrews and K. Peterson, "C-Span Takes a Star Turn in House Democrats' Sit-in." *Wall Street Journal,* June 24, 2016, A1.

PART III

Assessing Results

How do you know if your strategy and tactics are working? In a word, assess. Perhaps more important, how do you persuade social media skeptics that your strategy makes a difference? A good assessment plan, once again, provides the answer.

This section highlights an approach to assessment anchored in thoughtful inquiry and meaningful measurements designed to produce influential reports for organizational leaders. The following figure (Creating a Sound Assessment Plan) outlines a three-step approach starting with developing a protocol based on key strategy and performance questions and ending with how to craft a persuasive and useful assessment report. Let's start the journey of proving the value of your strategy!

Creating a Sound Assessment Plan

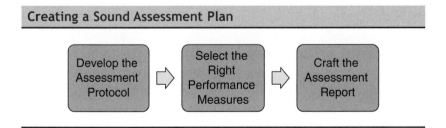

CHAPTER 12

Developing the Assessment Protocol

"Followers don't automatically equal influence. Succeeding is not a volume game because friends, fans, and followers don't directly translate to income on a profit-and-loss statement. Impressions don't convert but influence does."

—Amy Jo Martin

Richard Feynman is my favorite physicist. Professor Feynman was a slightly zany, deeply thoughtful contrarian who was a gifted visualizer of complex phenomena. And he was a Nobel Prize winner. One of his most memorable aphorisms was, "The first principle is that you must not fool yourself and you are the easiest person to fool."[1] If you assess your strategy and performance properly, then you are abiding by his principle. If not, then you are probably fooling yourself. Unfortunately, there are a lot of ways to fool yourself and mislead others.

HOW WE FOOL OURSELVES

Three of the more common ways are reviewed below.

First, we fool ourselves by focusing on one or a few metrics. Numbers can reveal important information, but they also inherently conceal underlying facts. Consider major league baseball Hall of Fame player Reggie Jackson who played for 21 seasons. A baseball player's batting average is the most frequently cited statistic measuring a player's value. Reggie's rather pedestrian lifetime batting average of .262 certainly doesn't begin to tell the story of his worth. Other statistics, such as slugging percentage (SLG) and runs batted in (RBI), provide a better picture of his athletic prowess. He was known as Mr. October for his legendary slugging during the playoffs. In fact, he helped the New York Yankees win the 1977 World Series by hitting three consecutive home runs in game 6. It was a truly amazing feat.[2]

Likewise, the total number of followers or even the number of "likes" reveals important information, but these totals also conceal other important metrics such as actions on the page, post engagement, and total page reach.[3] After all, certain celebrities have been known to "buy" followers and "likes" covertly to boost their perceived value.

Second, we fool ourselves by neglecting to identify underlying <u>actionable</u> issues. Over the last several decades, my associates and I have conducted hundreds of communication assessments in organizations. Our primary objective was to measure the effectiveness of the communication system. We can easily assess employees' general level of communication satisfaction by comparing the results to our databank norm. But this would be like comparing Reggie Jackson's batting average to the averages of other players. It reveals some important information, but it doesn't provide specific and actionable items that the executive coaches need to improve the communication in the organization. So we ask a series of other, more specific questions about issues such as supervisory communication, performance feedback, and information flows—questions that are related to overall communication satisfaction. Breaking the general question into its component parts allows us to make more targeted recommendations to improve the organization's communication system.

Likewise failing to identify other related, underlying, and actionable social media factors translates into playing a fool's game of chasing ephemeral numbers without understanding the dynamics of the game you are really playing. Fortunately, the 5 Cs approach provides the model for identifying the specific challenges social media managers need to master. More on this later.

Third, we fool ourselves by failing to take the situation into account. It almost goes without saying that all assessments take place within a situational context. Unfortunately, assessors often need to be reminded of this simple fact. Consider one administrator who managed three different departments at a midsized university and was required to do annual assessments. Normally, that makes perfect sense, but one of his departments had recently lost half of its faculty and was in the process of revising the entire curriculum. It would be a meaningless, valueless, and senseless exercise to conduct the typical assessment in this situation. Consequently, the administrator, using more diplomatic language, requested a waiver for the year by pointing out the limited value of any information gleaned from such a tedious exercise. It was not granted. This story demonstrates the all too typical and myopic bureaucratic focus on process over purpose.

We can extrapolate a general lesson about assessment from this incident. Namely, all evaluations are generated in a certain context, and those contexts need to be considered when interpreting the findings. Social media assessments can inadvertently fall into this trap by not taking into account how long it takes to master a platform, changes in who is responsible for the platform, and recent modifications in the platform. It's unrealistic, for example, to expect a newly launched social media strategy to perform as well as one tweaked over a number of years. Learning about the nuances of a new strategy or new responsibilities requires time. Even then, some external changes made by the platform provider, such as eliminating a feature, may alter your results. For example, Facebook announced in June 2016 that it would place higher priority on posts from friends and family in users' news feeds.[4] These issues need to be considered when making judgments about a social media strategy and performance. Of course, exercising good judgment also means distinguishing between "taking into account" reasonable issues and "making excuses" for poor performance.

The concept of good judgment surfaces in one form or the other in all three of these ways "we fool ourselves." Unfortunately, the notion of "good judgment" resembles the familiar aphorism about "common sense"; good judgment, like common sense, is not so common. Clarity of purpose is one of the best ways to foster good judgment. We turn to that issue next.

Purpose of Assessments

Why do we need assessments? Clearly, they inhibit our natural tendency to fool ourselves. Additionally, assessments help us achieve the following three related objectives.

Setting benchmarks. GDP (gross domestic product) numbers are widely reported in the media and highly influential to government officials, financial professionals, business leaders, economists, and investors. Economists created the measure after the hostilities of World War II to "reassure richer nations that the assistance they were providing under the Marshall Plan wasn't being misspent and was contributing to the growth of economies."[5] In other words, it served as a benchmark to judge growth. The beauty of any benchmark, the GDP included, is that, despite its flaws, it measures something: "when something is quantified and valued, and then written up in bright neon lights, it is more likely to be recognized and protected."[6]

The same kind of recognition and protective forces hold true for social media assessment numbers, or **benchmarks**. Routinely assessing your social media strategy and performance allows you to measure progress over time and across different platforms.

Orienting management processes. Measuring progress naturally evolves into identifying problems, opportunities, and recommendations for changes. Think of it this way: why should we go to the doctor for an annual physical? Even if we're feeling fine, the physical is a preventative measure designed to provide early warnings of potential problems before they become more difficult to manage. It's an advance warning that helps forecast potential challenges and prevents major health breakdowns in the future.

The social media assessment serves a similar function, helping to forecast potential problems and prevent major breakdowns in the future. For example, if your social media strategy lacks sufficient corrective mechanisms, all might seem to be going well until someone posts something objectionable to your core audience. A good assessment can help prevent that kind of breakdown as surely as routinely monitoring your blood pressure helps prevent heart attacks. If you are aware of the potential problem, you can put resources into place to address the potential hazards. In essence, with sufficient specificity, assessments help orient managerial attention, resources, and interventions.

Identifying continuous improvement opportunities. Professional athletes routinely pass their physical exams with flying colors. So they often turn to their physicians for improvements to maximize their performance, enhance their mental health, and optimize their energy. In other words, they are looking for ideas that will help them toward **continuous improvement**. Useful health or social media assessments not only protect us from the downside but also enhance our current performance. To extend on this example, assume that your social media strategy includes corrective tactics and your network of friendly spies is routinely identifying some potentially objectionable posts. Great. That protects you from the downside. But who is providing you with innovative ideas so you can potentially seize new strategic and tactical opportunities? That's where the continuous improvement opportunity exists. An effective assessment should identify such options.

DEVELOPING A SOCIAL MEDIA ASSESSMENT TOOL

Most social media managers monitor daily, weekly, and quarterly statistics about their social media performance. These may help with setting benchmarks, orienting management processes, and identifying continuous improvement opportunities, but they are unlikely to provide the necessary perspective for a strategic assessment. The **assessment tool** discussed in this section focuses on something more comprehensive than can be captured in the daily stream of numbers flowing across most social media manager's desks.

The tool assumes that candid judgments about the five strategic elements and their related performance indicators trump a single metric. Table 12.1 summarizes the key features of the tool built on this premise. Column one identifies the pivotal questions in each category that should guide judgments about the level of effectiveness. Note that all these questions are open to debate. They are not closed-ended questions with a simple "yes" or "no" answer or metric-driven solution. That's by design. A good debate spurs better judgments about complex issues. Yet debates should not go on forever; they need resolution. That's the

TABLE 12.1 Social Media Assessment Summary

Categories	Rating (1–10) 1 (NO!) 5 (Unsure) 10 (YES!)	Explanation
Coordinates • Our social media efforts help us meet our business goals. • We have the proper communication goals to support our business goals. • We are meeting our communication goals. • We have the right measures for our goals. • Our goals are aligned with one another.		
Channels • We have selected the proper platforms to meet our goals. • We have clearly defined roles for our different platforms. • Our core audiences consistently use our selected platforms. • We share the right type of content on our platforms. • We properly manage the logistics of our platforms.		
Content • Our content resonates with our core audiences. • We have the right mix of different types of content. • Our content creates a consistent brand image. • We have the right mix of in-house-created, user-generated, and curated content. • Our content syncs with our goals.		

Categories	Rating (1–10) 1 (NO!) 5 (Unsure) 10 (YES!)	Explanation
Connections • Our social media platforms logically link to one another. • Users can easily connect to our target site (e.g., website or blog) from our platforms. • We have the right internal organizational relationships to manage our platforms and related content properly. • Our social media platforms properly link to our other communication tools (e.g., flyers, billboards, table kiosk). • We are connected to the right communities (including competitors) to achieve our goals.		
Corrections • We have in place mechanisms to detect social media gaffes quickly and identify emerging opportunities. • We avoid making the same kinds of mistakes. • We consistently and quickly correct errors. • We have informal protocols in place to review performance regularly (e.g., daily, weekly) and to detect trends. • We have a formal process in place to review our strategy and performance on a quarterly or semiannual basis.		

role of column two. A numeric summary on a 0–10 scale forces the debaters to make a summary judgment that can be used to detect problems, set priorities, and identify opportunities. Column three provides the justification for the rating and should summarize key elements of the debate.

Next, we discuss some details concerning each of the key questions listed in Table 12.1. Note: the details we review are NOT intended to be comprehensive; rather they are meant to spark the conversation.

COORDINATES

Senior leaders will probably pay the most attention to this category because it is the one most clearly driven by readily available metrics. Fair enough. The metrics can guide answers to two questions, but not to the others. Here are some brief comments about each question:

- *Our social media efforts help us meet our business goals.* This may be the most important question in the entire chart because senior leaders want to know if they are getting a proper return on investment. Often, the answer cannot be easily quantified. However, some business goals, such as "lowering advertising costs while maintaining sales levels" can be more easily judged.

- *We have the proper communication goals to support our business goals.* This question forces us to separate out our communication goals from our business goals. One major assessment objective is to look back and tweak or reimagine the goals.

- *We are meeting our communication goals.* This is where the traditional social media metrics, such as audience size, traffic flow and engagement, can prove quite useful.

- *We have the right measures for our goals.* The next chapter explores some of the options you might consider.

- *Our goals are aligned with one another.* This question addresses the synergy issue that we have been stressing throughout the book.

CHANNELS

These questions should foster some intriguing discussion for the social media team:

- *We have selected the proper platforms to meet our goals.* The major discussion points should involve whether you should drop a platform and/or embrace a new one.

- *We have clearly defined roles for our different platforms.* This question presents more challenges. Each platform serves slightly different social needs. How well you tap into those nuances can make the difference between a great social media presence and a merely adequate one. For instance, you could focus Facebook on outreach efforts to your current users and use Twitter for real-time reporting of your events.

- *Our core audiences consistently use our selected platforms.* Certain metrics will help you gain insight into this issue.

- *We share the right type of content on our platforms.* Once again, metrics can be helpful, but it is also worth considering more qualitative judgments about the general type of posts that appear to be well suited to a particular platform. If you have a good grasp on this issue, then you should be able to identify the type of material that works best—and, likewise, what falls flat—on each platform.

- *We properly manage the logistics of our platforms.* This question focuses on the degree of attention you are devoting to the selected platforms. For instance, are you posting on a regular basis? Are you routinely responding to queries? Are you meeting your planned posting frequencies?

CONTENT

Queries in this category may well foster the most intense debate. They should because the answers are neither easy nor obvious:

- *Our content resonates with our core audiences.* Metrics can help with this question, but it can also be useful to examine what your competitors are doing and how they are faring with your core audiences.

- *We have the right mix of different types of content.* This question resembles one that a master chef would ask when creating a restaurant menu. It's really hard to discern an optimum mix, but we know that Iron Chef–like social media masters are always experimenting with different combinations. It's a red flag if you can't even identify the "content mix" you are providing.

- *Our content creates a consistent brand image.* Image consistency cultivates the kind of recognition and reputation that increases audience loyalty. It starts with using easily recognizable imagery or words, such as a logo or slogan, in all communication.

- *We have the right mix of in-house-created, user-generated, and curated content.* Simply identifying the current mix and looking at the related metrics can be helpful in answering this question.

- *Our content syncs with our goals.* The inclination might be to assume that, if you're meeting your goals, you've been sharing the right content. But this is like assuming that because you won the game, you excelled in all phases of the game. Excellent teams always look for improvements— even after a win.

CONNECTIONS

As we discussed in the "Connections" chapter, a thoughtful connections framework is probably the most overlooked and hidden component of a social media strategy. All too often, these decisions are driven more by happenstance than by thoughtful planning. The specific questions below help bring the issue into the limelight:

- *Our social media platforms logically link to one another.* Mapping out the current relationships with one-way or two-way arrows provides the starting point for answering this question.

- *Users can easily connect to our target site (e.g., website or blog) from our platforms.* Auditing user experiences can help you answer this question confidently.

- *We have the right internal organizational relationships to manage our platforms and related content properly.* Use an organizational chart as a guide to start this conversation about who should and who should not be part of the social media team's internal network. Then you can gauge the strength and responsiveness of those relationships. Hint: almost every department needs to have some kind of connection to your strategy, even if it's a minimal one.

- *Our social media platforms properly link to our other communication tools (e.g., flyers, billboards, table kiosks).* Creating an inventory of other communication tools provides a starting point for this discussion.

- *We are connected to the right communities (including competitors) to achieve our goals.* This is simply Audience Analysis 101. Most goals imply target audiences with different needs, desires, and constraints. Are we properly connected to those groups?

CORRECTIONS

These questions protect and optimize your social media strategy and performance. Some are part of a daily regimen; others are "maintenance items" to be regularly scheduled. Some brief remarks about each question:

- *We have in place mechanisms to detect social media gaffes quickly and identify emerging opportunities.* Answers might include routinely tracking metrics and/or regularly tapping into your friendly spy networks.

- *We avoid making the same kinds of mistakes.* Logging and categorizing the types of gaffes made could be a way to answer this query confidently.

- *We consistently and quickly correct errors.* The log discussed above could also report how quickly errors of commission are corrected.

- *We have informal protocols in place to review performance regularly (e.g., daily, weekly) and detect trends.* You can gain insight into this question by looking at how readily available metrics are managed on a daily and/or weekly basis.

- *We have a formal process in place to review our strategy and performance on a quarterly or semiannual basis.* If you've thoughtfully answered all the questions in Table 12.1, then you've aced this question!

So What?

The assessment framework outlined in this chapter suggests a number of important implications.

First, do your homework by collecting relevant metrics and holding discussions with a wide range of people. You could answer all the questions in the framework in a matter of minutes. But doing so would be like taking a test without reading the book or attending class. You might get some answers right, but you'd miss a lot, too. Let me suggest a better approach: collect all the relevant data, conduct the right analyses, and consult the right people. Then you've dramatically enhanced the chances that the process will move beyond merely jumping over another bureaucratic hurdle and venture into creating something of real value for the social media team. This implication is so important that we've devoted the entire next chapter to the issue.

Second, embrace the debate. By design, most of the questions defy clear, easy answers. The debate can be healthy because it surfaces different issues. Consequently, reasonable people might disagree on the number assigned in column two. That's fine if the issue is acknowledged in column three.

Third, acknowledge the relationships between the 5 Cs. Some people might desire clean, clear, unrelated assessment categories such as intelligence and height; your height has nothing to do with your intelligence.[7] Yet social media assessments works more like height and weight; they are discrete measures, but they are related. Taller people tend to weigh more than shorter people.

So when you make judgments about one of the 5 Cs, these judgments will often spill over into the appraisals in another category. That's fine if you recognize what's happening. For example, judging how well you are making use of a particular platform inevitably gets entwined with deliberations about content.

Another, more troubling relational dynamic is at work, as well. Namely, nice neat lists with five categories and five related questions might signal that all the categories are equally important. Wrong. Although all the categories are important, some are more important than others to particular people. In all likelihood, senior leaders will place far more emphasis on the coordinates section of the assessment. That's an unfortunate reality but one that savvy social media managers recognize. Yet smart and savvy social media managers recognize that you can stumble onto success almost as easily as you can slide into failure.[8] That's why they assess all of the 5 Cs: they don't want just to stumble onto success; they want to plan for and sustain it. And a proper assessment provides you with a deeper understanding of your social media strategic and tactical presence.

CONCLUSION

Useful assessments require good judgment, which hinges on collecting, interpreting, and reporting the right qualitative and quantitative data about the 5 Cs. Thus far, we've only touched on the utility of metrics. In the following chapters, we take the next step and fully embrace them.

KEY TERMS

Assessment tool 165

Benchmarks 164

Continuous improvement 165

DEEP DIVES

These exercises are designed to enhance your understanding of the chapter's key ideas, principles, and approaches.

1. Refer to Table 12.1.

   a. Identify which specific items can be easily answered with metrics. Discuss how the metrics help you answer the questions.

   b. Identify three specific questions that cannot be easily answered with metrics. Provide your rationale.

2. Describe three potential problems with benchmarks. Discuss how you could minimize those problems.

3. Create a chart with three columns and three rows.

   a. In column one, describe three potential tools (e.g., a survey, platform metrics, interviews, focus groups) a team could use to conduct an assessment as outlined in Table 12.1.

   b. In column two, describe three potential benefits of each option.

   c. In column three describe three potential problems associated with each option.

   d. Craft a summary argument explaining which option you think is best in most situations.

NOTES

1. I agree with Professor Feynman on this about 95 percent of the time. However, self-deception in the form of optimism energizes us to overcome barriers. That accounts for the 5 percent disagreement. Dr. Feynman would probably chuckle and likely agree with this observation.
2. Thanks to Rick Fantini for this example.
3. Here are more specifics about these metrics: a) actions on page = how many times users have clicked on action buttons (e.g., go to website, get directions, call a phone number); b) post engagement = number of likes, comments, and shares on page posts; and c) page reach = the number of people you reach when it's shown in News Feed on Facebook.
4. D. Seetharaman, "Facebook to Give Friends' Posts More Weight," *Wall Street Journal,* June 30, 2016.
5. E. Mason, *The Great Invention: The Story of GDP and the Making (and Unmaking) of the Modern World* (New York: Pegasus Books, 2016), 251.
6. Mason, *The Great Invention,* 242.
7. There was a time when some "scholars" argued that leaders were taller than their followers. More enlightened researchers have debunked this myth.
8. For a provocative discussion of this issue see R. Frank, *Success and Luck: Good Fortune and Meritocracy* (Princeton, NJ: Princeton University Press, 2016).

CHAPTER 13

Measuring Social Media Effectiveness

Laleah Fernandez

"Even the most carefully crafted and executed social media program in the world will crash and burn if both success and areas of improvement cannot be properly identified and measured."

—Olivier Blanchard

Though 92 percent of companies report that social media is important to their business, only 42 percent feel that they can accurately measure the value of their social media efforts.[1] This chapter is designed to help you use publicly available data from your social sites to increase awareness of your organization, grow your audience base, and help you achieve your goals. You can use the four-step process outlined in this chapter to select the right metrics for your assessment of the 5 Cs (see Figure 13.1).

STEP 1: MASTER METRIC LANGUAGE

If you want to master metric language, you will quickly find yourself knee-deep in a swamp of numbers, calculations, and often obscure

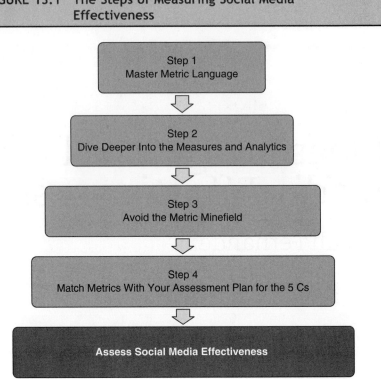

FIGURE 13.1   The Steps of Measuring Social Media Effectiveness

Step 1
Master Metric Language

Step 2
Dive Deeper Into the Measures and Analytics

Step 3
Avoid the Metric Minefield

Step 4
Match Metrics With Your Assessment Plan for the 5 Cs

Assess Social Media Effectiveness

terms. A little perspective can move your understanding to higher ground and help you select the metrics that best suit your purposes.

What is a **metric**? These are numbers that measure something we believe is important. Social media metric tools change over time. Features change. Options change. And accessibility and costs change. Thus, it is important to understand the concepts behind the metrics, so you can adapt to the inevitable shifts in the social media landscape. Rather than becoming overly dependent on a specific tool or metric, social media managers should focus on the four categories of metrics discussed below (See Figure 13.2).

AUDIENCE COMPOSITION

Audience metrics provide insights about the composition of your audiences and their preferences. Most social media platforms include some

FIGURE 13.2 Main Categories of Metrics

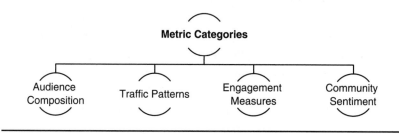

measure of **audience composition** in the aggregate. You can usually find information about an audience member's age group, gender identity, location, education, and occupation.

After you have identified demographic information, you can use these same tools to identify interests. Identifying the interests of your audience is arguably more important than the demographics because your audience preferences should guide your posting approach.

One other factor may be even more important than audience preferences. What is it? The influencers in your audience. **Influencers** are the people who sway others. By connecting with influencers, you can build connections exponentially.

TRAFFIC PATTERNS

Let's assume the followers on your platforms perfectly represent your target audiences. That's a good start, but what we don't know is whether those people are actually paying attention to your content and driving traffic to your website. That's what traffic pattern metrics will measure.

Three specific measures can help you understand traffic patterns: 1) **impressions**, 2) **reach**, and 3) **drivers**.

- *Impressions* are a measurement of exposure to your content. Impressions can also be thought of as views. For example, the total number of Twitter impressions refers to the number of times a tweet from your account has been delivered to the Twitter streams of other users, including tweets and retweets. A measurement of Facebook impressions refers to the number of times your posts were seen in user feeds (or ticker) or during visits to your page. These impressions can include views from fans or nonfans, whether the post is clicked or not. The number includes views from people who may see multiple impressions of the same post. A note of caution: the number of views does not necessarily equate with the number of different people seeing a post. In other words, you could have 1000 views from one person, or you could have 1000 people view the same post one time. Both circumstances would be measured as 1000 impressions. Most social media managers would prefer the second option!

- **Reach** is the number of *unique visitors* exposed to a message or who received impressions. This number might be less than total number of impressions because one person might have multiple exposures to your post. Reach is important because it is a measure of exposure to your content. It's a more accurate measure of your audience than fan or follower counts because not all of your fans or followers will see your posts.

- **Drivers** provide numeric indicators of what social media platforms push traffic to your website. For most organizations, social media is the largest traffic driver to their site. You can use metrics on your website to learn which social sources are sending new visitors, returning visitors, and engaged users.[2] Web analytic software can be used to understand the social channels that are driving traffic.

ENGAGEMENT MEASURES

Engagement means that viewers respond in some tangible way to your page, post, pin, or tweet. Engagement measures audience actions. Every platform has a unique way of measuring engagement. Even within the boundaries of each platform, there are multiple variations and levels of engagement. Facebook, for example, counts the number of people who have clicked on, liked, commented on, or shared a post (called **shares**). Depending on your social media goals, you may be interested in measuring this at the page level or post level. Twitter, on the other hand, measures engagement by totaling the number of clicks, retweets, replies, follows, **likes**, links, cards, hashtags, embedded media, username, or profile photo. However, you may decide to break down this comprehensive measure of engagement to focus on specific types of engagement, such as the number of likes or the number of retweets at the post level.

Successful social media efforts seek to increase not only the *amount* of engagement but also the *intensity* of engagement. The three basic levels of intensity in increasing strength are 1) observing, 2) participating, and 3) propagating. Twitter, for example, defines the intensity levels as follows:

- *Observation* occurs when followers look online and click through posts and links.

- *Participation* happens when followers are moved to action, such as following your Twitter account, liking a post, or commenting on a post.

- *Propagation* occurs when followers retweet, repost, repeat comments, share articles, or use your hashtags.[3] Propagation is a means of amplification. This is important in expanding reach because it essentially means that others are pushing your content into their networks.

Measuring engagement with your videos adds a deeper layer of specificity to traditional engagement measures. Video may be an especially effective way to broadcast content with high potential to go viral. Video posts have a 135 percent greater organic reach than photo posts.[4] Video metrics provide an additional set of engagement measurements, such as **total views** and short or full views, as can be seen in Table 13.1.

High levels of engagement represent "The Promised Land" for most social media strategists. Engagement is also the category most frequently debated by social media specialists because the true value of the current metrics remains relatively speculative.

COMMUNITY SENTIMENT

Community sentiment is focused on audience responses to your content. This approach looks for patterns in attitude, opinion, feelings, and

TABLE 13.1   Video Engagement Metrics

Video Metric	Definition
Exposure Time	• How long a visitor stayed on the site or post
Average Video Completion	• The portion of your video content that is viewed in an average watch session
Total Views	• The number of people who viewed any portion of the video
Autoplay Views	• The number of people who viewed a portion of your content by scrolling through the feed *Note: This measures how well the content captured the attention of your target audience*
Click-to-Play	• The quality of your caption, video title, or photo to compel your target audience to stop, click, and watch the video *Note: A high number of click-per-play views indicates that the content is worth their time*
Short Views	• The number of people who watched 3–30 seconds of your video
Full Views	• The number of people who watched the video from 31 seconds to the end *Note: If the count of short views is higher than that for full views (and there were no technical glitches frustrating viewers), it suggests that your content isn't resonating with your audience. If full views outnumber short views, your content retained most viewers.*

emotion based on social conversations and comment threads. In its most simplistic form, sentiment analysis seeks to determine whether the social conversation around your organization or brand is positive, negative, or neutral. Sentiment analysis is a way of learning the reactions of your audiences—whether audience members are happy or unhappy with your posts or are just ignoring you on social media.[5] It's a feeling, emotion, attitude, or opinion conveyed in a comment, emoticon, or mention.

Sentiment metrics are like a TV "color commentary" for an NFL game because they offer further context, nuance, and explanation concerning the other metrics. They allow you to measure your reputation, respond quickly to problems, or prevent a crisis from spreading. Measuring sentiments can help you understand what isn't working, so you can abandon those tactics and try again. For instance, Page Insights from Facebook Business allows you to see what content is not working through a hide post feature. You can track when someone hides a specific post from appearing in her or his news, when someone elects to hide all posts associated with your page, when someone reports a brand's posts as spam, and when a user chooses to unlike a Facebook page. When considered over time, peaks in negative feedback will quickly notify you when you're off track. By cross-referencing these spikes with the type of posts and content you published around that time, you may be able to identify the root cause.

STEP 2: DIVE DEEPER INTO THE MEASURES AND ANALYTICS

The four categories of metrics identified in Figure 13.2 provide a good starting point for understanding social media measurement possibilities. But we need to dive deeper into the specifics to create a useful measurement plan. Taking this deeper dive requires one further step: we should distinguish between **platform-specific measures** and non-platform-specific measures.

PLATFORM-SPECIFIC MEASURES

Every social media platform offers both free and paid analytics. In this chapter, we focus primarily on the freely available analytics for the largest social media platforms.

Table 13.2 outlines some of the specific metrics by platform based on our four categories of measurement. Each measurement cell in Table 13.2 identifies several measurement options. You must decide what is meaningful for your social media efforts and be consistent over time so that you can adequately gauge your effectiveness.

TABLE 13.2 Platform-Specific Metrics and Tools

Platform and Tool	Audience Composition	Traffic Patterns	Engagement Measures	Community Sentiment
Facebook Insights (Page Level and Post Level)	• Location • Age • Gender • Language *You may look at composition for fans, people reached, and/or people engaged.*	• Fans • Impressions • Page/Post Reach • When Fans Are Online	• Clicks • Likes • Shares • Comments • Actions on Page (People Engaged)	• Page/Post Likes (Thumbs Up) • Unlikes, Hide Posts, Report as Spam • Emoticons • Comments
Twitter Analytics	Followers'... • Gender • Income • Education • Lifestyle • Location • Mobile	• Followers • Follower Growth • Impressions • Link Clicks	• Replies • Retweets • Mentions • Clicks • Followers' Likes	• Favorites (Stars) • Comments

Platform and Tool	Audience Composition	Traffic Patterns	Engagement Measures	Community Sentiment
LinkedIn Analytics	• Seniority • Industry • Company Size and Function	• Followers • Impressions	• Clicks • Interactions • Likes • Comments • Shares	• Likes • Comments
Pinterest Analytics	• Location • Age • Gender • Metro Region • Language • Top Boards	• Profile Impressions • Daily Viewers • Traffic to Website	• Repins • Clicks • Impressions • Reach	• Likes (Hearts) • Comments
Instagram Insights	• Location • Age • Gender	• Reach • Impressions	• Top Posts • Engagement	• Likes (Hearts) • Comments
YouTube Analytics	• Location • Age • Gender	• Views • Subscribers • Traffic Sources	• Views • Watch Time • Shares • Audience Retention	• Likes • Dislikes • Favorites • Comments

Although some platforms do not currently offer analytic dashboards, some measures are freely available and accessible. For example, to measure audience sentiment on Google+, you can look at the comments or +1s. You can look at the number of likes (or hearts) on Tumblr to assess audience sentiment or at the number of reblogs to measure engagement.

MEASURES NOT SPECIFIC TO PLATFORMS

Many times, you're able to make meaningful comparisons by using measures that are not specific to particular platforms, measures such as word clouds and hashtag inventories. A **word cloud** can provide a qualitative tool for visually analyzing blocks of texts. With Wordle, for example, you can create word clouds by pulling the text from your profile pages and pasting it into the application. The size of the words projected in a word cloud correspond to the relative frequency of their use; the larger the size of the word, the more frequently it occurred. As a social media specialist, you want your profiles to emphasize the same words across platforms and to match your goals and mission. By selecting a sample of your posts, you can determine if you conveyed the same message across platforms and over time.

Hashtags also serve as keyword measures of interest across platforms. People use the hashtag symbol (#) before a relevant keyword or phrase to mark posts as relating to a topic. Twitter popularized the usage of hashtags, but they are now used on Facebook, Google+, Instagram, and Pinterest.

Optimizing keywords in your content and hashtags in your social media posts helps you increase your reach and social sharing among users who are interested in your content.[6] It makes it easier for people to find your posts and to follow the conversation. That's why assessing hashtag usage across platforms can be particularly helpful. When one team of students at our university compared the hashtag usage of two competing national retailers, they discovered considerable differences between the two. They found that one retailer was very disciplined in hashtag usage by frequently using the same ones across multiple platforms. The team judged this hashtag usage pattern to be more effective because the frequent use of the same hashtag acted like a branding mechanism for the company.

STEP 3: AVOID THE METRIC MINEFIELD

Oddly enough, one of the most important steps in creating a meaningful measurement plan is to avoid stepping on the many metric mines inadvertently planted by overly eager bloggers and platform providers. The often bewildering array of numbers, analyses, and reports may actually hinder you in finding useful measures. Specifically, you need to avoid the three mines discussed below.

RESIST BEING SEDUCED BY THE GLAMOUR METRICS

Celebrities, athletic superstars, and high profile politicians naturally garner lots of fans, likes, and social media buzz. These glamour metrics, like the number of fans, may or may not be relevant for your social media strategy. As we discussed in Chapter 9, if you have a reach strategy (i.e., seeking many weak connections), then the number of followers and views may be important. But if you have a depth strategy (i.e., seeking a few strong connections), these same numbers are virtually meaningless. Instead, you should look for metrics indicating you are reaching the right audiences.

DON'T ASSUME THAT METRIC LANGUAGE TRANSFERS ACROSS PLATFORMS

It can be tricky to compare metrics across sites. As we previously noted, Facebook measures *engagement* by looking at the number of people who have clicked on, liked, commented on, or shared a post; but LinkedIn calculates *interactions* by summing the number of times people have liked, commented on, or shared a post. Thus, engagement and interactions measure the same concept although the two platforms use different terminologies.

WATCH OUT FOR COMPARISONS ACROSS ORGANIZATIONS AND OVER TIME

What metrics work for one organization will not *necessarily* work for another organization. Decisions about content must be customized and personalized for your organization and target audience. Therefore, use *your* measurements as a guide to improve and refine rather than adopting another organization's measurement plan. Additionally, because the focus and interests of your audience will likely change over time, your measurements may indicate that something that worked for your organization in the past no longer works. Don't be surprised if your tried-and-true tactics fall short from time to time. Declining engagement and changes in sentiment often signal that it's time for new content.

STEP 4: MATCH METRICS WITH YOUR ASSESSMENT PLAN FOR THE 5 CS

Selecting the best measures is the final step in the process. As Albert Einstein is said to have noted, "Not everything that counts can be counted, and not everything that can be counted counts."[7] Table 13.3 embraces this wise advice. The table synthesizes the key questions posed in the previous chapter with the metric categories discussed in this chapter. Recall that your primary task is to make well-informed judgments about the effectiveness of your social media strategy in relation to the five categories (the 5 Cs). The right metrics help you come to reasonable and supportable conclusions. Your responses to the items italicized in column one should be strongly influenced by your metrics. Some of the metric category possibilities are identified in column two. This does not mean, though, that you must use all the items in column two or that you can answer all the questions with metrics. The discussion following provides some insights about how to use the metrics to craft a well-informed judgment.

COORDINATE METRICS

The right metrics can provide insight into two of the specific coordinate issues represented in Table 13.3:

- Our social media efforts help us meet our business goals.

- We are meeting our communication goals.

For example, if your business goal is to increase customer acquisition, traffic pattern measures such as the number of fans and followers and

TABLE 13.3   Social Media Assessment Metric Options

Categories	Metric Category	Rating (1–10) 1 (NO!) 5 (unsure) 10 (YES!)
Coordinates • *Our social media efforts help us meet our business goals.** • We have the proper communication goals to support our business goals. • *We are meeting our communication goals.* • We have the right measures for our goals. • Our goals are aligned with one another.	Audience Composition Traffic Patterns Engagement Measures	
Channels • We have selected the proper platforms to meet our goals. • *We have clearly defined roles for our different platforms.* • *Our core audiences consistently use our selected platforms.* • *We share the right type of content on our platforms.* • We properly manage the logistics of our platforms.	Audience Composition Engagement Measures Community Sentiment	
Content • *Our content resonates with our core audiences.* • *We have the right mix of different types of content.* • *Our content creates a consistent brand image.*	Engagement Measures Community Sentiment Audience Composition	

(Continued)

TABLE 13.3 (Continued)

Categories	Metric Category	Rating (1–10) 1 (NO!) 5 (unsure) 10 (YES!)
• We have the right mix of in-house-created, user-generated, and curated content. • Our content syncs with our goals.		
Connections • Our social media platforms logically link to one another. • *Users can easily connect to our target site (e.g., website or blog) from our platforms.* • We have the right internal organizational relationships to manage our platforms and related content properly. • Our social media platforms properly link to our other communication tools (e.g., flyers, billboards, table kiosk). • *We are connected to the right communities (including competitors) to achieve our goals.*	Audience Composition Community Sentiment Traffic Patterns	
Corrections • We have in place mechanisms to detect social media gaffes quickly and to identify emerging opportunities. • *We avoid making the same kinds of mistakes.* • *We consistently and quickly correct errors.* • We have informal protocols in place to review performance regularly (e.g., daily, weekly) and detect trends. • We have a formal process in place to review our strategy and performance on a quarterly or semiannual basis.	Community Sentiment Traffic Patterns Engagement Measures	

*The italicized issues can be directly measured by the right metrics.

the amount of follower growth can be helpful. If one of your communication goals is to increase user loyalty, then sentiment measures such as the number of likes and positive comments can be beneficial to track.

CHANNEL METRICS

Several metrics can be particularly helpful in evaluating three of the specific channel issues represented in Table 13.3:

- We have clearly defined roles for our different platforms.
- Our core audiences consistently use our selected platforms.
- We share the right type of content on our platforms.

Deciding to use different metrics for each platform is frequently an indicator that you've selected different roles for different platforms. The wide range of metrics offered by platform providers should help you answer the other two questions with a high degree of confidence. At a minimum, you should measure engagement for each platform. For most platforms, there is an analytic function available: Pinterest has Pinterest Analytics, LinkedIn offers the LinkedIn Analytics suite for its Company Pages, YouTube offers YouTube Analytics for your YouTube channels. You may want to start with these built-in platform analytics because they are free and are provided directly from the source.

CONTENT METRICS

You will probably find that some of the metrics you selected for channel issues can help you evaluate the specific content issues identified in Table 13.3:

- Our content resonates with our core audiences.
- We have the right mix of different types of content.
- Our content creates a consistent brand image.

Recall the prior discussion about levels of engagement. This matter should be ever present as you decide on the proper metrics in the content category. For the first level of engagement, you'll want to use a reach or impression metric. Reach without engagement is still important because a lot of people pay attention to your content but don't respond to it. For the second and third levels of engagement, you will want to look for measures of interaction or action, such as the number of retweets, shares, favorites, likes, replies, and comments.

You can sharpen your understanding by analyzing engagement at the individual page level. For example, by using Page Insights, you can easily quantify the number of likes, comments, and shares to compare individual posts and identify the most compelling content on your Facebook page. Page Insights generates reach and engagement metrics for individual posts and for the page as a whole.

CONNECTIONS METRICS

The right metrics can help you evaluate performance on several of the connections issues listed in Table 13.3:

- We are connected to the right communities to achieve our goals.

- Users can easily connect to our target site from our platforms.

Measuring your reach to the target communities is fairly straightforward for most social platforms. For a Facebook page, you can view how many people saw your posts by using Page Insights. On Twitter, you simply access your Tweet activity dashboard and look at the number of impressions for each tweet. On Pinterest, scroll down below "Pins" and "Repins" to the section with "Impressions" and "Reach." Metrics of audience composition on the platforms can help you determine if you are reaching the targeted demographics and interest groups (e.g., dog lovers). Looking at demographic information such as location, age, gender, and interests helps measure if you are reaching your target. Facebook provides additional metrics for demographic or lifestyle differences by comparing your fan base as a whole with those that engage with your posts. In addition, you should consider whether you are reaching the most influential followers. See Table 13.4 for some **influence analysis** tools that can help you make that determination.

TABLE 13.4   Influence Analysis Tools

Tool	What It Measures	Special Features
HowSociable	Brand influence through activity across networks	• Enter your brand or company name into the search field to see a magnitude score • The score indicates how well you are spreading your brand across all social sites and monitoring all followers' conversations around your brand
Klout	The size of your social media network	• Klout tracks your ranking over time to measure your influence • It is designed specifically to find influencers by providing social scores based on engagement
Talkwalker	Search queries for keywords or phrases	• Talkwalker searches for words and phrases; its alerts are free • The paid service provides a summary of mentions over time and sources of these mentions
Followerwonk	Twitter influence, so influencers can be used for targeted growth	• Finds targeted Twitter profiles to identify influencers and help generate content ideas and plan content promotion

When it comes to finding influencers, you have two options: 1) those within your existing network and 2) those outside of your existing network. Grab the low-hanging fruit first, those who are interacting with your current audience. This is the process of turning acquaintances into allies. For example, on Twitter you can navigate to the "Followers" tab for a list of handles followed by your audience. The Pinterest "Top Boards" metric will show you the boards people are seeing your pins from. Look for and create connections with people who are pinning your content, particularly if they have a loyal following.

You have several options for finding potential influencers outside of your network. To find out about potential influencers on Twitter you might try Followerwonk. Click on "Search Bios" to look for profiles and bios by category or keyword to identify the top people to follow. You can sort by "Social Authority" to find those people with the highest authority and click on "Follow" to see what they're talking about and what hashtags they're using. If you find that the influencer uses keywords or hashtags that are consistent with your audience's interests, reach out to that person and build a connection.

The second issue, user ease of connecting to the target site, can best be addressed by using tools designed to measure **traffic patterns**. For example, Google Analytics is a free tool that is particularly useful in monitoring traffic and assessing demographic information from your social sites. Google Analytics will provide a look at the overall social media traffic sources that deliver visitors to your site or blog. You can use the "Referral to site" function to see which social channels are sending you users. When you compare traffic from social media alongside the traffic from other channels, it's easy to measure the impact social has on your site's traffic.[8]

CORRECTIONS METRICS

The right metrics can help you evaluate two items listed in Table 13.3:

- We avoid making the same kinds of mistakes.
- We consistently and quickly correct errors.

Recall that sentiment analysis measures and reports on the tone or sentiment of a social conversation. You might look for changes in average sentiment to signal shifts in perception. Several social media management tools are especially useful: Followerwonk, Social Mention, Mention, Hootsuite, and Sotrender.

You can use a tool like Followerwonk to measure your own social authority. Check the social media sentiment over time to see changes in your reputation. Tools such as Social Mention, Hootsuite, and Sotrender allow you to detect sentiment across platforms. Hootsuite, for example, helps you keep on top of chatter in real time on platforms such as Facebook, Twitter, and LinkedIn.

You can use sentiment analysis to respond quickly to negative posts or mentions using a tool called Mention. In Mention, you can set the filter at the top of your unread mentions stream for negative comments first. Doing this is particularly useful if you are trying to minimize or prevent a crisis, or if you simply want to respond to negative feedback. The most effective tactic is to filter your analysis to respond to negative sentiments first.

All the tools can help answer the questions about how quickly you are correcting your errors and if you are avoiding the same types of errors.

CONCLUSION

Metrics can be confusing and complex, but the right ones can be meaningful and vital tools for making strategic and tactical improvements. This chapter presented a four-step process that allows you to move beyond confusion to illumination:

- Master metric language.

- Dive deeper into the measures and analytics.

- Avoid the metric minefield.

- Match metrics with your assessment plan for the 5 Cs.

If you follow that process, you will be able to make a sound assessment about the effectiveness of your social media strategy, an evaluation based on the five social media factors —the 5 Cs. Perhaps even more important, you can confidently, authoritatively, and persuasively present your assessment of social media efforts to others who may not share your passion for social media. However, you will need a protocol for effectively sharing your findings and assessment. That important issue is the subject of the next chapter.

KEY TERMS

Audience composition 177
Community sentiment 179

Drivers 177
Engagement 178

DEEP DIVES

These exercises are designed to enhance your understanding of the chapter's key ideas, principles, and approaches.

1. We reviewed a number of metrics in this chapter, and you may be familiar with others as well. Create a chart with three columns.

   a. In column one, identify the three most *useless* metrics for most organizations.

   b. In column two, identify the metric category for each metric.

   c. Provide your rationale for the designations.

2. Research three metrics that provide the typical organization with the *most* value.

   a. Provide a reason that you selected each metric.

   b. Based on your research, discuss how the metric has been tweaked over time.

   c. Speculate on how the tweaking has influenced the interpretations of the metric.

3. Refer to Table 13.3. Create a three-column chart.

   a. In column one, identify your three favorite Cs.

   b. In column two, select a metric that is a *mismatch* for each of your favorites.

   c. In column three, provide your rationale for deciding that each metric is a mismatch.

NOTES

1. M. A. Stelzner, *Social Media Marketing Industry Report* (Poway, CA: Social Media Examiner, 2015), 7, 9, www.socialmediaexaminer.com.
2. R. Gordon and R. Hlavac, "Measuring Engagement," Lecture 7 in the course *The Business of Social*, Northwestern University, 2016, https://www.coursera .org/learn/business-of-social/lecture/CfMx8/measuring-engagement.
3. K. Paine, *Measuring What Matters, Online Tools For Understanding Customers, Social Media, Engagement, and Key Relationships* (New York: John Wiley & Sons, Inc., 2011).
4. P. Ross, "Native Facebook Videos Get More Reach Than Any Other Type of Post," *Socialbakers*, Feb. 17, 2015, https://www.socialbakers.com/ blog/2367-native-facebook-videos-get-more-reach-than-any-other-type-of-post.
5. "Social Media Sentiment Analysis: The Spine of Social Media Marketing," *Mavis Edutech*, July 14, 2016, http://www.mavisedutech.com/blog/ social-media-sentiment-analysis/.
6. J. B. Hopson, "7 Marvelous Resources for Researching Trending Twitter Topics," *Inbound Marketing* [blog], November 4, 2015, http:// www.inboundmarketingagents.com/inbound-marketing-agents-blog/ bid/333604/7-Marvelous-Resources-for-Researching-Trending-Twitter-Topics.
7. These words are frequently attributed to Einstein because he repeated them often, so the story goes; some say he had them tacked up in his office (or written on his blackboard). But many also report that Einstein got the quotation from British physician Sir George Pickering. The first published record seems to be in William Bruce Cameron's *Informal Sociology* (1963).
8. K. Lee "How to Measure Social Media Using Google Analytics Reports," *Social Media Examiner*, April 21, 2016, http://www.socialmediaexaminer .com/how-to-measure-social-media-using-google-analytics-reports/.

Crafting the Social Media Assessment Report

Jena Richter Landers

After you have the strategy in place and begin to implement the plan, it is important to monitor your level of success. After all, measuring your effectiveness has been a guiding theme throughout this book.

Let's assume you've used all the correct tools and made your final judgments about the 5 Cs. One final step remains: you will want to craft an easily understood **assessment report**. People unfamiliar with social media and even seasoned professionals may find it difficult to assess the efficacy of social media and explain the return on investment (ROI). That's why crafting your social media assessment requires special care.

What do you need to know for this special assignment? First, you need to embrace a few key principles that will guide the crafting of the report. Second, you need to know how to craft the key sections of the report. These are the issues we address next.

KEY PRINCIPLES

This section highlights five principles to ponder while drafting the initial report.

First, analyze your audiences. When preparing your social media report, focus on who will be reading it or listening to the briefing. Think about these kinds of questions: What do they know about social media? What do they know about what you've been trying to achieve? Do they use social media? These questions can be helpful when deciding on how much and what kind of background information to provide. In any case, briefly review your organization's actively managed social media platforms. Although you do not need to provide analytical data for all the platforms, it is important to provide insight into the full scope of your organization's presence on social media.

As noted in the previous chapter, various social media platforms use similar terminology but often quite different methods of quantifying standard measures, such as reach. Therefore, when using quantifying terms to explain the reach or engagement levels of the social media content, be sure to define terms using easily understood language. For example, Facebook analytics refers to "reach" as the number of people who see your posts, including those who see posts on Facebook's news feed. Twitter, on the other hand, does not have a metric for this exact measurement. Instead, Twitter reports "impressions," a measure that quantifies the number of times users saw the content. Though both terms explain the extent to which social media content is distributed, they differ on how they measure the concept. For this reason a first step is precisely defining and explaining the social media technical terms that you use.

Second, establish the right comparison points. Even when you carefully define social media lingo, your audience may have difficulty processing exactly what the data mean. That is why it is important to provide the right **comparison points** and a context for the numbers that you share. The most effective ways to frame social media data are to a) show growth over time and b) compare your data to that of competitors or similar organizations.

Showing growth in percentages, instead of raw numbers, improves your readers' understanding of the underlying platform dynamics.

For example, "Followers increased by 17 percent in the last year" is more vivid and meaningful than "Followers increased by 452 in the last year."

Displaying your growth data alongside the data of a competitor or similar organization can be an effective way to show results. Keep in mind, though, that you will want to 1) select an organization of similar size and 2) one that devotes similar resources to its social media presence. Comparing your results to those of a company devoting twice the resources to social media probably won't be to your advantage; besides, this comparison is neither fair nor particularly useful. On the flip side, comparing your results to those of firms devoting limited resources can also create a false impression.

Third, spotlight the return on investment (ROI). In the broadest sense, **ROI** means the benefits gained compared to the costs incurred. You want a high ROI, which means you invested little compared to the benefits you received. Smiling at someone usually has a high ROI because, for very little investment, you usually get a nice return in terms of relationship building. It's often a bit tricky to calculate ROI for social media. You basically have two choices.

> ***Choice one***: Demonstrate that, for a certain number of dollars invested, you were able to generate a certain level of sales, donations, votes, leads, and so on. For example, assume your goal is to increase conversion rates. In that case, you will want to report how many of your posts resulted in actual sales, donations, or other target action. Note, however, that there may not be a direct correspondence between the number of click-throughs and sales because users may use other ways of purchasing, from store visits to phone calls. For example, a user might be prompted to buy a product because of a social media post but not even respond to the actual post. Therefore, watch for correlations between success on social media and a general increase in sales.

> ***Choice two***: Compare the social media investment to the dollars or energy spent on more traditional communication channels. Investments in social media can seem low when compared to the costs of traditional media, such as advertising fees, printing costs, mailing costs, and airtime.

The bottom line: the ROI that you report on depends on your organizational, communication, and social media goals. These frame all of your choices and orient your entire report.

When you report on ROI, it's important to note significant caveats. Platforms frequently change features or analytic reporting styles, so you will want your report to reflect these changes. For example, in early 2016, Facebook added "Reactions" to expand the ways that users could interact with content. Previously, engagement scores had been mostly positive because users could only click on content, share content, and "like" content. With the addition of "Reactions," Facebook expanded engagement by allowing the responses "love," "haha," "wow," "sad," and "angry" in addition to "like." Previous to this change, "high engagement" meant only positive responses; today, "high engagement" could indicate a variety of emotional responses to a post.

Fourth, highlight connections between social media platforms, other communication tools, and events. Social media does not occur in a vacuum, nor do other outreach initiatives in your organization. When you evaluate the success of social media efforts, it is important to consider what occurred on other channels, including your websites, email campaigns, and traditional media. Even national or local events can affect interaction and traffic on social media. Highlight potential correlations in your report because doing so provides an opportunity to replicate success in the future.

Likewise look for correlations between your various communication efforts. Did you see a spike in Facebook likes after distributing print material with a push to your Facebook page? Did you see a spike in Instagram followers after posting a link to your Instagram account on your Twitter account? It can also be helpful to outline the success of campaign hashtags in social media reports. Monitor and record the hashtag usage patterns for the brand being represented. Your success stories about branded hashtags demonstrate social media accomplishments as well as your brand's reach.

Fifth, focus on continuous improvement. Social media assessment reports should also grow and change to remain flexible to the reporting needs of your organization. As the needs of your audience change or the objectives of your social media strategy change, you will want to adapt your report. If an organization finds its audience responding positively to a social media channel that had not been previously featured in reports, future assessments should reflect that change. Assume, for example, that a company begins to rely more heavily on Instagram by adding additional accounts and including Instagram streams on its website. The report needs to reflect these administrative improvements to readers.

MAIN SECTIONS OF THE ASSESSMENT REPORT

The principles above should guide you as you draft the main sections of the report.

INTRODUCTION

In this section, prepare the readers for the assessment they are about to review. Let the reader know when the data were collected, the timespan the report covers, how the data were gathered, and how the summary ratings for the 5 Cs were developed. Also note what platforms are reviewed and why others are not. If your organization's social media presence is anything like the one I oversee, you may be on many platforms for defensive purposes—in other words, platforms to which you don't actively push content. In my case, I've simply reserved various usernames to conserve a brand. In short, you don't need to analyze every social media presence in the assessment.

LIMITATIONS

In this section, acknowledge what you don't know. This is an important section because it helps readers better understand the constraints of the analytical work. Three particular areas deserve special mention.

First, there are some data that you may not be able to collect with a platform's provided analytics. For example, currently, the Snapchat platform does not provide data other than the number of viewers per "story." What this means is that there is no way to know how many users have "added you as a friend" (essentially a "follower"). Other times, you may need specific data that are not reported in platform analytics but that can be calculated using what you know. For instance, Facebook provides historical reach, but only by day. So, if you want to summarize reach for an entire month, you must make calculations on your own.

Second, platforms continue to evolve, potentially causing year-to-year comparisons to be misleading. Algorithm changes alter the way content is delivered to users. As a result, you may no longer have data on items you once reported on. For example, in 2015, Instagram introduced algorithms that produce a feed that is "ordered to show the moments we believe you will care about the most." Previously, posts were chronologically ordered.

Third, you have a limited view of the social media analytics for your competitors. Though you see such data as their follower counts or likes, you are missing information such as the quantitative data on engagement levels, the demographics of their follower base, or their reach outside of their follower base. To begin to understand this sort of information about your competitors, you can only use your powers of observation or pay a third-party provider. You can watch such things as the content competitors circulate and observe the type of content to which users are responding, how they are responding, and how they are engaging with the content. These numbers are inexact, but they provide small slivers of information about your competition's social media success. By investigating this success, you might gain insight into your own strategy.

COMPARATIVE FRAMEWORK

This section frames everything else in the report and, to a large degree, helps readers make sense of the data. Start by noting similarities in missions, structures, budgets, and audiences. In my assessment report, I share the data I have on similar organizations. Although other organizations' data are often limited to what the average user can observe about social media presences as an outsider (follower count and growth in follower count since your last report), these statistics are still tremendously helpful. They suggest how your organization's social media followership "stacks up."

This section can include data beyond just social media–specific numbers. Providing background information on the comparable organization can be useful as well. Consider including information such as when organizations were established, how long their accounts have existed, follower counts, and growth rates.

DATA AND ANALYSIS

The main data section of the social media assessment will vary from organization to organization, but it typically reveals changes that have occurred since the last report. It focuses on the main platforms that the organization is utilizing. This means showing factors such as growth (or loss) in followership, reach, and different types of engagement. To better quantify growth, you can provide past data from a recent report. Or, in some cases, it makes sense to refer to the same time span of the previous year.

After reviewing each data set by platform, explain potential factors influencing the numbers. Was there a platform change? Did organizational goals shift? Did an event occur that could have impacted the numbers? Imagine you are reporting that a certain month stood out because it had noticeably higher numbers than did previous or future months. In doing research, you might find that there were several events in a particular month that generated a lot of attention for your organization. Including this background information will help show the synergistic nature of effective social media strategies.

SUCCESS STORIES

One of the main goals of a social media assessment report is to highlight what works. This allows you to replicate your successful strategies moving forward. When you highlight **success stories**, you can justify your strategy.

In each report that I compile, I first establish the criteria I will use to determine what makes a successful post. Using these criteria, I highlight the most successful post from each month on each platform mentioned in the report. Then I identify trends and lessons learned about topics, type of post, hashtag usage, and types of audiences. This approach fosters an understanding of what content worked best at accomplishing goals. If your criteria included the post with the highest reach, the most successful post will show what sort of post generated the most buzz and likely resonated with most users.

CONCLUSIONS AND RECOMMENDATIONS

The conclusion of a good social media assessment should highlight the main takeaways from the report. This is where you summarize and explain your rating of the 5 Cs reviewed in Chapter 12. You should weave in your data analyses and discussions about major successes and failures, if any. Remember: these are judgments made about your social media effectiveness. Finally, you should note how to replicate your successes, improve your strategy, and correct tactical errors. This approach not only embodies the continuous improvement mindset, it also bolsters your credibility and instills confidence in your organizational leaders.

APPENDIXES

Appendices supply the kind of detail that many readers crave. They furnish supporting material for the main findings in the report. You could, for instance, provide details on your analyses, raw comments from followers, and other supplemental material.

CONCLUSION

The assessment reports you generate may be as important as the strategies you implement. Assessing your strategy's effectiveness completes the feedback loop. It informs your leaders about what works and what does not. It fuels your decision-making process by helping you to stay on top of trends and react quickly to changes. It justifies the benefit of social media in the organization, while allowing you to take risks, try new ideas, and gain confidence in your strategic and tactical expertise. And that's a pretty good return on the investment!

KEY TERMS

Assessment report 197
Comparison points 198

ROI 199
Success stories 203

DEEP DIVES

These exercises are designed to enhance your understanding of the chapter's key ideas, principles, and approaches.

1. Identify three examples of inappropriate social media comparisons. Explain your rationale. (Remember that inappropriate comparisons are like comparing apples to oranges instead of apples to apples.)

2. Locate a social media assessment report from an organization.

   a. Identify and discuss three appropriate features of the report.

   b. Suggest and discuss three ways to improve the report.

   c. Provide your rationale based on the discussion in this chapter.

3. Craft three compelling arguments about why an organization that does a good job reporting on daily or weekly analytics should still develop a social media assessment report like the one described in this chapter. Provide specific examples and your rationale.

PART IV

Conclusion

The Mindset of a Strategist, the Sensibilities of a Professional, and the Zeal of an Enthusiast

When you hear the word "social," the last word that you would probably associate it with is "strategy." After all, "social" implies a kind of carefree, go-with-the-flow spirit. The word "strategy" sounds difficult, abstract, and challenging. It's like trying to visualize a Kardashian as a chess-playing grandmaster. It just doesn't work. But those are almost exactly the sensibilities that great social media managers find a way to fuse together. In fact, throughout this book, we've hinted at the underlying power of synthesizing a strategic mindset, professional sensibilities, and enthusiastic zeal. This chapter moves these issues out from the wings to center stage, spotlighting the **Social Media Aspirational Triangle** (see Figure 15.1).

STRATEGIC MINDSET

How do strategists think? What makes them different than tacticians? Next we highlight three of the more important insights related to

FIGURE 15.1   Social Media Aspirational Triangle

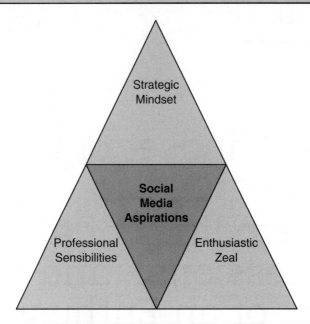

these questions, insights gleaned from a rich body of scholarly and applied work.

First, strategists are always grounded by the current reality even as they envision the next steps forward. Many people consider chess grandmasters to be *the* master strategists. We imagine them thoughtfully pondering the current array of pieces on the board as they plot their next moves. It's a perfect image even when we have little insight into what they are pondering. Here's a hint, though: they are looking for underlying patterns, contemplating the outcomes of various options, and weighing the amount of time they should put into the decision. They can do so because they've studied thousands of different scenarios and games.

These skills mirror those needed by a social media grandmaster. Social media strategists need to understand their current position thoroughly, as well as their competitors' position, in the social media cosmos. They also need to envision various channel and content options in order to move forward and make those choices considering how others might respond.

Like chess grandmasters, they need to think ahead—not necessarily ten moves ahead but, two or three—to win the social media game. A thought leader, for example, might avoid endorsing a politician because doing so might draw the ire, if not the condemnation, of audience members with different political views. That's thinking a couple of steps ahead, even if the thought leader has strong political views.

This mindset cultivates an organic approach to growth, one that encourages learning through experience and experimentation, which is necessary for someone seeking to choreograph a social media strategy most effectively. Professionals can cultivate this **organic growth** approach by tweaking tactics, developing people, and devoting energy to thoughtful experiments. This doesn't mean, though, that *everything* needs to be changed *right now*. What it does mean is that, because the social media world changes more quickly than other professional worlds, people without the flexibility to adapt, change, and grow will be left behind.

Second, strategists focus on making the right trade-offs. Grandmasters know when to sacrifice pawns and even rooks when necessary. These are the kinds of trade-offs they make to win the game. Effective strategists have a similar orientation. They operate by a simple basic principle: we can do virtually anything in the social media world but we can't do everything.

The following conversation stoppers often mask a hesitancy—or an inability—to make trade-offs:

- "We should have a presence on all the social media platforms." **Strategist's retort:** This assumes that all our social media platforms have similar value to our organization. We need to pick the ones with the most potential for us.

- "We should get approval from everyone before we post something." **Strategist's retort:** By the time we get everyone to sign off, we may have lost an opportunity. In the social media world, speed usually trumps perfectly crafted posts.

- "We should spread around our resources equally to all our content sources." **Strategist's retort:** Not all content has equal value. Certain types of content are more valuable to your audiences than other types.

Skillful strategists spot this type of mistaken thinking and know how to confront it effectively. One strategy expert put it this way: "Bad strategy flourishes because it floats above analysis, logic, and choice. . . . [It] is the active avoidance of crafting a good strategy. One common reason for choosing avoidance is the pain or difficulty of choice."[1] In short, strategists are equally proud of what they choose *not to do* as they are about what they choose *to do*. It's painful but rewarding.

Third, strategists cultivate synergies. Skilled, experienced surgeons have good outcomes regardless of the hospital in which they operate, right? Answer: Wrong. "The benefits of experience virtually disappear when surgeons treat patients elsewhere."[2] Why is that? "The surgeon's skill is tied to the experience of the entire surgical team."[3] Likewise, skilled social media strategists want all the social media elements (i.e., the 5 Cs) to work together. It's not just about "being on the same page"; that's just the starting point. It's more about how the strategic elements strengthen and enrich one another—about how to achieve **synergies**. Strategists tolerate task silos for efficiency's sake but remain skeptical of their value and actively seek to subvert their subtle illusions of stability, effectiveness, and power.

To be specific, a strategist might task one person with maintaining several platforms and another person with managing the website. But the strategist would make sure the relationships between the website and platforms were engineered to enrich all components and that those assigned with the responsibilities regularly coordinate with one another. It's not just about meeting together; it's about coordinating actions, policies, and purpose to achieve something neither person could while hidden away inside a silo. As my favorite strategic theorist put it, "Good strategy is not just 'what' you are trying to do. It is also about 'why' and 'how' you are doing it."[4] In fact, this orientation underlies the entire premise of the book.

PROFESSIONAL SENSIBILITIES

Developing professional sensibilities protects you and your company from overreaction while enriching your own and your company's effectiveness. Three issues deserve special mention.

First, professionals are committed to a core set of values and related ethical standards. Most professionals, like engineers, accountants, and military officers, adhere to a professional code of conduct that emerged from the historical experiences of veterans in the field. Educational institutions often explicitly and implicitly instruct new professionals on the code. This code cultivates both strong bonds and the necessary constraints. After all, we all want our engineers to build bridges based on sound construction principles. And if they aren't following the code, then we want people to blow the whistle, regardless of what employers might say.

Unfortunately, such rich traditions do not really exist in the social media cosmos. Instead, social media managers are often tasked with creating the codes and educating others about them. Thoughtful professionals eagerly take on this task because it provides them an opportunity to shape the social media space in ways that uphold their organization's values. Specifically, they address what kinds of information should be shared on social media and what kinds should not. And the codes of conduct provide guidance as to acceptable practices for their different audiences—senior leaders, employees, and users. Employees, for example, are representatives of an organization, and leaders should reasonably expect employees to represent organizational values and not disclose confidential information. It's probably a stretch to expect every employee to THINK (T: Is it *true?*, H: Is it *helpful?*, I: Is it *inspiring?*, N: Is it *necessary?*, K: Is it *kind?*) before they post, but it is worth mentioning the ideal. Some nursing homes, for example, have grappled with caretakers using Facebook to post humiliating images of patients coping with dementia and other maladies.[5] The posted images may well meet the "true" test but not the others.

Those same THINK expectations may not apply to platform users. That said, users might well post objectionable material; it falls to the social media manager to make the call as to whether something should be removed from the platforms. Therefore, many platform administrators post guidelines for removing objectionable content such as spam, threats, pornographic images, and derogatory language.

Second, professionals cultivate collaborative, respectful relationships with others in their organizations. Social media professionals, unlike the stereotypical chess grandmaster, cannot work in isolation. They not only rely on others but also must build respectful relationships to advance the business goals of their organization. Doing this requires a great deal of respectful listening, as they learn about the values, concerns, and goals of various areas of their organization. Then they can collaborate with others to use social media to move their organization forward.

The bonus: building these kinds of relationships helps social media managers educate others about their social media approach, constraints, and opportunities. Consider, for example, a manager who knows in some vague way about the speed of social media but fails to recognize how speed also allows for the rapid correction of erroneous information. This hazy understanding evaporates into thin air when a customer posts something the manager finds offensive. This post may well induce a furious exchange of internal emails and even a call to shut down a particular platform. Respectful, professional relationships built on mutual understanding often prevent the understandable but unnecessary overreaction. Sadly, professionals usually get more credit for problems solved than for those prevented. Happily though, over the long run, prevention engenders respect for the competence of the social media manager.

Third, professionals exercise good judgment. We all know people who have bad judgment. These are the people about whom we all too often find ourselves asking, "What were they thinking?" They seem to have a knack for making the wrong decisions. In contrast, people we know with *good* judgment consistently make the best decisions possible in a reasonable time frame based on the available information at the time. Think of it this way: what do we expect from good sports officials? We want them to make the right call at the right time. If it takes too long to make the right call, it slows down the flow of the game. Alternatively, if the referee quickly throws a lot of flags in error, it could undermine the integrity of the game. Do we expect the referees to get every call right? That's impossible, but we do expect them to respect the integrity of the game and keep it moving along.

People with good judgment don't overreact or underreact to situations because they have the good sense to weigh short-term and long-term goals properly. Consider, for example, the social media manager who has an employee who posted something that a group of people found offensive. Should the employee be fired? Reprimanded? Warned? Advised? This is a judgment call based on the track record of the employee, the employee's willingness to learn from a mistake, and the potential harm to the organization. The short-term and easy response would be to fire the person on the spot, but that would send chilling ripples through the organization. Other employees might just "play it safe" by avoiding future posts of anything remotely provocative, but potentially viral. On the other hand, if the offense is egregious, failing to act might signal organizational fecklessness and timidity. There is not an optimal choice in this situation; rather, choosing is about envisioning various options, weighing the alternatives, and calmly deciding on the best possible course of action in the situation.

Similarly, assume that you are tasked with surveying employees' level of satisfaction with the social media presence. Although quantitative data might be easy to collect and calculate, numbers alone rarely tell the whole story. Professionals would also include some interviews and focus groups to get a deeper understanding of employee insights and impressions. Exercising sound judgment in this case means realizing that not everything can be easily quantified.

The good news about good judgment is that it can be developed. That's one reason we included the word "exercise" in this action principle. Daily exercise protects your long-term health. Likewise, the daily routines of examining situations from various perspectives, calculating likely outcomes, and making choices will protect the long-term interests of your social media initiatives. The calmness and evenhandedness of professionals emerge from a confidence in the soundness of their approach to making challenging and timely decisions on a routine basis. Think of how an All-Pro quarterback calmly throws a winning touchdown with seconds on the game clock amidst a ferocious onslaught of 300-pound aggressors trained to destroy him. That's how professionals react and perform. We should expect nothing less from "All-Pro" social media managers when competitors and trolls attack them.

Of course, attending to all these options requires a certain degree of energetic zeal, which is the last cornerstone of the Social Media Aspirational Triangle.

ENTHUSIASTS' ZEAL

"Rah, rah" might come to mind when you hear the word "enthusiasts." Fair enough. But true enthusiasts don't need flashy pom-poms to let others know about their excitement. There are other ways, far more in line with the first two corners of the Social Media Aspirational Triangle. Consider the following ideas:

First, enthusiasts have fun, within limits. Social media should be fun, make us laugh, and lighten our mood. Enthusiasts structure the fun into their imagery and words; they can poke occasional fun at their organization and, perhaps, their competitors.

There are limits, though. Professional expectations set fuzzy boundaries that you need to consider. I use the word "fuzzy" because it depends on the degree of professionalism expected in your industry. For instance, the model Emily Ratajkowski tweeted about how thrilled she was to complete a photo shoot for *Harper's Bazaar*. Talk show host Piers Morgan tweeted his take on the photo: "Do you want me to buy you some clothes? You look freezing." Ratajkowski cleverly retorted, "@piersmorgan thanks, but I don't need clothes as much as you need press."[6] It's clever repartee, but the stream of tweets devolved from there. Maybe this kind of exchange is OK for people in the entertainment industry but probably not for those in other professions. In most cases, social media is not the place for trying out your "shock jock" routines. Instead, aim your fun at the PG level.

Second, enthusiasts devour the latest news and trends in their field. This may be the most important indicator of your degree of enthusiasm for any subject. The quest for cutting-edge information helps you refine your current approach and enrich your understanding of the field. At the core, it reflects a deep commitment to embracing the uncertainties of any field of knowledge. Robert Grudin probably best articulated this commitment when he said, " . . . the only thing forbidden should be to stand still and say, 'This is it.'"[7]

Third, enthusiasts experiment. It's not enough to just read what others are saying about social media trends. Enthusiasts take it one step further and try to contribute something new through experimentation. Social media firms, for instance, are experimenting with various messaging strategies to counter Islamic terrorist rhetoric.[8] For the experimentally minded social media manager, this could be as simple as tinkering with existing protocols or something as complex as embracing an emerging platform. Either way, the results, positive or negative, fuel the enthusiast's spirit with excitement and mind with new insights.

CONCLUSION

Embracing the Social Media Aspirational Triangle might not guarantee your instant social media success, but it can position you for sustained excellence. Realizing your potential requires aligning the five social media Cs into a coherent strategy supported by organizational leaders and implemented with thoughtfulness, thoroughness, and eagerness. If you can do that, then you may well embody the illusive image of a Kardashian-like grandmaster. As disturbing or hilarious as you might find that image, it surely suggests a path toward success.

KEY TERMS

Organic growth 211   Synergies 212
Social Media Aspirational
    Triangle 209

DEEP DIVES

These exercises are designed to enhance your understanding of the chapter's key ideas, principles, and approaches.

1. Rank order the three elements of the Social Media Aspirational Triangle in terms of difficulty to achieve and maintain. Provide your rationale.

2. Using your own social media network, identify three people or organizations that appear *not* to balance the three corners of the Social Media Aspirational Triangle properly. Provide your evidence.

3. Create a list of 10 daily or weekly habits that social media managers could use to cultivate a healthy balance between all three elements of the Social Media Aspirational Triangle.

NOTES

1. R. Rumelt, *Good Strategy, Bad Strategy: The Difference and Why It Matters* (New York: Crown Business, 2011), 58.
2. D. Dranove and S. Marciano, *Kellogg on Strategy: Concepts, Tools, and Frameworks for Practitioners* (Hoboken, NJ: John Wiley and Sons, 2005), 189.
3. Dranove and Marciano, *Kellogg on Strategy*, 189.
4. Rumelt, *Good Strategy, Bad Strategy: The Difference and Why It Matters*, 85.
5. See C. Ornstein and J. Huseman, "Social Media Abuse of Nursing Home Residents often Goes Unchecked," *Shots: Health News from NPR*, July 14, 2016, http://www.npr.org/sections/health-shots/2016/07/14/485293079/social-media-abuse-of-nursing-home-residents-often-goes-unchecked. Accessed July 15, 2016.
6. See O. Blair, "Emily Ratajkowski Responds to Piers Morgan's Quip over Nude Picture," *Independent*, July 8, 2016, http://www.independent.co.uk/news/people/emily-ratajkowski-nude-photos-piers-morgan-response-twitter-magazine-shoot-a7127111.html. Accessed July 9, 2016.
7. R. Grudin, *Time and the Art of Living* (New York: Houghton Mifflin, 1982), 2.
8. S. Schechner, "Social-Media Firms Target Terrorism," *Wall Street Journal*, August 1, 2016, A6.

APPENDIX 1

Social Media Platform Fact Sheets

Elizabeth Hintz

FACEBOOK

Value Proposition: Everyone you know is using it.

Founder(s) and Start Date: Mark Zuckerberg, 2004

Historical Milestones:

- Facebook.com was launched by Mark Zuckerberg in February 2004
- High school students began using Facebook in September 2005
- Facebook became open for anyone to use in September 2006
- Debut of Facebook "like" button in April 2010
- Facebook had more than one billion active users in October 2012
- Facebook replaced "likes" with various reaction options in February 2016

Source of Income: Facebook makes about $15 per user through various methods of advertising. The purchase of Facebook credits for use in apps and games also generates income for the company.

User-Generated Content: Users are able to post a variety of content, including status updates, photos and videos, and life events.

Benefits for Users: With over 1.55 billion users, Facebook is the largest social network in existence. In some ways, Facebook acts as a "Google" for people you know, making it an integral part of the fabric of the Internet.

Largest User Demographics: 45–54+, retirees, women

Analytics: Facebook provides a full range of "Insights" (the analytics suite) that cover ads and promotions, page likes, reach, page views, actions on page, posts, events, videos, people, and messages. Each of those categories, when selected, also offers options for further refining and filtering the information presented.

Further Reading:

- Carlson, N. "At Last: The Full Story Of How Facebook Was Founded." *Business Insider*, March 5, 2010. http://www.businessinsider.com/how-facebook-was-founded-2010-3/we-can-talk-about-that-after-i-get-all-the-basic-functionality-up-tomorrow-night-1.

- Bloomberg News. "Inside Facebook's Plan to Boost Ad Revenue by Turning Users Into Buyers." *Advertising Age*, July 13, 2016. http://adage.com/article/digital/facebook-turn-users-into-buyers/304474/.

- Zephoria. "The Top 20 Valuable Facebook." *Zephoria Digital Marketing*, updated monthly. https://zephoria.com/top-15-valuable-facebook-statistics/.

- Stinson, L. "Facebook Reactions, the Totally Redesigned Like Button, Is Here." *Wired*, February 24, 2016. https://www.wired.com/2016/02/facebook-reactions-totally-redesigned-like-button/.

- Kirkpatrick, D. *The Facebook Effect: The Inside Story of the Company that Is Connecting the World*. New York, NY: Simon & Schuster, 2012.

TWITTER

Value Proposition: Participate in the global conversation in real time.

Founder(s) and Start Date: Jack Dorsey, Evan Williams, Biz Stone, and Noah Glass, 2006

Historical Milestones:

- First sketch of Twitter completed in March 2006
- First tweet sent March 21, 2006
- Hashtag debuted in August 2007
- Promoted tweets, promoted trends, and promoted accounts launched in 2010
- Twitter launched Vine in January 2013
- Twitter announced IPO filing in September 2013

Source of Income: Advertising on the site accounts for 85 percent of Twitter's revenue. Advertising is offered in three ways: promoting a tweet, promoting a trend, or promoting an account.

Data licensing is Twitter's second highest source of revenue. Twitter refers to its public data as the "fire hose" and sells about 500 million tweets a day.

User-Generated Content: Users are able to post text, photos, videos, and live streams.

Benefits for Users: Over 316 million people are able to interact with friends, family, celebrities, politicians, and peers across the globe in real time. Global trending topics spark conversation, slacktivism (i.e., actions requiring little time or involvement that are performed via the Internet in support of causes), and often outrage among individuals, groups, and organizations.

Largest User Demographics: under 50, college educated, non-white

Analytics: Twitter has an analytics site that any user or organization can access. Tweet success is measured in *impressions*, or the number of unique viewers who were exposed to your tweet. Engagement, link clicks, retweets, likes, and replies can all be measured in detail.

Further Reading:

- Monica, P. R. "Twitter May Be the next MySpace." *CNN Money*, March 27, 2014. http://buzz.money .cnn.com/2014/03/27/twitter-stock-down/.

- Duggan, M., and A. Smith. *Social Media Update 2013*. Washington, DC: Pew Research Center, January 2014. http://pewinternet.org/Reports/2013/Social-Media-Update.aspx.

- Gadkari, P. "How Does Twitter Make Money?" *BBC News*, November 7, 2013. http://www.bbc.com/news/business-24397472.

INSTAGRAM

Value Proposition: Follow your friends' lives through photography.

Founder(s) and Start Date: Kevin Systrom and Mike Krieger, 2010

Historical Milestones:

- Instagram, originally released exclusively for the iPhone, was launched by Kevin Systrom and Mike Krieger in October 2010

- Facebook bought Instagram in April 2012

- Video capabilities were added to Instagram in June 2013

Source of Income: Currently, Instagram does not make money. It is supported through Facebook's revenue. In April 2014, Zuckerberg stated that "monetization isn't our near-term priority."[1]

User-Generated Content: Users can post photos and videos using a variety of filters and editing options.

Benefits for Users: 300 million people are able to follow visually the lives of their friends, family members, and celebrities.

Largest User Demographics: 18–29, women, minorities

Analytics: None provided by platform.

Further Reading:

- Luckerson, V. "A Year Later, Instagram Hasn't Made a Dime. Was it Worth $1 Billion?" *Time*, April 9, 2013. http://business.time.com/2013/04/09/a-year-later-instagram-hasnt-made-a-dime-was-it-worth-1-billion/.

- Rusli, E. M. "Instagram Pictures Itself Making Money." *The Wall Street Journal*, September 8, 2013. https://www.wsj.com/news/articles/SB10001424127 887324577304579059230069305894.

- Borow, J. "How Facebook Is Already Profiting From Instagram." *AdvertisingAge*, August 8, 2013. http://adage.com/article/digitalnext/facebook-profiting-instagram/243515/.

- Griswold, A. "Here's the Problem With That $35 Billion Instagram Valuation." *Slate*, December 19, 2014. http://www.slate.com/blogs/moneybox/2014/12/19/instagram_valuation_citigroup_says_facebook_s_photo_app_is_worth_35_billion.html.

- Harbour, S. *Instagram: How a Photo-Sharing App Achieved a $1 Billion Facebook Buyout in 18 Months.* N.p.: Hyperink Inc., 2012.

- Wong, J. I. "Instagram Likes and Comments are Plummeting." *Quartz*, June 15, 2016. https://qz.com/707819/instagram-likes-and-comments-are-plummeting/.

PINTEREST

Value Proposition: Plan for the future by collecting ideas.

Founder(s) and Start Date: Ben Silbermann, Evan Sharp, and Paul Sciarra, 2009

Historical Milestones:

- Pinterest was launched by Ben Silbermann, Evan Sharp, and Paul Sciarra in March 2010

- Pinterest acquired the recipe aggregator Punchfork in January 2013

- Pinterest acquired the custom keyboard company Flesky in June 2016

Source of Income: Pinterest currently offers promoted pins that allow businesses to pay to have certain pins show up on a potential buyer's main page. The company is researching additional features that allow businesses to analyze who sees and repins their pins.

User-Generated Content: Though users *do* have the ability to upload their own content, most of the content created by users are boards. Boards are aggregations of pins posted by other users, usually organized around a central theme: e.g., wedding ideas, home renovation, and outfits for summer.

Benefits for Users: Over 100 million people, mostly women, can bring ideas from across the Internet to one, completely customizable place. These collections of ideas may help others to utilize small spaces, plan a baby shower, or create the best handmade decorations. Often, the information about where to purchase the products needed for the projects are attached to each *pin*, making shopping by idea board effortless.

Largest User Demographics: women under 50

Analytics: One simple click from the Pinterest homepage takes you to analytics.pinterest.com, where a full array of analytics shows you data about your Pinterest profile and about the audience your pins reach.

Further Reading:
- DeAmicis, C. "Why Pinterest Makes No Money but Is Now Worth $3.8 Billion." *Pando*, October 23, 2013 https://pando.com/2013/10/23/why-pinterest-makes-no-money-but-its-now-worth-3-8-billion/.
- Goodwin, D. "You Now Have 3 New Ways to Target Pinterest Users." *SEJ: Search Engine Journal*, June 16, 2016. https://www.searchenginejournal.com/pinterest-ad-targeting-options/166167/
- Cooper, K. *How to Build a Huge Following on Pinterest.* N.p.: Hyperink Inc., 2016.

LinkedIn

Value Proposition: Maintain professional brands and networks.

Founder(s) and Start Date: Reid Hoffman, Allen Blue, Konstantin Guericke, Eric Ly, and Jean-Luc Vaillant, 2002

Historical Milestones:

- LinkedIn was founded by Reid Hoffman, Allen Blue, Konstantin Guericke, Eric Ly, and Jean-Luc Vaillant in Hoffman's living room in 2002; the site launched on May 5, 2003

- LinkedIn opened its first office overseas, making the company global, in 2008

- LinkedIn went public in 2011 and purchased SlideShare in 2012

- LinkedIn reached 300 million members in April 2014

- Perkins v. LinkedIn was filed in 2015; this class-action lawsuit held the site accountable for sending millions of unsolicited emails to potential site users

- Microsoft purchased LinkedIn for over $26 billion in 2016

Source of Income: In 2014 LinkedIn had revenue of $568 million: 61 percent from talent solutions ($345 million), 20 percent from premium subscriptions ($114 million), and 19 percent from marketing initiatives ($109 million).

User-Generated Content: Users of the site create a profile that serves as a digital résumé. Projects, awards, certifications, publications, skills, and endorsements can all be posted on this profile.

Benefits for Users: LinkedIn is the world's largest professional social network. Over 300 million users can connect with leaders in their industry, receive recommendations and endorsements, be scouted by major organizations, and search and apply for jobs.

Largest User Demographics: college graduates, high-income households

Analytics: Each LinkedIn business page has an analytics section, which details post reach and engagement for that page. Follower demographics and trends are also available, in addition to information about competitors.

Further Reading:

- Pepitone, J. "LinkedIn Stock More Than Doubles in IPO." *CNN Money*, May 19, 2011. http://money.cnn.com/2011/05/19/technology/linkedin_IPO/.

- "Perkins v. LinkedIn." Gilardi & Co. website ©2017. Available from Gilardi & Co., P.O. Box 808012, Petaluma, CA. http://www.addconnectionssettlement.com/.

GOOGLE PLUS

Value Proposition: Increase your search engine rankings.

Founder(s) and Start Date: Google (especially Vic Gundotra), 2011

Historical Milestones:

- Started by Google in June 2011

- Google+ pages launched for organizations to join Google+ in November 2011

- Google+ Photos and Hangouts were launched in May 2013

Source of Income: Google has invested over $500 million in Google+.

User-Generated Content: Google+ allows users to create a profile, add information, photos, video, and post links and updates. Circles allow users to add friends to groups, and Hangouts allow for instant messaging, videoconferencing, and the sharing of files and photos. Much of the Google+ user base consists of YouTube users because YouTube made them create a Google+ account to sign in to YouTube. This network is also useful for nonprofit organizations, as it offers an inexpensive means of doing some of the tasks of member and client relations management.

Benefits for Users: For a business owner, using Google+ may improve search engine rankings. As Google is the most widely used search engine, it makes sense to create and publish content to Google+. Over 90 million users, mostly young men and IT Engineers, have accounts on the site.

Largest User Demographics: young men 25–34

Analytics: Google has always had analytics capabilities, with Google Analytics serving webmasters for years. Google+ has a simplified version of this software that produces easy-to-understand results for the average user. Metrics such as total +1s, likes, shares, comments, and engagement are available from this view.

Further Reading:

- Bullas, J. "22 Social Media Facts and Statistics You Should Know in 2014." Blog from jeffbullas.com, April 10, 2015. Retrieved February 27, 2017, from http://www.jeffbullas.com/2014/01/17/20-social-media-facts-and-statistics-you-should-know-in-2014/.
- Sauer, J. "Google Plus Analytics: Measuring Activity within Google Plus." *Jeffalytics*, n.d. Retrieved February 27, 2017, from https://www.jeffalytics.com/google-plus-analytics/measuring-activity-within-google-plus/.
- Jostes, L. "How to Discover Analytics with the Google Dashboard." *Social Media Examiner*, March 11, 2015. http://www.socialmediaexaminer.com/analytics-with-google-dashboard/.

SNAPCHAT

Value Proposition: Share memories with minimal commitment.

Founder(s) and Start Date: Evan Spiegel, Bobby Murphy, and Reggie Brown, 2011

Historical Milestones:

- Snapchat (originally called Picaboo) was launched in July 2011; its name was changed to Snapchat in the fall of 2011.

- Total users hit 100,000 in April 2012.
- Snapchat was launched on Android and released video chat in 2012.
- Snapchat launched Snapchat stories in October 2013.
- Snapchat added timestamps, filters, temperature and speed overlays, and the ability to replay snaps in December 2013.
- Snapchat added text conversations, Snapcash, and video in 2014.

Source of Income: Snapchat currently makes no money. It survives on funding from outside investors.

User-Generated Content: Snapchat allows users to take photos and videos, add filters (including location-specific filters), effects (face swapping, for example), write messages, add stickers, and draw on these photos and videos. The user can then send that photo or video to friends whom they select, or they can create a story (which is visible to all friends for 24 hours). Users also have the option to create a photo or video and then send it to a public story, which is available for anyone in the area to see.

Benefits for Users: Over 150 million people use Snapchat to connect with friends and family, send embarrassing photos, document vacations, parties, concerts, and other events. The app is valuable because 1) photos and videos do not have to be downloaded or saved to be sent to family and friends, which saves space on mobile devices, and 2) the photos and videos disappear within 10 seconds of their having been viewed.

Largest User Demographics: young men and women under 24

Analytics: No formal analytics are provided by this platform. You can, however, see how many times a story has been viewed, who has viewed your story, whether or not the story has been replayed, and whether or not any screenshots have been taken.

Further Reading:

- Crook, J., and A. Escher. "A Brief History of Snapchat." *Tech Crunch*, October 15, 2015. https://techcrunch .com/gallery/a-brief-history-of-snapchat/.

- Ballve, M. "Snapchat's Explosive Growth among Teens and Millennials Means It's Emerging as a Powerful Brand Platform." *Business Insider*, August 15, 2014. http://www.businessinsider.com/a-primer-on-snapchat-and-its-demographics-2014-7.
- Delaney, J. "How Does Snapchat Make Money?" *Money Morning*, January 19, 2017. https://moneymorning.com/2017/01/19/how-does-snapchat-make-money-3/.
- MacMillan, D., and E. M. Rusli. "Snapchat Fetches $10 Billion Valuation." *The Wall Street Journal*, August 26, 2014. https://www.wsj.com/articles/snapchat-fetches-10-billion-valuation-1409088794.

NOTES

1. V. Goel, "Facebook Profit Tripled in First Quarter," *New York Times*, April 23, 2014, https://www.nytimes.com/2014/04/24/technology/facebook-profit-tripled-in-first-quarter.html.

Dealing With Anger Online: Strategies for Social Media Managers

Ryan Martin

Anger is the most commonly expressed emotion online,[1] and social media managers routinely find themselves dealing with various forms of online hostility from angry customers. In this chapter, I will discuss the origins of online anger, some relevant research, and some general strategies for how social media managers can handle online anger when it is directed at them or their organization.

WHAT IS ONLINE ANGER?

Anger is an emotional state associated with being insulted, having one's goals blocked, or being otherwise provoked.[2] It is different from aggression, a behavior that has the intent to harm someone or something.[3] This is an important distinction as aggression is often misunderstood as being just the outward, harmful expression of anger when in reality there are lots of ways to express anger (e.g., crying, politely asserting oneself). This distinction gets a little confusing in an online environment, however, where we are dealing only with outward behaviors. In other words, anger (the emotion), is likely behind a hostile tweet or Facebook post (the behavior), but anger also might be behind a politely assertive tweet or Facebook post. If we think of online anger more broadly than just the aggressive or cruel behaviors often associated with it, we recognize that anger is expressed in a multitude of ways on the social web.

IMPORTANT RESEARCH ON ONLINE ANGER

There are four main findings regarding online anger. First, it's very common. Recent data suggest that nearly half of Twitter users say they tweet "often" as a way of dealing with anger.[4] Second, anger spreads faster online than any other emotion. Fan and colleagues categorized millions of "tweets" on Weibo, a Twitter-like social media site in China, and found that, although happy tweets were shared by those in close relationships, angry tweets were shared by people in both close and distant relationships. Researchers described anger as the most "viral" online emotion.[5] Third, online anger has some fairly severe consequences. In one recent study, those who vented online were angrier than the general population, were more likely than the general population to express that anger in maladaptive ways, and frequently experienced negative consequences for their anger.[6] That same study, though, also shed some light on why people are so likely to rant online. Specifically, participants in the study reported that, after they had expressed their anger via some sort of online rant, they felt calm, relieved, and relaxed. Thus, because their anger dissipates for the short term, people often feel rewarded for their online anger expressions, despite the long-term consequences.

WHY WE GET MAD

To really understand how to respond to someone's online anger, you need to understand why people get mad at all, whether online or offline. The types of situations in which people most often get angry were outlined by Dr. Jerry Deffenbacher in a 1996 article on anger. In it, he described three overlapping factors that lead to anger: (1) a stimulus,

(2) the person's appraisal of the stimulus, and (3) the person's pre-anger psychobiological state. The stimulus is the event that people often point to as the cause (e.g., a decision made by a service provider, politician, or other public figure). These stimuli do not cause the anger directly, though. What matters as much as the stimulus itself is how the person appraises or interprets that stimulus. Imagine, for example, that your favorite sports team decides to raise ticket prices. That event alone, which is the stimulus, does not cause the anger directly. First, you need to appraise that event as being negative, unfair, unacceptable, or something that will be difficult for you to handle. If your interpretation of the raised ticket prices was, "I wish the games were cheaper, but I understand why they are raising the prices," you'll have a very different emotional response (e.g., disappointment) than if you interpret the raised ticket prices with this attitude: "That's completely unfair. I've been a loyal customer for a long time. They can't do this to me."

The types of appraisals that are most likely to lead to anger are those in which people feel they were treated poorly (e.g., poor customer service) or in which their goals have been blocked (e.g., they were unable to obtain a product they want or attend an event they want to attend). Further, people tend to get angry when they feel the stimulus is so negative that they can't cope with it. For instance, a flight being canceled will likely always be frustrating, but if the travelers' interpretation is that they will now miss an important part of their trip and, consequently, "everything is ruined," they will likely become even angrier.

Deffenbacher's third factor, the pre-anger state, refers to our psychobiological state right before the stimulus. If people are already fatigued, tense, sleepy, hungry, or in some other negative state when provoked, they are more likely to become angry. For instance, customers who have waited all night for a product, and are therefore tired, are much more likely to become angry when they fail to obtain the product than another customer who is not fatigued.

Tips on Dealing With Online Anger for Social Media Managers

Finally, here are some practical tips for social media managers who find themselves dealing with angry customers via the social web.

1. Understand what is driving the anger. When confronted with customer anger, social media managers need to consider where the anger is coming from. Using the model described above, ask yourself how the customer is feeling and thinking. Are they angry because their goals were blocked? If so, perhaps you can help them meet their goals somehow. Are they angry because they feel they were treated unfairly? In that case, perhaps you can help them feel better about their interactions by better explaining a policy that has upset them. Or, if they were genuinely wronged in an interaction, you can take steps to right that wrong.

2. Understand your goals too. Much of what social media managers should do depends on what their own goals are in responding. If your goal, for example, is to minimize the visibility of a customer who is making a scene, you likely want to try and get the angry customer offline into a private conversation. If your goal, though, is to demonstrate to others how willing you are to listen and be responsive to customers, you likely want to keep that conversation online where others can witness it.

3. Model kindness in your interactions. One of the best things social media managers can do is model kindness in their interactions with customers. By being polite, kind, and courteous, even when customers are rude, you demonstrate to all who are following along what kind of customer service experience they can have with you. Also, by taking the high road, you send an important message about how to behave online.

4. Don't reward incivility. As noted in the Fan and colleagues study, anger online is rewarded with retweets, likes, shares, and replies. Those responses serve as positive reinforcement to the perpetrators of online anger, so an important thing we can do is to avoid rewarding such incivility ourselves.

5. Promote positivity. In contrast, we can promote positivity by making a point of retweeting, sharing, liking, and replying to positive tweets and posts. Obviously, you only want to do this when it is consistent with the image of your organization that you are promoting via social media, but by promoting positivity, you send an important message to your customers and others about how you want people to communicate online.

NOTES

1. R. Fan, J. Zhao, Y. Chen, and K. Xu, "Anger Is More Influential Than Joy: Sentiment Correlation in Weibo," *PLoS One* 9, no. 10, 2014. Reprint submitted to Elsevier, September 10, 2013, http://arxiv.org/abs/1309.2402.

2. C. D. Spielberger, *State-Trait Anger Expression Inventory–Revised* (Odessa, FL: Psychological Assessment Resources, Inc., 1999).

3. J. L. Deffenbacher, "Cognitive-Behavioral Approaches to Anger Reduction," in *Advances in Cognitive-Behavioral Therapy*, edited by K. S. Dobson and K. D. Craig, 31–62 (Thousand Oaks, CA: Sage, 1996).

4. Martin [Online anger consequences]. Unpublished raw data, 2016.

5. R. Fan et al., "Anger Is More Influential."

6. R. C. Martin, K. Coyier, L. M. Van Sistine, and K. L. Schroeder, "Anger on the Internet: The Perceived Value of Rant-Sites," *Cyberpsychology, Behavior, and Social Networking* 16 (2013): 119–122.

APPENDIX 3

Case Studies

Using Social Media
to Recruit New Employees

Amy Martin

> *"No one wakes up in the morning saying, 'I want to work for a packaging company!'"*
>
> —Rick Fantini

Established in Menasha, Wisconsin, in 1849, Menasha Corporation is one of the oldest family-owned manufacturing companies in the United States. Menasha has a long history as a market leader in the packaging industry; it is also known for innovation in its field, social responsibility, and its people-first culture. The engaged leadership team fosters an atmosphere in which every employee can make an impact and contribute to this midsized company's success. And employees have opportunities to grow, develop, and move into roles of increasing responsibility across this growing organization. This long list of positive attributes sounds like a recruiting manager's dream, right?

As Menasha's senior human resources representative, however, I can tell you a different story. The reality is that the very nature of our business—the manufacture of packaging, transport materials, and in-store product displays—presents a challenge to our recruiters despite these compelling factors. As a member of our leadership team often bemoans, "No one wakes up in the morning saying, 'I want to work for a packaging company!'" The fact is that packaging is not exactly a sexy industry in a high-tech world. Further, Menasha Corporation is a business-to-business organization with little name recognition outside of our field. Although we provide materials and services that are essential to protecting, transporting, and promoting products manufactured by some of the world's largest companies, few people know who we are or what we do. The need to overcome these recruiting challenges by sourcing, screening, and hiring many talented employees in a short time frame became critical in 2013 when the company suddenly experienced unprecedented growth after landing major contracts with several key customers. Following a comprehensive review of our recruiting practices, the Menasha Talent Acquisition Team initiated a six-step integrated recruitment process (see Figure A3.1) that has allowed us to refine continuously how we bring our open positions to market, react more quickly and effectively to changes in technology, and ultimately increase our visibility in the market. Social media plays a significant role in each of the six steps. In the following case study, I will discuss how our social media strategy has been successfully integrated into each step of the process, ultimately increasing our ability to bring top talent into our organization in a quick and cost-effective manner.

STEP 1: JOB POSTED IN MENASHA CORPORATION APPLICANT TRACKING SYSTEM

The first issue our human resources team tackled in 2013 was to assess the system we were using to post our open positions. The research was telling us that 34 percent of candidates between the ages of 18–29 were using a smartphone to apply for jobs[1] and that was a key demographic that we knew we were going to need to attract to address on our recruiting needs. After an in-depth analysis, the team decided that the applicant system we had in place did not provide a strong user experience for online applicants, particularly those on a mobile device. The application form was long, the text boxes were small, and, most important, the system was not at all optimized for mobile devices. These realizations persuaded us to discontinue our contract with our current system provider and begin working with a younger company that had an applicant

FIGURE A3.1 Menasha Corporation's Recruitment Process

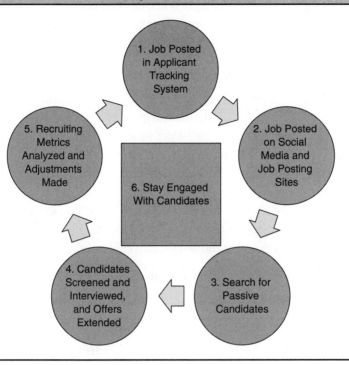

SOURCE: Copyright © CanStock Photo/mybaitshop.

tracking system (ATS) that met many of these needs. After a short implementation cycle, we found ourselves with a system that allowed candidates to view and complete applications on mobile devices and even log in and import their profiles from LinkedIn and other social networks to allow for easy access. We also spent time increasing our knowledge about search engine optimization (SEO) keywords and how to improve our job postings so that they were easier to read and would grab the candidate's attention more effectively. Our new system allowed us to customize the look and feel of our job postings, which in turn increased our candidate pools.

STEP 2: JOB POSTED ON SOCIAL MEDIA AND JOB POSTING SITES

As we went through the implementation of our new ATS, the human resources team also started learning more about the world of social media. "Be where the candidates are, each and every day": this was the advice we received, and it became a key component of our new system. Our team realized that we were missing some key opportunities to advertise our open positions. And these resources were free, as well. Previously, open positions were posted only on Monster and CareerBuilder. These sites were considered the key job posting boards available, but each posting had to be entered manually and came with a heavy price tag for each month that the job was posted. With the implementation of our new ATS, we began to explore other channels where we could post our positions. And with this exploration came some key questions we began to explore. If Facebook was where everyone lived, why not be on Facebook? And what about Twitter? And what other sites are out there that we're not considering? And do we just post jobs or do we try to engage candidates with our content? Oh, and how do those darn hashtags work, and what can they do for us?

We began experimenting by posting our open jobs on a variety of social media channels, and this process of trying new sites and venues to reach our candidates continues today. We created careers pages on Facebook, Twitter, and Google Plus, and the functionality of our new system enabled our jobs to feed to these free social media resources automatically. We worked hard to build a following on these pages, encouraging our own employees to connect with us on those pages. We also implemented "career alert" functionalities; these enable us to segment lists of job seekers by employee function and location and to send any potential candidates email or text alerts whenever a new job is posted in our system. Our recruiting team also did some experimenting with one of our key channels, Twitter. By incorporating hashtags into our postings on Twitter (e.g., #JoinMenasha, #hiring, #TweetMyJobs) and investing a small amount of money to target our campaign further, we found that we significantly enhanced our candidate reach.

And finally, we began experimenting with where we were posting our jobs. We discovered that CareerBuilder and Monster, formerly the giants in the job posting world, were less applicable to us and that we had better returns on job aggregators such as LinkedIn and Indeed, where you could move your jobs in and out of slots, sponsor key positions, and use a pay per click model. These changes not only increased our visibility but helped us to manage our costs more effectively.

Our recruiting team has also partnered closely with the marketing and communications functions in our organization to ensure that the branding we portray on our job postings and social pages are consistent with the image the organization is working to portray. These strong partnerships are key to our success and allow us to leverage the knowledge and expertise of others in our organization.

STEP 3: SEARCH FOR PASSIVE CANDIDATES

Sourcing for passive candidates has also been a key dimension of our recruiting strategy. At any given time, only approximately 10 percent of the potential job pool is actively looking for a job, leaving 15 percent as tiptoers (people exploring potential job options but not actively searching) and 75 percent as passive job seekers.[2] Technically, a passive job seeker is someone who is currently employed but is open to learning about new career opportunities. To augment our recruiting efforts beyond the candidates who apply to our jobs via our posting efforts, the recruiting team began leveraging social media tools to source passive candidates. Because so many professionals put their job information, educational background, and skills out on LinkedIn, sourcing for candidates using this tool has become another key aspect of our recruiting strategy. By leveraging functionality in LinkedIn, our team can send messages directly to qualified candidates who may not currently be looking for new positions and encourage them to apply to our open position. This strategy has been very successful for our team, and a large percentage of our recent hires have come from the passive candidate searches conducted by our recruiting team. We are also able to collect information about candidates who have previously applied to positions in our company, and we find this particularly valuable when we have candidates who were very strong but ultimately were not offered the job for which they applied. By leveraging this information in our system, we can reconnect with these runner-up candidates at a later date when we have another position open that matches their qualifications. We are currently working to enhance our abilities to mine these data in our system even further, as they are a key source for enhancing our candidate pool.

STEP 4. CANDIDATES SCREENED AND INTERVIEWED, AND OFFERS EXTENDED

As our economy has continued to grow and unemployment has decreased, competition for top talent has become much tighter. The Menasha recruiting team put a great deal of effort into facilitating the speed with which we can screen, select, and make offers to candidates, including streamlining our interview processes, encouraging our hiring managers to make swift decisions, and putting together market-competitive offers. Developing a video interviewing tool, along with making other small changes, increased our speed and ability to be quick and agile when we find a strong candidate, and we continue to explore other ways to enhance our processes and educate our hiring managers.

STEP 5: RECRUITING METRICS ANALYZED AND ADJUSTMENTS MADE

With the implementation of our new applicant tracking system, we found ourselves equipped with a robust set of metrics, which allows us to track the hits, views, and applicants to a position. By enhancing our understanding of how and where we are reaching our candidates, we have been more effective at refining and understanding where to spend our advertising dollars. For example, when sourcing for an operations director in the Toronto, Canada, region, we could identify that our top three sources for applicants were LinkedIn, direct views to our careers site (menasha.com/careers), and sponsored postings on Indeed.

These data have given us the information to make educated choices as to where to post our positions and how to minimize our cost per hire. We are also able to look in real time at a job that has a low applicant flow and make decisions as to whether it would benefit from additional postings.

The metrics that we obtain from our system also provide us with some other critical information. According to a 2014 talent acquisition survey, 60 percent of job seekers feel that job applications are challenging to fill out, rating the application process more difficult than filling out mortgage applications, college applications, and loan applications.[3] We can see from these metrics that, although we have large numbers of applicants completing our applications (e.g., 73 percent of those who find us through LinkedIn and 67 percent of those who find us on Jobillico), we are losing a large segment of applicants during the process. This understanding has encouraged us to continue to refine our application process to increase its usability and minimize our drop-off rates.

Some of the additional functionality of our ATS allows us to dig further into our job postings to get a better understanding of the timing of views. Gaining a better understanding of when our posts are being viewed allows us to target the timing of our posts and tweets more effectively so as to even further optimize our reach.

STEP 6: STAY ENGAGED WITH CANDIDATES

Ensuring a positive candidate experience for anyone who engages with our postings of open positions is critical to the success of our recruiting function. Thirty-three percent of candidates who have a negative experience when applying to a company will share their experience with friends; 12 percent will share this information on social media.[4] Our team has made it a top priority to ensure that we provide the most positive candidate experience possible. Through functionality in our ATS, we can easily send messages to candidates when they first apply, throughout the application process, and when they receive their final disposition. Staying in close contact with our candidates has become a critical component of our recruiting strategy. Our careers page also has an easy way for candidates to submit support requests. These requests for assistance go directly to a member of our staff who reaches out within hours to candidates to assist them with their questions. Just as shoppers review products on Amazon, candidates share information about their job search experience on sites such as Glassdoor, Indeed, and LinkedIn. Members of our recruitment team are engaged in reviewing these pages and have protocols in place about how to respond to unfavorable reviews. They also work to correct issues that appear to be occurring frequently.

Our recruitment process has continued to change and evolve over the past several years as we have learned more, incorporated new tools and techniques, and striven to stay ahead of the ever-changing world of social media and candidate preferences. Our days-to-fill average is currently hovering around 54 days, which is lower than the industry average, and at approximately $3,400, our cost per hire is far lower than it has ever been.

Although we continue to experiment with different messaging and formats to convey our brand externally, we are finding that taking a "culture-forward" approach is key. We work to ensure that all of our external job postings, websites, and social media posts lead with information about our culture and feature engaging images of employees from across the organization. We try to minimize our text and have as much white space as possible on our websites and social pages to present a clean, modern image. We also find that focusing our text and images around items that showcase how our employees are making a difference in the environment, in their communities, and in the workplace makes the largest impact on our audience, as it gets to the heart of our company's culture and values.

Social Media Marketing for Small and Midsize Businesses

Julie Sadoff

- "I *need* a website, but do I have to update it all of the time?"

- "My Facebook page doesn't have enough likes—what should I do?"

- "Do you think I need a Twitter account? What about Snapchat?"

As a marketing and communications consultant, these are the most common questions I get from small and midsize businesses. Twenty years ago, clients wanted fancy PowerPoint presentations with lots of effects flying in and out, and cool brochures that would stand out from the crowd. Today, they expect the same thing from social media.

I often explain to my clients that social media has its place in the marketing mix but cannot be relied upon to do everything. I also emphasize the need for a social media marketing strategy and plan to be developed *before* a business goes online. Furthermore, as newer technology replaces older technology, businesses need to get back to fundamental marketing and communications principles to reach their audiences effectively, rather than just relying on the cool new tech trend.

THE MARKETING MIX

Social media marketing, like all marketing, is used to persuade your target audience to take action—buy your product, use your service, or support your cause, for example. It is one of the tools in your marketing mix and must support your business goals, not the other way around. In other words, marketing shouldn't be driven by the technological tools that are available but instead by what you want your business to achieve.

Before integrating social media marketing into your mix, you need to decide what your goals are and how social media can help you reach them. Common goals include

- Increasing sales or market share
- Building brand awareness
- Redefining or repositioning your company or product in the marketplace
- Launching a new product or service

Once your business defines its goals and gets buy-in from all the key influencers, the correct marketing tools can be chosen and placed into a strategic plan.

Social Media versus Traditional Tools

Social media differs from traditional marketing tools, such as print and broadcasting tools, because of its capability to build a two-way relationship with your audience. Just as they do on the telephone or in face-to-face meetings, companies can connect with customers and other target audiences online, in real time. In this way, both a business and its customers help craft the company's messages, and people can feel that they have a stake in the business.

According to James Runkle, principal and owner of Drummond St. Strategy, "It's important to understand that marketers are no longer solely in control of the message. It's not easy for some people to relinquish control, but social media marketers have to be quick, adaptive, and able to change things daily, or even hourly, depending on the conversation."[5]

Companies can also learn why their loyal customers like them, use their products or services, and, on the flip side, what people don't like about them. This is a key reason that there needs to be a person or people dedicated to online vehicles before a business launches them to the public. So choosing the correct professional to run your social media is critical.

Take JetBlue for example. This company set itself apart from other airlines because its employees prioritize their customers' experience and deal with any online comments or complaints in a timely and patient manner. In one case, a JetBlue customer tweeted that it was his first text at 34,000 feet in the air, and it took only six minutes for an employee to respond and tell him to have a great flight. JetBlue also has three separate departments working on customer service, including the marketing team, the communications team, and the customer commitment team. With these three departments aligning themselves to serve customers, JetBlue has broken the mold on customer service, and it has earned the airline over 2 million loyal online followers.[6]

On the other hand, American Airlines has not quite figured out how to respond to customers online. In one case, when a customer tweeted that American Airlines was the largest and worst airline in the world, the company responded with an automatic reply—"Thank you for your support! We look forward to a bright future as the #newAmerican." Though everyone wants to see an uplifting and positive message, that message doesn't mean a lot when it has nothing to do with the comment or complaint to which it is responding.[7]

As marketing professionals develop their plans, they need to consider these seven things:

1. What social media vehicles make sense for the business (channels)?

2. What information will the business post (content)?

3. How often will the company post on social media (content)?

4. How will the various communication channels work together (connections)?

5. What infrastructure needs to be put in place to take care of the company's online needs (connections)?

6. How long will the company take to respond to customer comments and questions (corrections)?

7. How will the business react to posts or take care of negative publicity (corrections)?

Recently, a restaurant owner in Milwaukee, Wisconsin, responded to a negative review of his establishment on yelp.com, an online application that consumers use to find and review local businesses. The reviewer stated that he had been to the restaurant several times and found the drinks overpriced, the service hit or miss, and the menu very basic. Instead of letting this review go unanswered, the owner went on to yelp.com and Facebook and gave a 1,300-word rebuttal describing his establishment. He also asked that customers speak to staff directly instead of going online with their complaints. Afterward, the restaurant owner received nationwide media coverage because of his reaction, which went viral and actually helped put his business on the map.

Although this direct and somewhat confrontational approach may not be the best way to handle every issue, it does highlight the need for a company's social media managers to be aware of all the things that are said and done online as they relate to that company. Because consumers have a lot more power online, businesses must be savvy enough to manage their brand online, as well.

EFFECTIVE SOCIAL MEDIA MARKETING

Social media marketing employs the same fundamentals as traditional marketing—know your audience, deliver a compelling message that ensures action, create a loyal audience, and use that audience to influence other people positively, so they also become lifelong customers. Social media often trumps traditional options because of its ability to

- Reach a global audience

- Generate user input

- Connect target audiences with like-minded people

- Track and analyze audience interest and action

GLOBAL INTEREST

Never before were businesses able to reach as many people as now with such little cost. There are literally no borders that can't be crossed because social media as a mechanism has almost infinite possibilities. Whereas, before, marketers were concerned with buying media in several outlets or sending mailers out to millions of customers to reach a mass audience, now, social media allows a company and its customers to share publicity information with everyone at one time.

One concern, however, is controlling the message and how it gets communicated across all technology. As many of us have seen, it isn't always easy to control what people say about a business. Many companies go on the defensive because their message has been misconstrued or taken out of context. A key way to avoid this problem is by understanding your target audiences and always being true to your brand. You must also examine your marketing content to make sure it communicates what you want to all audiences around the world. Nuances can get lost in translation, but messages should transcend physical borders.

A good example of a social media campaign gone wrong is Starbucks #RaceTogether promotion. In March 2015, Starbucks wanted to enter the conversation about race relations after several black men were killed by white police officers. Starbucks President Howard Schulz thought that employees and customers could hash out their differences at Starbucks and make progress on this issue. Unfortunately, the entire well-intentioned initiative backfired. Within 48 hours, the company had received 2.5 billion tweets, most of them negative. For example, customers wondered whether a barista was the best person to deal with the complexity of race relations and how the company was training its employees to deal with all of the issues that surround this divisive topic. Starbucks eventually pulled the campaign, but Schulz still stands by his decision to enter the national forum on race and admits that, although the campaign didn't go the company's way, it did create a national conversation on the topic.[8]

USER-GENERATED CONTENT

Marketing is no longer based solely on what a company says about itself, its product, or service. People can now research products and services at the click of a button, compare companies with each other, and check out endless competitors in most industries. So how can businesses define themselves in this type of climate? The answer is, "With the help of customers." They can give feedback, like or dislike something, and, perhaps most important, find other people with similar interests. Companies can augment this organic process by launching campaigns that promote people's interactions with their brands. For example, Chobani, a Greek yogurt company that was founded in 2005, decided to use its customer base to improve its image and boost sales. The company asked customers to submit videos and images praising its yogurt and then shared the content on the company website, billboards, and other social media outlets. These videos were then shared with users, and the company increased its revenue by 225 percent while the campaign was running, attributing most of its success to the promotion.[9]

Another brand, Lululemon, the athletic apparel retailer, launched an online lifestyle campaign to engage customers called #thesweatlife. The company used Twitter and other social media outlets to ask customers to send in pictures of themselves working out or doing something active and include the hashtag #thesweatlife. They then put these images on their website, allowing potential customers to review the photos and decide if they would like to purchase Lululemon products online. In this way, the company rewarded current customers by showcasing them on their website and rewarded new customers by giving them more information with which to make purchasing decisions.

BUILDING CONNECTIONS

It used to be that people met other like-minded people through clubs or organizations. Now, all they need to do is go online to find others like them with which to share their stories, opinions, concerns, and recommendations.

Businesses can leverage this social media peer-to-peer network because people are more likely to listen to and trust someone whom they feel is like them, as opposed to trusting a self-promoting company. Just look at the proliferation of websites such as TripAdvisor, which is a search engine that finds travel information from all over the Internet and conglomerates it so it can be accessed from one website. Users can rate hotels, excursions, and destinations and share that information, and much more, with everyone who visits the site. The consumers are in control, not the companies, and customers are relying on others in the online community to help them in their decision making.

Another way people build connections to businesses is through the value-added services that companies can create on social media. These services can be resources for information, continuously engaging their target audiences with new solutions, products, and updates that keep the company relevant and on top of customers' minds. For example, starting in 2015, Domino's Pizza let customers request delivery of their favorite pizza by tweeting a pizza emoji to the @Dominos Twitter account or by using the hashtag #EasyOrder. This new way of reaching customers earned the company national media coverage as well as increased market share. Domino's estimates that half of its orders now come from digital media, and the company is constantly adapting to new methods of doing business to stay ahead in the ultra-competitive fast-food market.[10]

ANALYSIS AND TRACKING

Of all the marketing tools available, social media gives us the best tracking and analysis tools. Even the most basic websites can provide information about who visits, precisely when they visit, and what they look at and search for. Utilizing this valuable information helps you determine, down to the time and day of the week or month, when you will best reach your audience most effectively.

These statistics are wonderful to know, but it is more important to find out how social media marketing translates into action. As social media strategist Marnie Lawler explains, "For me, it doesn't matter how many 'likes' a brand accrues if the dialogue and interaction happening isn't meaningful. I use the quality of the interaction taking place—who is saying what, tagging what, mentioning the products, posting pictures, etc.—to measure the overall impressions of the brand."[11]

A great example of a brand departing from its traditional ways to earn increased brand recognition is seen in the #BallotBriefcase Journey campaign of auditing firm PricewaterhouseCoopers (PwC). The company, which has been managing ballots for the Academy Awards for 82 years, wanted to highlight this role and increase public recognition. So for the 2016 ceremony, the firm decided to direct a marketing campaign at the millennial generation by using Snapchat, Twitter, and Instagram— all social media applications that allow companies to track their mentions and views. In the first two weeks of the campaign, PwC's Snap Story on Snapchat received over 700 views, and within three weeks, the campaign received 1,062 related tweets on Twitter and 406 Instagram mentions. From these data, the company knew that it had broken through the clutter to claim a place at the Oscars and had gained recognition among an important segment of consumers.[12]

As part of your strategic marketing plan, it is important to list guidelines to measure the effectiveness of a social media campaign or tool. For example, a client of mine, Freedom Physical Therapy, has an active online blog that contains several articles on different issues that clients face while offering therapy advice and guidance. At the end of each entry is contact information for the therapist who authored the article and a menu of services offered at the clinic. The company is also able to track the views for each article to see which ones are most popular and gain feedback from viewers so its therapists and employees can start a dialogue. Because these articles are so specific, Freedom Physical Therapy can find out what patients are looking for and work to fill those needs. It also uses Instagram ads that pop up on a person's screen if that individual is searching a topic that relates to physical therapy.

THE FUTURE OF MARKETING

Marketing will never disappear, but new technologies, cultural trends, and consumer tastes will change over time. What marketers need to remember is that they must rely on their brand's essence—what an organization stands for and its relationships with customers. Companies will always need to adapt to new ways of doing business, but if they have a strong relationship with their target audiences and a solid brand foundation from which to communicate, they will be better equipped to handle the future.

No matter what technological trends enter the marketplace, human nature remains the same. As James Runkle puts it, "One thing marketers can count on—for better or for worse—is that people will always want to feel connected to a brand, will always want to feel that they have exclusive information about a brand, and will always want a brand to make them feel special."[13]

Flexibility and adaptability should be a company's watchwords in the social media age, but this doesn't mean jumping on the bandwagon of the latest buzz. What it does mean, though, is that social media managers should be aware of what is available in the marketplace and utilize what works for their companies and their customers.

Building Brand Awareness
Katelyn Staaben

INTRODUCTION

Today, public relations professionals have an array of options to disseminate their messages. Social media has grown to become one of the primary methods by which people receive their news, and it is a crucial part of any communications strategy. But still, social media is often an afterthought. It is viewed as a tactic, instead of as part of the larger strategy. If social media is incorporated earlier in the process, organizations can benefit by reaching a large audience in an interactive and personal manner.

As a social media specialist at an advertising agency, my job involves writing marketing or public relations messages so that our audiences will identify with them. To create captivating advertising, you need to find more personal ways of communicating. Online audiences have grown to mistrust corporate advertising; therefore, using other methods, such as personal testimonials and brand advocates, can be very powerful ways to get your message across.

THE SITUATION

Our client, a producer of home gardening products, had several goals: 1) increase knowledge of its products throughout the industry, 2) drive traffic to its website so users could learn more about the products, and 3) increase sales.

The company was new to social media and wanted to increase awareness of its products throughout the space. We wanted to get the products into the hands of as many gardeners as possible.

This market was already saturated with competition. Gardeners don't want to risk using a product that could harm their plants, so they often stick with what they know works well. We needed to provide our audiences with examples from people they trusted to encourage them to try something new on their plants.

So we established relationships with a network of bloggers. We provided some bloggers with the product, asked them to write several posts, and that was it. We paid other bloggers for their work, as well as giving them product. Some agreed to create videos or to broadcast live about the product on Facebook. With one blogger, we participated in a Twitter chat. Each relationship was different, but the result was that we were provided many opportunities to showcase the product to different audiences.

In addition to creating relationships with bloggers, we established connections to community gardens in our target markets. We partnered with local hardware stores to provide free bags of the product to community gardeners and encouraged them to share on their social platforms the results of using this product. We posted their photos with the client's products on the client's Facebook page.

Our Approach

Each blogger used a different method to share information about our client's brand and products. The following is a brief look at how content was shared across various social channels.

FACEBOOK

We shared blog posts on the brand's Facebook page as the bloggers posted them. This gave the bloggers a boost in views to their sites and more eyes on the content we wanted a large audience to see. We also posted photos from community garden events to which our client donated product and shared updates about the growth of these gardens. One of our bloggers also used Facebook's live streaming capabilities to show how she used the product when planting a container garden. In the video, she planted several herbs and vegetables in containers and spoke about how the product helped in that process.

TWITTER

We participated in a Twitter chat with one of our bloggers. The brand did not have a Twitter account, so we relied on our blogger to represent us in the chat. We drafted ten questions, and throughout a one-hour period, the blogger posed the questions to her audience. The gardeners responded to our questions with advice, helpful tips, and questions of their own. Our blogger managed the conversation and added comments about what our client's product could do to help resolve these common garden problems. At the end of the chat, we gave away two bags of the product to several participants and encouraged those in the chat to visit the client's website. Approximately 35 users participated in the chat, and 11 people visited the website from the link provided in the chat.

YOUTUBE

One blogger created several short how-to videos that showcased our client's product. The videos were not directly focused on the product but instead solved problems that gardeners often had or showed them how to plant their crops in new or interesting ways. In the videos showing the blogger using the product, she briefly discussed why she liked using it. She also uploaded the videos to her other social platforms and used them in her blog posts.

INSTAGRAM

Several of the affiliated community gardens used Instagram to share quick looks at the growth of their crops. They also shared on Instagram photos of the gifts our client made to them. In addition, several of our bloggers used Instagram to help promote their new blog posts.

The cornerstone of this campaign involved connecting the brand to bloggers in the industry and their audiences. Much of the conversation and information that was being produced about our client's brand was not being posted on our client's own social channels. The connection that tied these channels and voices together was our client's website. Each blog post sent readers back to our client's website for more information. The posts often contained links that directed fans to the website. One of our goals was to increase website traffic, so we wanted to provide plenty of opportunities for that to happen.

This approach helped us to increase the conversation about the products online, generate more engagement on the company's Facebook page, and promote the work of the affiliated bloggers across social platforms.

CHALLENGES

When you work on a project that involves many different people with varying interests, there are always adjustments to be made. We had a blogger misspell our company's name in a post. One blogger wrote about our client's product and later in the blog also promoted a competitor's product. Situations like these were expected and sometimes required conversations with bloggers to go over what our expectations were.

We also had to find new ways to make the posts interesting to our fans. Often, more "corporate" or "marketing" style posts don't do as well on social media compared to more conversational or tip-based content. Our fans wanted to know that they were benefiting from following the page, not just because they knew what was going on with the company but also because they were receiving helpful information. There were only so many times that we could share photos of community gardens receiving a check and free product before the posts became tiresome and ineffective. To combat this, we shared the content in different ways. Sometimes we shared the post directly from the community garden and added a line of text to it. Other times we created a short video, slide-show, or photo album. By posting the information in a variety of ways and across multiple channels, we reached different audiences and kept similar posts interesting for our fans.

By analyzing our success after each set of posts, we could see which blogs were giving us the best return on investment and what types of content were helping us to achieve our goals. This program is constantly changing; either we add new bloggers or change the types of content we, or our bloggers, are posting.

SUCCESSES AND LESSONS LEARNED

After each of the bloggers posted once to their sites, we analyzed the success of the initial phase of the campaign. One of our main goals was to send readers of the blogs to the company website to learn more information and to find out where they could purchase the product near them. The six blog posts drove 182 visitors to the website, 133 of which were first-time visitors. The average visitor spent two minutes twenty-nine seconds on the site, one minute fifty-six seconds longer than typical site visitors. The visitors that came from blogs viewed more pages on the site than typical viewers, as well.

This relationship continues to be a win-win for both parties. It achieves our client's goals and allows us to reach a greater social audience than we could by simply using our own or the company's channels. In return, the bloggers receive free products to use in their garden and help in promoting their own sites.

This client was one of my first major ones in my position at this advertising agency. I was the first social media specialist to post on the client's Facebook page, and I was involved in the creation of the social strategy and social voice. During that process, and this social blogger campaign, I discovered three takeaways for new strategists:

1. *Social media should be thoroughly integrated in your public relations strategy.*

     Oftentimes, a public relations strategy is created and a social media plan is added in as an afterthought. Social media is bigger than that. There are endless possibilities that can be achieved with social media, so throwing it in at the end of the process doesn't allow you to take full advantage of everything you could accomplish.

2. *Don't be afraid to try something different or new.*

     The social media world is constantly changing. Don't wait to see how everyone else is using new technologies; instead, be at the front of the pack and let others learn from you! When a new social media tool comes out, don't be afraid to try it. The social algorithm often favors these new releases and will show your content to a wider audience. Users may have grown accustomed to seeing a text post or a photo, but when a new feature such as live video comes onto their timeline, it will grab their attention. We told one of our bloggers about Facebook Live soon after it was released, and she decided to try it with one of our client's products. She did a live stream as she planted several new container gardens and held the product up to the camera, talking about why she liked using this product on her plants. The video was viewed by almost 200 people, and it required very little effort to create.

3. *Be willing to give up control.*

Social media is about creating a conversation, and sometimes that conversation can turn sour. When we were dealing with the bloggers, we didn't know what they were going to say about the product. We can tell them about all of the product's benefits, but we have no control over their opinions on the product. These bloggers have very large, trusting audiences. One negative impression of the product can be shared with a large group of potential consumers very quickly. When a third party is creating content about your product, you should accept that you do not have control over what is being posted—and you should have a plan in place to deal with criticism if it comes up.

I am a new social media strategist, so this campaign has opened my eyes to the opportunities that are available when you coordinate your public relations and social media strategy. So rather than just tweeting a link to your newest press release, think about how you could use social media earlier in the process. Can you create a social graphic that tells your audience about your news in a visual way? Can you use social media to connect with journalists, or bloggers, and share news about your organization? The possibilities are endless; you just need to look for them.

Starting Up a Student Organization

Karli J. Peterson and Taylor (Thomson) Schroeder

In January 2014, The University of Wisconsin–Green Bay (UWGB) officially established a chapter of the Public Relations Student Society of America (PRSSA). This organization is dedicated to students who want to pursue a career in public relations and communications. Its goals are to enhance students' education, broaden their networks, and help them launch their careers.

We had six founding members when we started the chapter. We knew that it had the potential to grow very quickly because of the number of students majoring in public relations. We created an executive board, publicized the chapter in every communication course, and spread the word about PRSSA every chance we could. Not only did we want UWGB's attention, we were seeking PRSSA's national attention. We soon determined that social media was going to be a key factor in growing our membership and establishing a national reputation.

We used the social media 5 Cs (i.e., coordinates, content, connections, channels, corrections) that we learned in our "Social Media Strategy" class to craft the PRSSA's social media strategy.

COORDINATES: OUR GOALS

We started by determining the goals we had for our student chapter of PRSSA and used those to craft our communication goals:

Organizational Goals	Communication Goals
Grow membership	• Highlight benefits of PRSSA membership to students • Publicize opportunities for students to get involved in activities • Focus our communication efforts on students studying communication, marketing, and general business
Gain national attention	• Send representatives of our chapter to national events • Participate in and advocate for national PR initiatives • Publicize our chapter's dedication to community involvement
Cultivate a professional network for our members	• Reach out to local PR professionals and inform them about our chapter • Foster and maintain a relationship with the Public Relations Society of America (PRSA) sponsor chapter

CHANNELS: OUR SOCIAL MEDIA PLATFORMS

Our first step was to create a social media committee tasked with managing and maintaining our social media presence. Based on our research we selected Facebook, Twitter, Instagram, and a WordPress blog as the most appropriate platforms for achieving our goals because these are most likely to be accessed by our target audiences. After selecting our platforms, we determined how much time we would dedicate to each specific platform. We focused our attention on Twitter (60 percent) and Instagram (20 percent) because these two platforms encouraged time-sensitive interaction with PRSSA members and allowed us to share the "success stories" of our members.

Once we had chosen the platforms, we circled back to our goals and crafted more platform-specific objectives such as those below:

Communication Goals	Platform-Specific Social Media Goals
Highlight benefits of becoming a PRSSA member	Create a Twitter campaign that posts *five times per week* about the benefits of membership (example: #PRogressions)
Focus on gaining the membership of students studying communications, marketing, and general business	Invite at least *20 students* from specific majors *within the first two weeks of the semester* to like our organization's Facebook page
Participate in and advocate for national PR initiatives	Have *five members* participate in the *monthly* national Twitter discussions

We turned to Hootsuite to manage and update different platforms. But we soon discovered that you can't just set it up once and let it run. Someone must be responsible for tweaking content before it's automatically posted! A great social media strategy requires regular monitoring, evaluating, and fine-tuning because of ever-changing world events along with a rapidly changing social media landscape.

CONTENT: WHAT WE SHARED

Our social media team focused on creating and curating content that gave us the "biggest bang for the buck." We thought about the "BBFB" issue with the aid of the common journalistic questions: who, what, when, where, why, and how. These questions forced us to be audience focused and to look at our content from several different perspectives.

We concluded that "why" and "how" issues needed to be addressed first to achieve our membership goal, so we focused on answering these questions: "*Why* should I join?" (e.g., What's in it for me? What are the personal and professional benefits I'll derive from joining PRSSA?), and "*How* do I become a member?" Because our chapter had yearly fees, it was especially important for us to prove that members would get a return on their investment and that there were solid reasons for getting involved. The answer to another question was important to our existing members, especially to those who were nearing graduation: "*How* can I apply this to my life and college career?" Discussing issues such as internships, networking, and résumés became a focal point of our messaging when we addressed this "how" question.

After answering the "Biggest Bang for the Buck" question, we turned to the issue of which platform was best for different types of content. We came up with the following:

Facebook	Twitter	Instagram
• Include photos in most of the posts • Feature members' successes	• Share meeting time and location updates • Highlight information from meetings • Provide event updates • Participate in national chats and conferences • Link to other PRSSA chapters • Share articles with professional success tips	• Provide action photos of student presentations, working groups, activities, conferences, and events • Post images with creative #hashtags to encourage member participation

CONNECTIONS: HOW WE LINKED OUR NETWORKS

We are trained in our coursework to think strategically; this means that we needed to think as much about what we chose *NOT to post* as we did about what we chose *TO post*. This approach, in turn, suggested various questions:

- Should our PRSSA chapter be present on "all" social media?

- Should our PRSSA chapter be present only on the same platforms as competitors?

- Should our PRSSA chapter have a traditional, paper-style newsletter?

- How does our PRSSA chapter's website link up with the national PRSSA's website and social media presence?

- Should we contact professors and ask them to announce events?

- Should we write announcements about PRSSA events on classroom whiteboards?

As noted previously, we used a limited number of social media communication platforms (e.g., Twitter, Facebook, and Instagram), but we always linked back to some of the more traditional communication channels. For example, we wrote announcements on the classroom whiteboards while highlighting our social media sites. Then, we asked our professors to direct students' attention to the whiteboards at the beginning of class. In some cases, we coupled this with a personal "elevator pitch" to the class.

CORRECTIONS: WHAT DID WE LEARN?

Our main problem area was a lack of consistency, which stemmed from student officer turnover and academic breaks. More specifically, we found that, during times of transition between officers and during semester breaks, these things were difficult:

- Finding a consistent way to transfer the login and password information, especially if there was no training or overlapping time from one officer to the next

- Being consistent with posting frequency

- Having a consistent message style and organization (as an example, some officers used the "I" pronoun while others spoke in the "we" voice)

These everyday challenges, coupled with the feedback from our posts, helped us formulate a list of "lessons learned" to pass on to the new social media managers:

- *The student organization profile is NOT your personal profile.* The organization's social media presence may reflect your voice or writing style but not your content.

- *Consistency is vital*
  o Use a similar voice on each platform, regardless of who actually crafts the post
  o Maintain a consistent messaging theme throughout all posts
  o Avoid lulls in posting or activity
  o Don't ignore your key platforms; adhere to your strategic plan for the percentage of time spent on different platforms
  o Don't let the lulls in the academic year influence the frequency of your posts

- *Feature members and encourage them to share PRSSA posts with their non-PRSSA friends*

- *Proofread social media posts to ensure solid info and proper grammar*

- *Be aware of local, regional, and global surroundings when posting so as not to offend, post out of context, or accidently come off as unaware of other events*

Our year-to-year plan was a partial success. The glitches that beset our best-laid plans were semester breaks, constantly changing schedules, and new members who wanted to get involved. So we switched to a semester-to-semester social media plan. This decision fostered better posts, greater personnel stability, and more member engagement. On a practical level, it helped with handing off passwords and sharing lessons learned during key transition points. We relied on Google Drive and a generic Gmail account to pass information from member to member directly. This decision kept our chapter's information in one location, even during times of turnover.

RESULTS

Did our strategy work? Yes! The UWGB PRSSA chapter grew from the initial group of 6 in 2014 to 14 in 2015 to nearly 30 in 2016. In the 2015–16 academic year, our chapter placed a bid to host a regional PRSSA conference at UW-Green Bay. We were in competition with many other regional schools applying for the conference. We won the opportunity and held the conference in April 2016. The event had over 70 attendees, supportive faculty, and local speakers who presented on the theme: "PRactice: A Community ApPRoach to PR." We used live-tweeting and posted photos on the conference-specific Facebook page and website for members who were unable to attend. One highlight was a keynote address from Green Bay Packers' Director of Public Affairs Aaron Popkey.

The UW-Green Bay PRSSA chapter also won the Star Chapter Award for the 2014–15 academic year. This award is based on criteria such as ethics, high school outreach initiatives, membership drives, and national representation. The PRSSA also received the recognition of "Student Organization of the Year" for the 2015–16 academic year at UWGB. In short, we are thrilled with the outcome of our strategy. We not only met our initial goals but exceeded them. Much of that success was due to our social media strategy guided by our classroom experience and our advisor, Danielle Bina.

Managing an Algorithm-Induced Social Media Crisis

Elizabeth Hintz

INTRODUCTION

Social media marketing is the backbone of businesses, ranging from multibillion-dollar corporations like Target and Walmart to small town, family-owned shops. Though a website should be neat and orderly, social media allows an organization to have personality, to have conversations with customers in real time.

The firm I work for in Wisconsin, Laura Mitchell Consulting, provides marketing services for a wide range of organizations. The primary reasons these firms use our social media marketing services are to increase sales and profits; provide quality customer service; and create top-of-mind awareness, establishing the brand in the minds of consumers.

BACKGROUND

Businesses participate in social media to have a voice in the conversations that take place about them online. Many business leaders believe social media marketing is simple and inexpensive. That is a misconception. Digital advertising costs money, and many platforms will not allow unpaid posts to reach large audiences. Companies spend millions of dollars hiring social media managers, crafting marketing strategies, and paying customer service representatives to handle online feedback. But everything marketing departments work so hard to create can come crumbling down when they hear two dreaded words: "algorithm change."

So, what is an algorithm? Technically, it is a mathematical formula or set of rules used to calculate something of value. In the social media world, an algorithm is a mathematical process of ranking content for distribution, often by predicting its relevance to a specific user. Facebook's algorithm is very complex, as this blogger explains:

> When picking posts for each person who logs on to Facebook, the News Feed algorithm takes into account literally hundreds of variables—and can predict whether a given user will like, click, comment, share, hide, or even mark a post as spam. . . . This prediction is quantified into a single number called a "relevancy score" that's specific both to you and to that post. Once every post that could potentially show up in your feed has been assigned a relevancy score, Facebook's sorting algorithm ranks them and puts them in the order they end up appearing in your feed.[14]

Algorithm changes for social media marketers are like economic recessions. One simple change in a formula could mean uprooting several years' worth of marketing strategy and content creation.

For instance, at one time, Charlie Hintz, founder of the Facebook page and website Cult of Weird, had a page with over 136,000 organic (unpaid) likes. After Facebook released an algorithm change in 2014, he saw that number plummet in one day. How could this be? Could one algorithm change on Facebook really have drastically reduced the number of people who saw his content from Cult of Weird? Why even change the algorithm at all? According to Nick Mitchell, web developer and digital strategist at Laura Mitchell Consulting,

> Facebook tweaks the algorithm every so often to either quash any gaming of the system or to promote a new feature. For example, when Facebook introduced and started heavily promoting native video, they tweaked the algorithm to strongly prefer this video over links to external sites like YouTube. Marketers who noticed that their video posts were reaching more users than other posts responded by promoting a ton of video content to provide awareness for their brands.[15]

Could Facebook begin to favor paid and self-serving content over grassroots, homegrown content? The answer—in short—is *yes*. Marketers no longer make the rules; the platforms we use do. Many large corporations make major decisions based on Facebook-generated analytics. Properly understanding the inner workings of the algorithms improves the decision-making process. All posts are not created equal, so understanding the algorithm behind the "likes" metric will increase the probability that your messages will reach your target market.

OUR CHALLENGE: HOW DO WE MANAGE ALGORITHM CHANGES?

My team and I were faced with this challenge with one of our firm's clients, a company that provided senior citizens health-care technology products, such as hearings aids and home monitoring systems. During a client campaign, we noticed a sharp decline in our organic reach and engagement. At first, we blamed our content. Maybe we weren't posting enough, or we weren't posting during the right times each day; perhaps our post captions weren't good enough, or our blogs needed to be more exciting. We had never seen such low engagement on posts for this client, so we did some investigating. Sure enough, Facebook had just released another algorithm change that favored paid content.

Many of our clients did not allocate a large budget for paid digital advertising and sponsored content, making it incredibly difficult to reach their target audiences. Unfortunately, paid social media advertising is usually the only way to gain a following. We needed to create a strategy for producing quality content, completely resistant to the ebb and flow of algorithm changes, while still reaching our target markets.

OUR RESPONSE

We needed to rethink the client's social media strategy by reorienting our client's coordinates (goals), channels, connections, content, and corrections policy.

The Challenge

Our challenge was to create high-quality content that

- was favored by Facebook
- engaged our target market organically
- was resistant to algorithm changes

COORDINATES

Because our client was a senior health-care technology provider, we identified the target markets as senior citizens as well as their middle-aged children who are often decision makers for their parents. Therefore, we targeted people aged 35 and older. To best serve our client, we determined that our efforts would focus on the following organizational and communication goals.

Organizational Goals	Communication Goals
• Increase sales, sell products • Increase booth participation at trade shows	• Create awareness of our products • Establish the brand as an industry thought leader

CHANNELS

We chose Facebook as our primary channel for social media marketing because seniors represent one of the fastest-growing demographics on the site. Our client also used Instagram, Twitter, and LinkedIn, which we used to publish blogs from our WordPress site.

CONNECTIONS

We explored connecting third-party accounts such as WordPress, Instagram, and Twitter to Facebook to see if our organic engagement improved from those automated posts. It didn't. In addition, third-party scheduling platforms such as Hootsuite, when connected to Facebook, have very little organic post reach. To test this hypothesis, we posted the same content twice, once from Hootsuite and once natively. Native posts go directly to Facebook instead of to a scheduling platform (like Hootsuite) that indirectly posts the material to Facebook. The Hootsuite post reached 6 people, and the native post reached 56. We stopped using Hootsuite to schedule posts shortly thereafter.

Our social media efforts were centered on our blog, which was a WordPress-based site. Each week, a blog was published and then pushed through to all existing social media for our client. This meant boosting the maximum visibility for the post while sending users to the organization's website.

CONTENT

The 4/1/1 rule provided us a good benchmark. This rule suggests that, for every six posts a Facebook page publishes, four of those posts should be educational, lighthearted, funny, or human interest stories, one should be a soft promotion, and one should be a hard promotion. The four weekly "fun" posts attracted people to our page initially and kept them engaged. No one is going to like and follow your page if it consists merely of advertisements. The 4/1/1 rule provides a good mixture of entertaining content while still allowing product and service promotion.

4/1/1 Rule

- 4 weekly educational/fun posts
- 1 soft promotion (e.g., event/activity promo)
- 1 hard promotion (e.g., watch a video, read our press release)

Audiences will not engage with stiff, robotic, and overly promotional social media content. For instance, we were not afraid to share a photo of a hamster in a sweater.[16] We also prided ourselves on our agility in curating content. Knowing how to read the analytics properly helped us to identify whether our content was working or not. If we found that some posted content wasn't doing well, we pivoted to something else.

As each generation becomes increasingly diverse, traditional marketing tactics that rely on demographic data become less and less useful. We learned to transition from *marketing to demographics* to *marketing to values*. Specifically, our content was designed to target the interests, attitudes, values, and lifestyles of our target audiences. By targeting the values of your audience, you are approaching them in a way that feels familiar, not foreign. Values transcend arbitrary categories of age, gender, and socioeconomic status.

CORRECTIONS

As Mitchell puts it, "Constantly evolving and refining your social media strategy is a surefire path to success and will insulate you from future Facebook algorithm changes."[17] Weekly reviews of the Insights feature on Facebook helped us to better understand what engaged our users and what didn't. Then, based on what we found, we adjusted our strategy. Facebook also provided us with a plethora of tips, informative articles, and step-by-step tutorials that allowed us to work with the site to curate effective, engaging content. Facebook was essentially telling us what we were doing wrong, and all we had to do was listen and read.

We realized that posting too frequently caused reach and engagement numbers to plummet. If we saw that certain types of posts or media were doing more poorly than the average post, we took a closer look and moved in a different direction.

RESULTS

We began posting less frequently and saw our organic reach improve dramatically as a result. The algorithm was no longer penalizing our page for posting more than once or twice each day, meaning that more eyes and more potential customers were once again being exposed to our content.

We read many blogs, news releases, and articles from Facebook about the algorithm changes. We soon discovered how they would impact our page and how best to work around them. For instance, we decided to produce our own high-quality videos on-site. Our Insights page told us that video reached and engaged more users than any other type of content, so it made sense to spend time focusing on sharp, clean, quality videos for our client. In addition, we knew that Facebook was debuting a new video feature. All signs pointed to a Facebook initiative that strongly favored video content.

We began curating images that related to our client's industry, using quirky hashtags to reach our 35-and-older target market. This image reached 857 people organically, with 89 reactions, comments, and shares. This meme reached eight times more users than average, with four times more users than average liking, commenting, or sharing.

SOURCE: Copyright © CanStock Photo/mybaitshop.

Once our audience started paying attention again, we created a network of blogs and posts focused on our client's campaign and the upcoming industry trade show that the company was going to attend. We promoted giveaways and other activities through social media, which increased booth attendance and, ultimately, sales. The extra attention garnered by the success of the trade show, in addition to collaborations with other industry insiders through networking events promoted on social media, established our client as an industry thought leader.

LESSONS LEARNED

To recap, here are our lessons learned that could help other social media specialists:

1. *Focus on the quality of your posts, as opposed to the quantity, timing, or specific wording.* By creating valuable, original content, instead of clickbait, you will grow an audience of dedicated, engaged viewers.

2. *Monitor your Insights page on Facebook and remove less engaging content.* Why continue a marketing strategy or content style that isn't working? Decades ago, marketers relied on surveys to determine how effective campaigns were. Today, those analytics are now merely a click away.

3. *Create content that resonates with your target market, even if that content does not focus on promotion.* Human interest stories and seemingly tangential, peripheral pieces can add immense value to a social media profile. If your business is posting "Buy! Buy! Buy!" all day, you may not see satisfactory engagement.

4. *Follow the 4/1/1 rule, and stop posting excessively.* We posted four fun, lighthearted stories, one soft promotion, and one hard promotion each week. This way, we weren't overloading our followers with information or being flagged as spam by the sorting algorithm.

The sorting algorithm that caused challenges for my consulting firm has not gone away. Even though we got past this hurdle, the algorithm will change again. In fact, Facebook tweaks the algorithm almost daily. For this reason, it is important to pay attention to what is happening on your page and to be agile. Learn to work with platforms such as Facebook to create content that your audience—and Facebook—will love.

NOTES

1. Indeed, by 2014, 53 percent of those 18–29 reported having used a smartphone in one way or another as part of a job search; see A. Smith and

D. Page, *Searching for Work in the Digital Era* (Washington, DC: Pew Research Center, November 2015), 3.

2. L. Adler, *Performance-Based Hiring* (Irvine, CA: The Adler Group, 2016).

3. Jibe, *2014 Talent Acquisition Survey*, September 2014, http://www.jibe .com/wp-content/uploads/2014/09/2014-Talent-Acquisition-Survey.pdf.

4. CEB, *Q4 2011 Global Labor Market Survey* (Arlington, VA: CEB, 2012); L. Stevens, "Improve the Candidate Experience," *ERE*, July 15, 2008, http://www.ere.net/200B/07/15/3322/.

5. Personal communication with J. Runkle, July 12, 2016.

6. B. Kepes, "JetBlue and the Power of Some Simple Social Engagement," *Forbes*, May 1, 2015, http://www.forbes.com/sites/benkepes/2015/05/01/ jetblue-and-the-power-of-some-simple-social-engagement/#303062057a 87. Accessed February 8, 2017.

7. H. Abramyk, "Online Reputation Management Fails," *Vendasta* [blog], August 2, 2016, https://www.vendasta.com/blog/online-reputation-man agement-fails. Accessed February 12, 2017.

8. A. Carr, "The Inside Story of Starbucks's Race Together Campaign, No Foam," *Fast Company*, June 15, 2015, https://www.fastcompany .com/3046890/the-inside-story-of-starbuckss-race-together-campaign- no-foam. Accessed February 5, 2017.

9. S. Balderson, "4 Startups' Social Media Marketing Campaigns That Big Businesses Can Learn From," *Company Formations 24.7* [blog], July 22, 2016, https://www.companyformations247.co.uk/blog/4-start-social-me dia-marketing-campaigns-big-business-can-learn/. Accessed February 2, 2017.

10. E. Schuman, "Domino's Tweet-to-Eat Campaign Is Sneaky Social Media at Its Best," *ComputerWorld*, May 21, 2015, http://www.com puterworld.com/article/2925500/retail-it/dominos-tweet-to-eat-cam paign-is-sneaky-social-media-at-its-best.html; B. Snyder, "Domino's Growth Driven by Digital Orders," *Fortune*, July 16, 2015, http://fortune .com/2015/07/16/dominos-digital-orders/. Accessed February 1, 2017.

11. Personal communication with M. Lawler, July 13, 2016.

12. J. A. Gallegos, "The Best Social Media Marketing Campaigns of 2016," *Tint*, December 31, 2016, https://www.tintup.com/blog/the-best-social- media-campaigns-of-2016-so-far/. Accessed January 29, 2017.

13. Personal communication with J. Runkle, July 12, 2016.

14. L. Kolowich, "How the News Feed Algorithms Work on Facebook, Twitter & Instagram," *HubSpot* [blog], April 14, 2016, https://blog .hubspot.com/marketing/how-algorithm-works-facebook-twitter-insta gram#sm.0001qpr0ca74bdzxrd11w0gc5ivpj.

15. N. Mitchell, "Quality Content Is King in Latest Facebook Algorithm Change," *LMC: Laura Mitchell Consulting* [blog], May 4, 2016, http://

lmcllc.us/2016/05/04/quality-content-facebook-algorithm-change/. Accessed February 12, 2017. See also M. Blank, "News Feed FYI: More Articles You Want to Spend Time Viewing," *Facebook Newsroom*, April 21, 2016, http://newsroom.fb.com/news/2016/04/news-feed-fyi-more-articles-you-want-to-spend-time-viewing/. Accessed February 12, 2017.

16. See Facebook post from April 21, 2014 (reposted August 31, 2016), https://www.facebook.com/LauraMitchellConsulting/posts/1197009647008017. Accessed February 12, 2017.

17. N. Mitchell, "Quality Content Is King."

Glossary

5 Cs: The five components of a social media strategy: coordinates, channels, content, connections, and corrections. See also *channels*, *connections*, *content*, *coordinates*, and *corrections*.

A/B test: The process of monitoring two versions of the same post—using, for example, different images, words, calls to action, and even the timing of the posts—to determine which has the most traffic.

Abundance strategy: This strategy is representative of a "many and rich is more" approach; there are many user relationships to maintain and those relationships are strong in nature.

Actively managed platforms: The channels in which you invest significant time and energy by, for example, actively pushing out content.

Analytical anchors: Objective statements about important patterns regarding the competitive environment. These are the key insights the social media strategist extracted from the facts collected about the organization, competitors, and the social media environment.

Assess and respond strategy: An approach in which you *assess* posts and *respond* in an appropriate manner. The responses could range from directly replying to the post to ignoring it.

Assessment report: A document that presents an in-depth look at the effectiveness of an organization's social media strategy. A social media assessment report typically reveals changes that have occurred since the last report, focusing on the main platforms that the organization is utilizing. It could reveal factors such as growth (or loss) in followership, reach, and different types of engagement and an explanation of potential factors influencing the numbers.

Assessment tool: An instrument or a means of monitoring daily, weekly, or quarterly statistics about performance. This tool may help with setting benchmarks, orienting management processes, and identifying continuous improvement opportunities.

Audience composition: Metrics that provide insights about the composition of your audiences and their preferences.

Benchmarks: Gauges against which performance is measured.

Bull's-eye node: The *target* node that you designate for your network. For example, it could be the "Buy" button or the "Apply here" button on your website. Or it could be "Tap to view products" or "Shop now" on a social media platform.

Centralized network: A network of connections with minimal hubs, hinge points, and short path links. It maximizes a "command and control" orientation.

Channels: The mediums through which messages pass. This would include Facebook, Twitter, and Pinterest but also websites, email, and the telephone.

Cocreated content: Content created with your followers' or customers' input.

Community sentiment: Patterns of responses to your content, such as attitude, opinion, feelings, and emotion based on social conversations and comment threads.

Comparison points: The criteria or standards against which you can measure something.

Confirmation bias: The tendency to look for, favor, and remember information that confirms preexisting beliefs and to interpret all we discover in light of these beliefs while giving less consideration to alternative possibilities.

Connections: The links between various social media platforms, websites, non-digital channels, people, and departments. For example, a print ad that makes reference to a company's Twitter account would be considered a connection.

Connections matrix: A strategic thinking tool that underscores key decision points for the social media strategist. The horizontal axis measures the raw number of links in the network, from few to many; the vertical axis measures the intensity of connections that emerge from those links, from weak to strong.

Content: The material posted on social media sites or platforms.

Continuous improvement: An ongoing effort to enhance processes, performance, and/or service.

Coordinates test: A check to determine if your strategic goals are aligned with your channel choices, content selections, connection decisions, and correction plan.

Coordinates: Points of connection between big-picture goals (for example, between organizational and communication goals). In other words, coordinates are your strategic goals and their relationship to one another. In the social media cosmos, they represent goals that are strongly linked, interconnected, and mutually reinforcing. They answer the question, "What do I have to get right to end up where I want to be?"

Corrections: Tweaks and major changes made to a firm's social media strategy and tactics.

Corrections matrix: A tool that helps social media managers manage the correction process actively. It identifies 1) the level of severity of an error—whether it is strategic or tactical—and 2) the type of error—whether it is an error of omission or commission. The results point to errors ranging from minor oversights to major blunders.

Curated content: Content drawn from other sources and repurposed by the social media strategist.

Decentralized network: A network of connections that has many hubs and hinge points as well as a potentially large number of path links.

Depth strategy: This strategy is representative of a "quality trumps quantity" approach; there are few user relationships to maintain, but those relationships are strong in nature.

Distributed network: A network of connections in which many or all nodes are connected to each other.

Drivers: The social media platforms that push traffic to your website or target node. See also *nodes*.

Dynamics perspective: Approaching social media by examining how users make use of a platform rather than by looking at an inherent characteristic of a platform. Factors such as time sensitivity (How important is the timing of the post?), word selection (How important are the words chosen in the post?) and image choice (How important are images in the post?) represent the underlying *usage patterns* that typically emerge from a platform's attributes.

Engagement: Measures of audience actions in relation to social media.

Experiential perspective: Approaching social media by critically examining your own social media practices.

FAJV: An acronym that represents a fact-based approach to assessing social media's competitive environment. The approach includes the following four stages:

1. Facts—Collect relevant *facts*,
2. Anchors—Isolate the essential *analytical anchors* implied by the facts,
3. Judgments—Make *judgments* based on the analytical anchors, and
4. Validation—*Validate* your judgments.

Five Cs: See *5 Cs*, at the start of the glossary.

Form (category of content): The choice among options for transmitting content on social media sites. The options include a picture, text, video, sound clip, or graphic.

Friendly spy network: An informal group of people who watch over your posts and your competitors' posts. Their role is to quickly alert you to possible miscues and missed opportunities.

Functional perspective: Approaching social media in terms of the unique functions it performs, taking into account what your tools are *intended* to do and how they are *actually* used.

Goldilocks zone: Positioning the message at just the right level of detail or abstraction—not too much and not too little. The zone is the "sweet spot" that *guides* but does *not dictate* actions.

Hashtags: Relevant keywords or phrases marked with the symbol #. Hashtags mark posts as relating to a topic and can also serve as keyword measures of interest across platforms.

Hinges: Nodes that connect otherwise separate groups in the network. Hinges are the linchpins of the network. If a hinge node goes down, then two groups will not be able to connect.

Hubs: Nodes that play a role in more than one network.

Impressions: A measurement of exposure to your content, or views of your posts.

Influence analysis: Finding people within or outside of your network who have high potential for swaying your target audience; the goal is to connect with those influential individual or entities.

Influencers: People who sway others.

Insight pods: Related or connected insights gleaned from the competitive analysis.

Likes: A measure of engagement that indicates positive sentiment. A "like" function usually lets social media users share their appreciation of content without having to make a written comment.

Links: A link is a direct path between two nodes. The more links in the chain, the greater both the path length and the likelihood of distortion.

Major blunder: A strategic error of commission. The committed error is severe and has the potential to harm a firm's image and long-term viability.

Metric: A system or standard of measurement or a number that measures something we believe is important, e.g., the engagement performance of a post.

Minor oversight: A tactical error of omission. This type of error, which involves not doing something that should have been done, can be quickly rectified.

Missed opportunity: A strategic error of omission. Nothing "wrong" may have occurred, per se, but the organization, by not doing something, may have missed out on some innovative idea.

ML+- thinking: "Most like (ML) plus or minus" is a formula for understanding social media platforms. This approach has the strategist answer the following questions:

1. What familiar tool or activity is the social media *most like*?
2. What is a feature that is *added* to the familiar tool or activity?
3. What is a feature that is *subtracted* from the familiar tool or activity?

Modest gaffe: A tactical error of commission. The incident, which involves doing something wrong, may be moderately annoying to users, but the mistake can be easily corrected.

Niche platforms: Social media channels that are less publicized and less well known but that might hold more innovative and edgy appeal.

Nodes: Points of reference in a network. The most obvious nodes in the social media world include social media sites, websites, and the email system. Some less obvious nodes include traditional media (e.g., brochures, kiosks, menus, and advertisements) and partner advertisements.

Observation: Looking online at social media content and clicking on posts and links.

Organic growth: Using internal resources to boost social media performance naturally, such as by reaching out to already established friends.

Participation: Being moved to action. In the social media world, participation might involve following a Twitter account or liking, sharing, or commenting on a post.

Passively managed platforms: The channels in which you invest little time and energy. Managing these platforms might involve, at a minimum, securing the platform names that some audience members might access or stumble across, as well as regularly monitoring these.

Path length: The number of links that separate any two nodes in the system. The more links in the chain, the greater both the path length and the likelihood of distortion.

Platform job description: The role that a specific social media channel is to perform in the organization, or in other words, the *aspiration* that the channel is seeking to fulfill in a *specific circumstance*.

Platform-specific measures: Analytical tools offered at the platform level of various social media, such as Facebook Insights, Twitter Analytics, LinkedIn Analytics, Pinterest Analytics, Instagram Insights, and YouTube Analytics.

Propagation: Amplification of content when followers retweet, repost, repeat comments, share articles, or use your hashtags.

Reach: The number of unique visitors exposed to a message.

Reach strategy: This strategy is representative of a "quantity trumps quality" approach; there are many user connections but the relationships are weak in nature.

ROI: Return on investment. In the social media realm, this financial measurement compares the benefits gained to the costs incurred by following a social media strategy or tactic.

Shares: A measure of engagement that indicates how many times social media users have shared your content. The number of "shares" can be used to identify which content was the most relevant for your audience.

Simplicity strategy: This strategy is representative of a "less and lean is more" approach; there are few user connections to maintain, and those relationships are weak in nature.

Social Media Aspirational Triangle: This illustration highlights three qualities that can position a social media strategist for success and sustained excellence: a strategic mindset, professional sensibilities, and enthusiastic zeal.

Social media: An electronic form of communication for users to share images and text within their selected communities. This communication is governed by the rules of platform providers.

Social media strategy: Coordinated big-picture choices that form a coherent path forward and result in an orchestrated set of tactics.

Social media tactics: The specific actions that implement the strategy.

Success stories: Examples of content that produced the intended effect and accomplished your social media goals.

SWOT: An approach to strategic planning that involves identifying a firm's *s*trengths, *w*eaknesses, *o*pportunities, and what potentially *t*hreatens it.

Synergies: These describe how the strategic elements strengthen and enrich one another.

Synergy test: A check to determine if your channel choices, content selections, connection decisions, and correction plan are aligned with one another.

Tease and seize strategy: An approach in which you *tease* different audiences with several different kinds of posts, monitor the results, and then *seize* the opportunities implied by the feedback.

Test-post content strategy: An approach that helps regulate what content to post and when to post it. For example, a person might ask these questions before posting content: "Does it need to be said?" "Does it need to be said by me?" "Does it need to be said now?"

Thinking biases: Systematic patterns of thinking that deviate from rational judgment. See also *confirmation bias*.

Thinking routines: The regular ways or approaches we take to reason through problems, challenges, or situations.

Total views: A measurement of exposure to your content. This is the total number of times content was seen, so if your content had only two viewers, one who saw your content 17 times and another who saw it twice, the number would be 19.

Traffic patterns: Metrics that help determine if people are paying attention to your content and if that content is driving traffic to your target node or website.

Translation test: A check to determine if your strategy has been effectively transformed into action plans and tactics.

Type (category of content): The choice among options regarding the kind of content that gets posted on social media sites. Examples include content featuring news and information, events, calls to action, and inspirational messages.

Unequal dialogue: The term refers to the tenor of the discussion between organizational leaders and social media managers; the former have more dialogic power than the latter. Social media managers should argue vigorously for their point of view, but, in the final analysis, organizational goals always trump the social media goals.

User-generated content: Content that fans develop. This content may include a clever or funny use of a product that catches the eye of social media managers.

Word cloud: An image composed of words used in a text. As dominant words and phrases are visual proportional to their frequency of occurrence in the text, a word cloud provides a qualitative tool for visually analyzing blocks of texts.

Index

About the Author

Phillip G. Clampitt received his PhD in organizational communication from the University of Kansas. He holds the Blair Endowed Chair of Communication and was previously the Hendrickson Professor of Business at the University of Wisconsin-Green Bay, where he is a full professor. Dr. Clampitt is the chair of four units at UWGB: Information and Computing Science, Communication, Computer Science, and Information Sciences. SAGE Publishing recently published the sixth edition of his best-selling book *Communicating for Managerial Effectiveness*. He coauthored two books with Robert J. DeKoch (president and COO of the Boldt Company): *Embracing Uncertainty: The Essence of Leadership* and *Transforming Leaders into Progress Makers*.

Phil's work on "decision downloading" was featured in the *MIT Sloan Management Review* and the *Wall Street Journal*. Additionally, he has published in numerous journals, including the *Academy of Management Executive*, the *Journal of Communication Management*, the *Journal of Business Communication*, and *Management Communication Quarterly*. He has contributed chapters to numerous works including the *Handbook of Communication Audits for Organisations*, *Communication Audits*, and the *International Encyclopedia of Organizational Communication*. He also is on the editorial board of many professional journals. Over the past thirty years, he has worked on communication and leadership issues with many organizations including Nokia, PepsiCo, Schneider National, the Boldt Company, Dental City, National University, and the Menasha Corporation.

Phil has been a guest speaker at the U.S. Army War College, where they use his books in their Strategic Leadership class. In addition to having had many guest-speaking opportunities in the United States, he has also been invited to speak internationally at places such as the University of Pisa, the University of Aberdeen, and the University of Ulster, as well as to address numerous multinational businesses and professional organizations.

His students have heard him ask, "So what?" so often that they started calling him "Dr. So What." Subsequently, he developed a related website (www.drsowhat.com) that highlights his passionate commitment to critical thinking and thoughtful inquiry.

About the Contributors

Laleah Fernandez is an assistant professor in the Department of Information and Computing Science at the University of Wisconsin-Green Bay. Her research interests include network analysis and the role of new and emerging media in community-level and global mobilization efforts. Laleah has published research and reviews in the areas of advertising, economic development, mobilization, and science communication. She earned her PhD in media and information studies, her MA in advertising, and her BA in journalism, all from Michigan State University.

Elizabeth Hintz is a graduate student and teaching assistant in the Brian Lamb School of Communication at Purdue University. She also works as a freelance consultant specializing in digital strategy for health-care technology organizations. Most notably, her social media skills were commissioned for the Digital Health Summit at CES 2016.

Jena Richter Landers is social media specialist at the University of Wisconsin-Green Bay and serves as a campus expert on social media. She received her bachelor of arts in communication from UW-Green Bay. Jena resides in Green Bay with her husband, Troy, and her English bull terrier, Floyd.

Amy Martin, talent maximizer and juggler-in-chief, is the manager of Talent Acquisition and Talent Management at Menasha Corporation in Neenah, Wisconsin. A native Floridian, Amy earned a master's degree in human resources and industrial relations from the University of Illinois at Urbana-Champaign and has worked in multiple corporate human resources roles for the past 15 years. You can connect with Amy at https://www.linkedin.com/in/amyjoymartin.

Ryan Martin is a psychologist and anger researcher at the University of Wisconsin-Green Bay. His research interests include the study of healthy and unhealthy anger in a variety of contexts (e.g., the assessment and treatment of anger problems, understanding how anger is expressed online). He received his PhD in counseling psychology from the University of Southern Mississippi.

Karli J. Peterson is a marketing, graphic design, and communication professional in Eau Claire, WI. Her bachelor of arts degrees were in communication and English literature from the University of Wisconsin–Green Bay. She currently resides in Eau Claire. Contact: petersonk06@gmail.com.

Julie Sadoff is the principal of Sadoff Consulting, a marketing and communications firm. She specializes in market research, brand development, customer experience management, and strategic development. She received her MS in integrated marketing and communications from Northwestern University. Her company's website is www.sadoff consulting.com.

Taylor (Thomson) Schroeder is a community affairs assistant for the City of Troy, Michigan. Her bachelor of arts degrees were in communication and Spanish and Latin American studies from UW–Green Bay. Taylor currently resides in Troy, MI, with her husband Lucas and their Alaskan Klee Kai husky, Pippin. Taylor served as president of the PRSSA for two years and was part of the founding executive board. She can be contacted at taylormarieschroeder@gmail.com.

Katelyn Staaben is a social media specialist in the B2B advertising industry. Her clients represent industries ranging from golf turf products to specialized sealing solutions. See LinkedIn.com/in/katelynstaa ben for more information.